"Since Cynthia Enloe analysed the militarisation of Campbell's soup cans, feminist scholars have been revealing a variety of previously invisible ways that (gendered) militarisations pervade everyday life across the globe. *Bulletproof Fashion* is an important contribution to this work, both empirically and theoretically. Starting at the tragic reality of the rise of children's bulletproof clothing responding to American school shootings, Barbara Sutton demonstrates that the *fashion of fear* has become a norm not an exception. Sutton links this militarised fashion to the security state in a book as important as it is fascinating, as innovative as it is timely."

Laura Sjoberg, *British Academy Global Professor of Politics and International Relations, Royal Holloway, University of London, UK*

"This book is a must-read for anyone concerned with understanding individualized approaches to gun violence prevention specifically and violence prevention more generally. Sutton lays out the stark choices that we as a society face. Do we move in the direction of guns everywhere and citizens including small children attired in body armor that purports to protect them or in a more collectivist direction of mutual care that addresses the underlying causes of gun violence? Sutton's book will help us to understand the powerful interests pushing us in the direction of a militarized society where we are all responsible for our personal safety rather than looking out for one another."

Mary Bernstein, *Associate Dean of The Graduate School and Professor of Sociology, University of Connecticut, USA*

"Barbara Sutton provides an unflinching consideration of the grim collision of unfettered violence and marketized fear. In civilian-marketed bulletproof fashion, Sutton identifies the quintessential commodity fetish, the object imbued with mystical meaning above and beyond its mere use value. While the Kevlar vest or backpack is not likely to protect us from the onslaught of firearm violence, we spend billions for a taste of invulnerability, for a symbolic bulwark against the unbearable burden our bodies are asked to bear in 21st century America. In accessible, cogent prose, this book exposes the stark emotional and political implications of an increasingly armored body politic."

Caroline Light, *Senior Lecturer and Director of Undergraduate Studies, Harvard University, USA*

"How do fears of gun violence influence not just our emotions, but our bodies and even clothing choices? How do desires for maximizing personal security take shape through fashion? Barbara Sutton's important and timely book examines the new phenomenon of bulletproof clothing—from leather jackets to women's corsets to young children's backpacks—to show how fashion helps Americans manage their fears of becoming the next victim. Bulletproof clothing turns the systemic problem of gun violence into an individual consumer choice, and exacerbates social inequalities of race, gender and class. Anyone who wants to understand the effects of excessive gun violence in the US should read this surprising and compelling book."

Elisabeth Anker, author of *Ugly Freedoms*

BULLETPROOF FASHION

In the context of gun proliferation and persistent gun violence in the United States, a controversial security strategy has gained public attention: bulletproof fashion. In this book, Barbara Sutton examines concerns about security focusing on armored clothing and accessories for civilians.

Available for children and adults, such ballistic products include colorful backpacks, elegant suits, sports jackets, feminine dresses, trendy vests, and medical lab coats. These products are paradigmatic of a "fashion of fear"—the practice of outfitting the body with apparel aimed at maximizing personal security. This fashion encourages the emergence of both a fortress body and an armored society.

Sutton also explores the wider social factors influencing the bulletproof fashion phenomenon, including the inequalities associated with neoliberalism and the militarization of civilian life. The book sheds light on the role of emotions in relation to discourses and perceptions of security, and encourages feminist and sociological studies to pay attention to the linkages between security, bodies, and dress. It is ideal for students and scholars interested in security and gun violence, culture and politics, neoliberalism and consumption, and bodies and emotions.

Barbara Sutton is a Professor in the Department of Women's, Gender, and Sexuality Studies at the University at Albany, SUNY. She is interested in body politics, multiple forms of violence, and intersecting inequalities, among other sociological issues. Her book *Bodies in Crisis: Culture, Violence, and Women's Resistance in Neoliberal Argentina* (2010) received the Gloria E. Anzaldúa Book Prize from the National Women's Studies Association. She is also the author of *Surviving State Terror: Women's Testimonies of Repression and Resistance in Argentina* (2018), which received Honorable Mentions for the Distinguished Book Award by the American Sociological Association Sex & Gender Section and for the Marysa Navarro Book Prize by the New England Council of Latin American Studies. She co-edited the book *Security Disarmed: Critical Perspectives on Gender, Race, and Militarization* with Sandra Morgen and Julie Novkov (2008) and *Abortion and Democracy: Contentious Body Politics in Argentina, Chile, and Uruguay* with Nayla Luz Vacarezza (2021).

Fashion Sociologies

The *Fashion Sociologies* book series speaks acutely and creatively to both fashion studies and sociology. It aims to make advances in the sociology of fashion, and sociology in general, clear to the broad community of fashion studies scholars worldwide. At the same time, it aims to showcase fresh thinking and research innovations in fashion studies to sociology and sociologists worldwide. This series stimulates and exhibits the productive synergies which arise when fashion and sociology are brought into explicit dialogue with each other.

Series Editor:
Anna-Mari Almila, Sapienza University of Rome, Italy
For proposal submissions please reach out to Series Editor Anna-Mari Almila at anna-mari.almila@uniroma1.it or Routledge Commissioning Editor Emily Briggs at emily.briggs@tandf.co.uk

Bulletproof Fashion
Security, Emotions, and the Fortress Body
Barbara Sutton

For more information please visit: https://www.routledge.com/Fashion-Sociologies/book-series/FASHSOC

BULLETPROOF FASHION

Security, Emotions, and the Fortress Body

Barbara Sutton

Routledge
Taylor & Francis Group
LONDON AND NEW YORK

Designed cover image: Moda Blindada. Illustration by Mariana Riquelme Pérez

First published 2023
by Routledge
4 Park Square, Milton Park, Abingdon, Oxon OX14 4RN

and by Routledge
605 Third Avenue, New York, NY 10158

Routledge is an imprint of the Taylor & Francis Group, an informa business

© 2023 Barbara Sutton

The right of Barbara Sutton to be identified as author of this work has been asserted in accordance with sections 77 and 78 of the Copyright, Designs and Patents Act 1988.

All rights reserved. No part of this book may be reprinted or reproduced or utilised in any form or by any electronic, mechanical, or other means, now known or hereafter invented, including photocopying and recording, or in any information storage or retrieval system, without permission in writing from the publishers.

Trademark notice: Product or corporate names may be trademarks or registered trademarks, and are used only for identification and explanation without intent to infringe.

British Library Cataloguing-in-Publication Data
A catalogue record for this book is available from the British Library

Library of Congress Cataloging-in-Publication Data
Names: Sutton, Barbara, 1970- author.
Title: Bulletproof fashion : security, emotions, and the fortress body / Barbara Sutton.
Description: Abingdon, Oxon ; New York, NY : Routledge, 2023. | Series: Fashion sociologies | Includes bibliographical references and index.
Identifiers: LCCN 2022057552 (print) | LCCN 2022057553 (ebook) | ISBN 9781032354316 (hardback) | ISBN 9781032354323 (paperback) | ISBN 9781003326854 (ebook)
Subjects: LCSH: Fashion—Social aspects—United States. | Ballistic fabrics—Social aspects—United States. | Body armor—Social aspects—United States. | Firearms—Social aspects—United States. | Security (Psychology)—United States.
Classification: LCC GT525 .S88 2023 (print) | LCC GT525 (ebook) | DDC 391.00973—dc23/eng/20230209
LC record available at https://lccn.loc.gov/2022057552
LC ebook record available at https://lccn.loc.gov/2022057553

ISBN: 978-1-032-35431-6 (hbk)
ISBN: 978-1-032-35432-3 (pbk)
ISBN: 978-1-003-32685-4 (ebk)

DOI: 10.4324/9781003326854

Typeset in Bembo
by Apex CoVantage, LLC

CONTENTS

Acknowledgments   *viii*

1   Security and the Fashion of Fear   1

2   Emotions and Security   31

3   Emotions and the Commercialization of Bulletproof Fashion   61

4   Aesthetics of Security: Emotions, Bodies, and Bulletproof Fashion   86

5   Feeling and Thinking About Bulletproof Fashion: Stakeholders' Perspectives   117

Conclusion   149

Index   *157*

ACKNOWLEDGMENTS

The ideas in this book developed, changed, and matured for more than a decade. My interest in bulletproof fashion emerged as an outgrowth of diverse research interests: on body politics, violence, militarization, and inequality. My research in Argentina, published in my book *Bodies in Crisis* (2010), traced how macro social processes, such as economic crises, get imprinted on individual bodies, including via beauty practices and clothing. Through my exposure to feminist critiques of war and militarization, I also became intrigued about how militarism finds its way to civilian bodies. For instance, popular education materials developed by the Women of Color Resource Center—the CD-ROM, *The Runway Peace Project* (2006)—encouraged me to think about the militarization of bodies manifested in clothing and fashion. I pursued this interest through an exploration of security matters more broadly, including in relation to gun violence in the United States. I am grateful to the work of scholar-activists such as Margo Okazawa-Rey and Gwyn Kirk, who inspired me to interrogate dominant meanings of security and to envision other possibilities. Collaborative work with Julie Novkov and Sandra Morgen, for our co-edited volume *Security Disarmed* (2008), also left a mark on how I think about security in relation to power and inequality.

I thank Erynn Masi de Casanova and Afshan Jafar for encouraging my research on bulletproof fashion when they invited me to contribute a chapter for an edited volume on globalization and the body. That study, published in 2013, turned out to be my first exploration of what I termed a "fashion of fear." In this book, I build on and expand that earlier research (sections of this work were first published in the following chapter and have been adapted and reprinted here with permission: Sutton, Barbara. 2013. "Fashion of Fear: Securing the Body in an Unequal Global World," pp. 75–99 in *Bodies Without Borders* edited by Erynn Masi de Casanova and Afshan Jafar. New York: Palgrave Macmillan). In 2013, I also participated in an international conference at the University of Cologne, Germany: "The Dilemmas of Security: How State and Non-State Actors Negotiate the Concept of Security," organized by Barbara Lüthi and Olaf Stieglitz. The feedback I received at the conference encouraged me to continue deepening my research, including in response to the conference organizer's invitation to contribute to a journal special issue on security and visuality. Thanks to that invitation, I embarked on a collaborative study that resulted in the following co-authored publication: Sutton, Barbara and Kate Paarlberg-Kvam. 2017. "Fashion of Fear for Kids." *InVisible Culture: An Electronic Journal for Visual Culture 25*, https://ivc.lib.rochester.edu/ready-fashion-of-fear-for-kids/. My thinking on bulletproof fashion in relation to children has been greatly influenced by my joint work with Kate Paarlberg-Kvam, to whom I am indebted.

The specific research for this book commenced in 2020 during the COVID-19 pandemic, amid major social upheaval and dislocation. I thank the participants in this study for their willingness to dedicate their time and share their experiences and perspectives on security with me—especially in that difficult context. I am also grateful for the research assistance tasks performed by Jem Lituchy, Siobhan Hansen, Eric Warren, and Alex Perry at different stages of the project. During the writing process, I benefited from my participation in various writing groups that met over Zoom to work together, including those hosted by Sociologists for Women in Society, the Gender and Feminist Studies Section of the Latin American Studies Association, and the Asociación Argentina para la Investigación en Historia de las Mujeres y Estudios de Género. These collective spaces of concentrated work and camaraderie sustained me throughout the project. Words of gratitude also go to colleagues and friends who provided valuable comments on drafts of specific chapters, including Kari Norgaard, Gwen D'Arcangelis, Oscar Pérez, Lisette Balabarca, Silvia Mejía, Alec Dawson, Liz Borland, and Erynn Masi de Casanova. I am particularly grateful to Ron Friedman and Nayla Vacarezza, who read and offered thoughtful feedback on multiple chapters and discussed with me ideas, questions, and observations throughout the project. This work was also strengthened by the constructive comments and suggestions offered by anonymous reviewers as well as by Routledge editor Emily Briggs, "Fashion Sociologies" series editor Anna-Mari Almila, and sociologist and researcher of gun violence prevention advocacy, Mary Bernstein.

The concentrated time for research and writing during my sabbatical was crucial to my ability to conduct this project. I am grateful to the University at Albany for making my sabbatical possible, and in particular to my colleagues in the Women's, Gender, and Sexuality Studies Department, Rajani Bhatia and Janell Hobson. I thank Alexandra Adams for her valuable suggestions when I was crafting my project proposal and applying for funding. My gratitude also goes to Jennifer Burrell, who encouraged me to apply to the Gerda Henkel Foundation and who shared valuable input during this process. My application was ultimately successful, and the funding I received from the foundation's "Special Programme Security, Society and the State" was vital to this work. I am extremely grateful for such support. Finally, I thank Mariana Riquelme Pérez for the illustration on the book cover, which helps to visually convey the blending of fashion and security concerns.

I wholeheartedly thank everyone who became interested in this project, asked pointed questions, offered critical perspectives, shared their expertise, listened to my ideas, and inspired me in myriad ways to write this book.

1
SECURITY AND THE FASHION OF FEAR

Guns and Armor

In the wake of persistent gun violence in the United States, news headlines have featured a controversial "back-to-school" item: the bulletproof backpack. Interest in this type of gear tends to rise after mass shootings, as communities across the country grapple with the grief, anger, and fear that such events generate. Companies in a growing security industry are offering not only ballistic backpacks but a wide array of bullet-resistant garments.[1] While some people see these products as a pragmatic response to security concerns, others decry this solution. In 2019, then-senator and presidential candidate Kamala Harris tweeted: "Parents shouldn't have to buy a bulletproof backpack for their child just to keep them safe at school. This shouldn't be normal."[2] Children's bulletproof apparel and accessories include hoodies with contemporary designs, colorful vests and jackets, and school-themed backpack inserts. Ballistic garments have also captured the attention of educators, advocates, and artists concerned about gun violence. A play called *Bulletproof Backpack*—drawing on interviews with students in Florida—sought to address the topic of school shootings. Similarly, a New York City art installation, *Back to School Shopping*, included garments that look like bulletproof vests for children.[3] As these examples reveal, bulletproof gear for everyday civilian use has become more than just a security object; it is a potent symbol of the unresolved problems, controversies, and emotions surrounding guns in U.S. society.

While in the United States armored attire for children has received particular attention after the deadly Sandy Hook Elementary School mass shooting in 2012,[4] this line of products joins a broader array of garments for adults, many of which blend ballistic protection with fashionable appearance. These items include elegant suits and trendy vests for men, stylish leather jackets and travel bags for women, and a range of backpacks and accessories for all genders. Furthermore, people in

DOI:10.4324/9781003326854-1

certain occupations can also find bulletproof garments for their daily work, such as armored lab coats for medical personnel and "discreet covert vests"[5] for teachers. In other words, ballistic gear has crossed the bounds of military and law enforcement fields and moved into a wider set of occupations and everyday civilian spaces.

These garments gain their protective features from bullet-resistant materials such as Kevlar, an extremely strong synthetic fiber developed by scientist Stephanie Kwolek in the mid-1960s while working for DuPont. Other materials are also used to produce different types of body armor, ideally combining strength and light weight to make it comfortable for civilian use.[6] Bulletproof apparel websites often refer to the National Institute of Justice (NIJ) ratings and standards of body armor performance, indicating different levels of protection against varying types of ammunition.[7]

One well-established producer of bulletproof fashion is Miguel Caballero, the founder of the eponymous Colombian-based company.[8] Speaking about his bulletproof clothing line for civilians, Caballero described the products as combining "discretion, comfort, and security in a single idea."[9] These types of garments are for people who fear for their lives, but as a reporter for the *New Yorker* put it, "don't want to dress like members of a SWAT team."[10] Over the years, the company has sold jackets, undershirts, polo shirts, tunics, and other clothes meant to protect users from bullets while also preserving style. Though originally focused on responding to security threats in Colombia, the company has exported products to numerous countries, including the United States, where the company MC Armor sells its products. Miguel Caballero's clientele includes wealthy people, but he also speculated that bulletproof fashion might be the way of the future: a time in which "everyone," and not just elite customers, would seek this protection.[11] Although this dystopian vision has not quite come to fruition, certain types of bulletproof products, such as armored backpacks, have been increasingly mainstreamed through their sale in popular retail stores.[12] Bulletproof garment companies also sell to the general public through their online sites. Armored apparel tends to be more expensive than their regular counterparts, yet various companies aim to reach a non-elite clientele as well, striving to make bulletproof items "more accessible to all."[13]

Why pay attention to bulletproof attire and accessories for civilians? What might following the trail of these objects reveal about contemporary social life, public fears and anxieties, and prevalent ideas about security? Bulletproof garments are paradigmatic of what I call a *fashion of fear:* the move to outfit the body with apparel and accessories aimed at maximizing personal security. While fear is not the only emotion associated with these items, it is a central one. This line of products can be conceptualized as a strategy to manage fear of violent attacks, whether the protection offered is effective or not. Attention to the fashion of fear also helps illuminate the attendant logics of militarization and neoliberalism, which shape countless policies and practices around the world. The fashion of fear integrates militarized technologies and civilian aesthetics, offers a market-based approach to security, and flourishes in the context of gun violence and gun proliferation. In the mode of a fortress, armored clothing creates a barrier between self and other, seemingly separating safety from danger.

This book explores an array of discourses, practices, and perceptions of security, and particularly examines the role of security-oriented clothing and accessories marketed as an appropriate response to certain forms of violence, from individualized gun violence to mass shootings. The focus on such products provides a unique entry point into larger debates about the meanings of security, the personal and political dimensions of social inequalities, and the centrality of emotions to experiences and perceptions of security/insecurity. The study delves into security cultures in the United States, moving from the broad realm of national security, and its militarized apparatus against external threats, to a narrower focus on the domestic civilian sphere, where debates about guns have been at the center of political controversy. At the same time, there are linkages between militarization for the purpose of national security and the militarization of everyday life on the "home front."[14] Versions of bulletproof attire meant for war zones—often imagined as foreign lands from a U.S. vantage point—have found their way closer to home, to be used in "normal" times. Hence, this study explores not only the creeping of militarized tactics into the space of civilian bodies but also the individualization of security as a personal responsibility in line with a neoliberal ethos. In this sense, this book's focus on the United States is particularly relevant, given how these products fit with this nation's cultural emphasis on the individual, its widespread reverence toward the military, and its permissive access to guns based on interpretations of the right to bear arms per the U.S. Constitution.[15]

Bulletproof apparel is connected to the question of guns in various ways: (1) It fits with contemporary *gun culture* in the United States, specifically its marked emphasis on self-defense.[16] In that sense, bulletproof fashion complements other security-oriented technologies used to "fort up" the body, including guns;[17] (2) It is a response to persistent *gun violence*, including mass shootings as well as targeted attacks linked to particular identities, social statuses, relationships, or occupations; (3) It raises the specter of *insecure security* in ways that overlap with the pitfalls of security strategies based on gun proliferation. While justifications for gun ownership often rest on self-defense arguments, guns can also be deployed for outright aggression (and they can be linked to self-injury and unintentional harm). In the case of intentional attacks, body armor has on occasion been part of the perpetrators' gear, bolstering the aggressor's destructive power. Among other cases, the perpetrator of a mass shooting targeting Black people in Buffalo, New York, in May 2022 was wearing body armor.[18]

To situate the commercialization of bulletproof fashion in the United States, it is important to consider the place of guns in U.S. society, including their social, legal, cultural, and political dimensions. Feminist scholars Cynthia Enloe and Joni Seager describe the United States as a "gun-toting nation," noting that it has the "most heavily armed civilian population in the world" and is the "largest global exporter of small arms."[19] According to global-level findings by the Small Arms Survey, the "United States has 4% of the world's population, but its civilians hold almost 40% of the world's firearms."[20] The same study also reveals that there are more firearms than people residing in the United States. This trend toward firearms acquisition has been exacerbated in recent times, especially during the COVID-19 pandemic, and characterized as a "domestic 'arms race.'"[21] When it comes to firearms, U.S. culture and legislation stand out for their notably permissive stance: "This is a country where civilian gun ownership is widely considered a 'right,' in contrast to many other countries, in which it is considered a 'privilege.'"[22]

While there is variation regarding gun policies, gun ownership, gun violence incidence, and attitudes about guns in different parts of the United States,[23] guns permeate various aspects of social life and significant political debates across the country.[24] In public discussions about guns, there are those who point to the propagation and lax regulation of guns as central to the problem of gun violence versus those who argue that more guns—for example, arming educators—would help prevent further harm.[25] Key social and political actors aiming to shape debates and policies about guns include "gun rights" organizations, such as the National Rifle Association, versus organizations associated with "gun control" advocacy, later "reconstituted [as a] 'gun violence prevention movement,'" as Kristin Goss explains.[26]

A nationwide debate about guns has raged in the United States as mass shootings in schools, universities, businesses, health care settings, sites of prayer, government buildings, and entertainment facilities have accumulated.[27] While these incidents rightly cause alarm, they are a minority of gun violence cases, and their reported prevalence varies according to the criteria used to define what constitutes a mass shooting. For instance, Rosanna Smart and Terry L. Schell noted that "depending on which data source is used, there were between six and 503 mass shootings in the United States in 2019."[28] According to the Gun Violence Archive, which defines mass shootings as events in which four or more people are shot or killed (excluding the shooter), there were 3,393 mass shootings between 2014 and 2021 in the United States, 690 of which occurred in 2021.[29] Beyond the numbers, mass shootings present disturbing features that have captured widespread media attention and public outcry. At the same time, more common forms of gun violence, especially impacting communities of color, do not seem to garner the same level of public concern.[30] Off the radar for many is also how the presence of firearms increases the risk of death of women experiencing intimate partner violence,[31] as well as the risks for children. In comparison to other countries, the United States presents heightened risks with regard to the victimization of women and children through the use of firearms.[32]

Whereas "concealed carry" is one of the ways in which guns are present in public life, guns have also become increasingly visible, not only during gun rights activist demonstrations but in other political events, adding a measure of volatility and danger to already tense situations.[33] In recent times, the presence of groups of heavily armed demonstrators at political rallies or at protests against COVID-19 public health measures heightened the need to critically address the role of firearms in U.S. society and ask to what extent they are compatible with democratic deliberation and expression.[34] Yet, based on the Second Amendment of the U.S. Constitution—on the right to keep and bear arms—guns are often naturalized in U.S. society, and attempts at regulation can be contentious.[35] For instance, at the policy level, litigation on gun rights made its way to the U.S. Supreme Court, successfully challenging New York State's statutory limitations on the ability of individuals to carry guns outside the home.[36] In this context, it is pertinent to consider how the commercialization of ballistic garments appeals to both unarmed civilians and those who see armor as a complement to their guns.

This book examines bulletproof fashion in the context of gun proliferation and gun violence in the United States. It also intervenes in broader conversations about security. Indeed, the fashion of fear needs to be understood in relation to the prominent role that concerns about security play in contemporary social life. Whether reliant on guns or bulletproof attire, personal security strategies are part of a wider landscape of security discourses and practices. The following section, then, turns to the contested and varied meanings of security to later consider the implications of the fashion of fear from this broad perspective.

Security Meanings, Discourses, and Practices

Security has become a dominant framework in contemporary societies, or as Didier Fassin put it, our current times can be characterized as "an age of security."[37] A yearning for security in an uncertain and often chaotic world has translated not only into the promise of state protection against the threat of violence[38] but also into a veritable industry of security products such as surveillance cameras, biometric technologies, alarm systems, tracking devices, policing software, and all manner of weapons purportedly for self-defense. Body armor for civilians adds to that list. Powerful institutions—whether the corporate media or the state—often raise alarm in relation to certain types of threats such as mass shootings or international terrorist attacks. Still, other insecurities threatening lives and bodies, including chronic food deprivation and health problems linked to systemic inequalities, might be taken for granted or receive less attention. Lately, the social devastation and massive loss of life associated with the COVID-19 pandemic starkly brought into the public eye the unequal vulnerabilities experienced by different population groups,[39] making the question of how we define security—and whose security seems to matter—ever more urgent.

Security is a common topic in political, scholarly, and media debates, but the concept can be hard to pin down. The notion of security is multifaceted and encompasses collective as well as individual aspirations and strategies to avert violence, coercion, and harm. In dominant discourse, certain forms of security, such as "national security," emphasize the approaches of the armed state apparatus, particularly the military. In contrast, international critiques of militaristic conceptions of security foreground more holistic understandings. The concept of "human security," for example, shifts our attention from state-centered militarized security to the security of people, including "personal," "food," "health," "economic," "environmental," "political," and "community" security.[40] Feminist activists' notions of "genuine security" endorse this broadened meaning, connecting it to "justice and respect for others across race, class, gender and national boundaries."[41] They also highlight the multiple insecurities that militarization in the name of national security generates. In that vein, critical scholars and activists have emphasized the costs of war and militarization: from the diversion of economic resources away from human needs (e.g., food, shelter, and education) and into military budgets, to the pollution of the environment, the destruction of vital infrastructure, and widespread and needless loss of lives.[42] Rampant inequalities have threatened the sense of security of large swaths of the population in many parts of the world, and these insecurities complexly intersect with militarization, beyond active war zones.[43]

These definitions hint at the breadth and multilayered dimensions of security. They also point to how different forms of insecurity do not necessarily stem from the armed attacks envisioned by governments bolstering the military apparatus or by civilians demanding gun rights. Rather, more widespread insecurity may derive from "slow violence,"[44] including the dumping of toxic waste into the environment, disease and malnutrition linked to economic programs that tear down social safety nets, and the bodily harm that so many workers encounter in the sweatshops of capitalist globalization. Yet in public discourse, security matters are often associated with technologies and policies that cannot alleviate most forms of insecurity, including structural forms of violence that result in serious bodily injury or loss of life. Obviously, bulletproof fashion cannot guard against these threats, and in fairness, they were not designed or intended to do so. However, one may wonder how a public focus on "self-defense"—whether with bulletproof garments or guns—obscures pervasive security threats that especially affect underserved populations and get in the way of more collective solutions.

Among other things, security measures aim to manage vulnerability. Judith Butler points out that vulnerability is "one central dimension of what might tentatively be called our embodiment";[45] it includes the possibility of being injured, but more broadly, it "may be a function of openness, that is, of being open to a world that is not fully known or predictable."[46] Individuals face specific vulnerabilities at different points of their lives, and vulnerability exposure varies across groups. These differences, however, are not necessarily inherent. On the contrary, vulnerability is affected by power relations that can increase or decrease risk of harm. We may ask: How do different approaches to security alleviate or increase vulnerability? Bryan S. Turner argues that institutions are one attempt to "reduce our vulnerability and attain security, but these institutional patterns are always imperfect, inadequate, and precarious."[47] Furthermore, institutions can create insecurity for some populations even when their stated mission is to provide protection (e.g., police and militaries). Technology has also been enlisted to the security cause—body armor is one example—but as with technological fixes for other social problems, such solutions may leave much to be desired and can have ambiguous or outright negative consequences.[48]

Human dependency on other people, material objects, the environment, and social institutions reminds us that security is "not a thing-in-itself; it is relational."[49] These considerations also mean that we need to think about security and vulnerability in the context of inequality and power. Inequalities in access to economic resources, justice systems, social standing, and political representation can affect the security of individuals and communities. Power is also implicated in various dimensions of security,[50] for instance, the power to define danger and determine who deserves to be protected, or the power to demand or implement forceful security measures that may displace harm to others. We can see this displacement at play in governmental initiatives to fortify and militarize national borders, which have pushed migrants to their death as they try riskier travel routes or border-crossing methods;[51] in politicians' racially coded calls for "law and order" that are likely to intensify state violence against people of color and marginalized communities;[52] or in how the U.S.-led "war on terror" produced massive civilian casualties, particularly in countries directly targeted, such as Afghanistan and Iraq.[53] No matter the definition of security, power and inequality should be considered. In this study, these types of issues emerged in conversations with different stakeholders about bulletproof fashion and security more broadly defined.

In political discourse, we often hear about security matters that include terrorism, wars, drug cartels, gangs, and cyber-attacks, for example. One way of responding to issues deemed a threat has been through "securitization." Barry Buzan, Ole Wæver, and Jaap De Wilde argued that a public issue is securitized when it "is presented as an existential threat, requiring emergency measures and justifying actions outside the normal bounds of political procedure."[54] Security concerns then can become the grounds for irregular detentions, increased surveillance, and declaration of states of exception. Political and social priorities bow to security, and extraordinary measures might be more likely to be accepted in its name. Many physical and social spaces became increasingly securitized after the September 11, 2001, terrorist attacks in the United States. Heightened security concerns have marked the design of public buildings, transportation systems, and the policies that govern us.[55] Yet private individuals do not necessarily trust the state to effectively protect them or may be afraid of being unfairly targeted by authorities as "security threats" on account of race, ethnicity, religion, nationality, or gender. Depending on the nature of risk and other factors, individuals may look for solutions in the private, non-governmental organizations, or community sectors.

State and non-state actors have played a role in security. In discussions about security, the state often appears as a principal actor framing security threats and implementing security measures, usually involving various degrees of militarization and policing (e.g., patrolled borders, military budgets, new weapons, and surveillance technologies). Non-state actors have also intervened in the security arena, including private militaries; non-governmental, charity, and media organizations; and international institutions.[56] While the interventions of some non-state actors may be alternative or oppositional to hegemonic state policy approaches, others may complement and bolster what Inderpal Grewal calls the "security state."[57] As we shall see, bulletproof fashion echoes aspects of militarized and law enforcement approaches to security, but as part of a wide range of private security initiatives it thrives under a neoliberal logic of individualized protection.

Militarization, Neoliberalism, and Bulletproof Apparel

As a security strategy, body armor traces back to the history of warfare, and as bulletproof fashion illustrates, it has percolated into civilian spaces not directly affected by war.[58] Ballistic products have also moved beyond security-related occupations. In the United States, it is generally legal for civilians to buy, own, or wear body armor, although some federal- and state-level restrictions apply to specific cases.[59] Notably, New York State passed legislation in 2022 that bans the sale, delivery, or purchase of body armor for civilians, except those in certain professions such as police officers, peace officers, military personnel, and those approved by the Department of State. Governor Kathy Hochul signed this legislation as part of a package of measures to address gun violence in the aftermath of two high-profile mass shootings: one resulting in the death of ten Black people in a grocery store in Buffalo, New York, and one in Robb Elementary School in Uvalde, Texas, which left 19 children and two teachers dead.[60] As mentioned, the accused mass shooter in Buffalo was wearing body armor. In the wake of these mass shootings, as in others, media coverage addressed body armor, particularly as businesses reported a rise in interest amid a heightened sense of insecurity.[61]

Much of the security apparatus, whether it is state- or market-based, operates under the logic of fortressing.[62] As a military structure, the fortress guards against "the enemy" by way of fortified fences and walls. However, in civilian society, fortresses of sorts also proliferate, addressing security concerns through enclosure/separation. They offer a sense of protection without having to address the structural conditions undergirding the violence and insecurity associated with certain spaces. Instead, fortress-like structures—national border walls, gated communities, guarded mansions, secured residences—often reinforce social privilege while fending off "the other," usually racialized and economically marginalized individuals and communities.

This tendency toward fortressing also reaches the body: Bulletproof clothing functions as a kind of mobile fortress at the micro-scale. We can think of various levels of fortressing as concentric circles with the body at the center, from the walled-off country to the gated community to the bulletproof vest. In fact, the name of one of the ballistic fleece vests sold by the company Bullet Blocker is as literal as it can be: "Fortress."[63] In that vein, the goal of bulletproof fashion is to achieve security through what can be thought of as a "fortress body" (even as many of these garments hide the militarized components through aesthetic devices).[64] The use of armor has been a common way of fortressing military bodies, and bulletproof fashion reflects how civilian bodies can also become militarized through everyday technologies of security. This approach resonates with what Elisabeth Anker calls "*mobile sovereignty*," in reference to citizens who arm themselves in a quest for security amid an "era of uncertainty in the United States."[65]

Bulletproof fashion fits with the privatization of security and the role of non-state actors as agents identifying and responding to insecurity in the context of neoliberalism.[66] As an ideology exalting the "free market," neoliberalism is associated with policies that reduce the role of the state in social welfare provision, and instead promotes private initiative, personal responsibility, and entrepreneurship.[67] In practical terms, neoliberal governance has helped exacerbate the inequalities derived from unbridled capitalism, producing multiple forms of "precarity,"[68] while expecting citizens to be responsible for their individual well-being. Still, with respect to militarized security and policing, the United States does dedicate enormous financial resources, often at the expense of investment in other areas such as education, housing, and environment.[69] Strong military and police investment is apparently not in contradiction with the neoliberal goal of reducing state expenditures, and in fact, armed forces are sometimes deployed to protect private property, elite interests, and U.S. business abroad. Private contractors partaking in overseas wars, private security companies operating domestically, and individual citizens involved in providing their own security are all part of the complex configuration of contemporary security apparatuses.

The United States' heavily armed security state, with militarized expenditures well above other countries,[70] coexists with an ethos of individualism and legally upheld ideas about armed self-protection. The latter notion has materialized, among other things, in the proliferation of guns owned by private citizens ("mobile sovereigns" in Anker's terms). In this sense, rather than the sole purview of the state, security has become another privatized commodity, reflected not only in widespread civilian purchase of guns but also in the form of civilian armor for sale. As civilians acquire guns and these circulate in U.S. society, both legally and illegally, it would not be surprising if more people expected that, at some point, those guns might be turned against them. Bulletproof garments in the United States need to be understood in relation to the massive presence of guns, the cases of gun violence that garner public attention, and civilian spaces that are experienced as war zones of sorts.

As private contractors and weapon manufacturers know, war can be profitable, and in civilian milieus with security concerns, clothing companies can also carve out a market niche even in "peace times." Miguel Caballero found inspiration for his line of clothing in Colombia, a country with a prolonged history of state, guerilla, and paramilitary violence. In a media interview, Caballero expressed that "a product like this, can only be created in a country like this,"[71] alluding to pervasive violence in Colombian society. Yet it was in response to school shootings in the United States that his company started producing bulletproof products for children.[72] Companies that specialize in bulletproof apparel sometimes refer to the expertise or product quality stemming from linkages to security and military-oriented spaces, people, and occupations. ArmorMe boasted connections to militarized Israel as a mark of quality, emphasizing that "Israel has amassed the world's most renowned expertise in self-defense and terrorism countermeasures."[73] According to media reports, the CEO of Leatherback Gear had law enforcement experience in the Department of Homeland Security,[74] and the founder of Bullet Blocker drew on "the knowledge he gained while training as a R.O.K. Ranger in the United States Army, along with his experience as a Deputy Sheriff and firearms instructor."[75] In these ways, we can trace the path of militarization into civilian households, schools, and bodies through the commercialization of bulletproof garments and accessories.

Borrowing from Cindi Katz—who has written about the pervasiveness of security measures in the post-9/11 urban landscape[76]—we can think of bulletproof clothing and related products for civilians as "banal" security objects that may be fulfilling various functions besides offering protection.[77] Their implicit message is that security is available via purchase, militarized security is necessary, and security is a personal responsibility.[78] This connects to an overarching politics of fear, from fear of terrorist attacks to mass shootings in everyday spaces.[79] The promotion of these products also fit with what historian Caroline E. Light referred to as a "DIY [do-it-yourself] security ethos" that encourages individuals to take charge of their own security, particularly in the face of a state perceived as incapable of protecting law-abiding citizens.[80] While Light analyzes this ethos in reference to the increased promotion and appeal of gun ownership for self-protection, and in the context of older patriotic—and exclusionary—narratives about "the heroic armed citizen,"[81] there are some resonances when it comes to body armor. Not only is the emphasis of bulletproof products on self-defense, but this type of DIY-security is promoted in the marketplace. Furthermore, the strategy is in line with a neoliberal capitalist ethos that devolves to individual citizens the responsibility for their well-being. "Law-abiding" citizens are to find solutions to insecurity in the marketplace, where not only are products sold but also emotions, desires, dreams, fantasies, and—pertinent to bulletproof products—the promise of security and peace of mind.

Whereas a number of bulletproof garment companies cater only or mainly to military and law enforcement sectors—which is where much of the body armor industry's profits are located—some companies specialize in civilian garments, including for private citizens not employed in security-related jobs. According to Goldstein Market Intelligence, the "defense sector accounted for the largest revenue of 60% in global bullet proof clothing market in 2016."[82] The specialized "civilian/VIP" market is also profitable and predicted to grow according to reports, but Goldstein Market Intelligence pointed out that "[t]here are very few companies around the world that design a range of fashionable bulletproof clothing for a variety of clients."[83] The global bulletproof garments market has been expected to "reach USD 5.8 billion by the end of the forecast period [2035] owing to government funding programs and advanced technologies for the production of bullet proof clothing."[84] Two of the companies included in this study, Aspetto and Miguel Caballero, are mentioned as global players in the Goldstein report. While the defense and law enforcement markets are in many ways distinct from the one geared toward private citizens, there are products that cross over sectors in modified form, blurring the lines between military, police, security personnel, and civilians.[85] Different market research assessments mention factors such as social and political unrest, rising violence, armed conflict, terrorist activities, and an abundance of arms circulation as important elements in the growth of the bulletproof garments market globally.[86] These types of phenomena certainly can trigger public anxiety, fear, and concern, and it is not just governments that seek body armor to secure their forces. Among the civilians who fear for their physical safety, there are those who have turned to body armor for protection as well.

Interestingly, in reflecting on his bulletproof vest during war reporting in the Middle East, journalist Kenneth Rosen troubles the promise of security associated with this object. He makes a point to recall the words of the garment's salesperson before his trip to a conflict zone: "Nothing's bullet*proof*. The thing's only bullet *resistant*."[87] Other people in the industry echo such observation,[88] and so do governmental analyses of the value of body armor.[89] For instance, bulletproof vests have saved the lives of law enforcement officers, or protected them from serious injuries, in over 3,000 cases since the late 1980s;[90] however, many officers were also killed while wearing their vests (this can happen for a variety of reasons, including being shot in parts of the body not covered with ballistic materials, or being shot with weapons that body armor is not specifically designed to resist).[91] In *Bulletproof Vest*, as we follow Rosen through his travels in armed conflict areas, we learn that his body armor operated more like a talisman—the symbol of protection—than what might actually keep him safe. In fact, throughout Rosen's journey, we learn about the occasions in which it would not have been wise to wear the armored vest, and the many ways in which it would be ineffective against plausible threats, such as hitting a landmine, being kidnapped, or other kinds of attacks for which this gear would be practically useless. He mused: "That which is meant to make you invincible is rarely certain to work and most definitely will not be painless or without damage."[92] If the utility of body armor was rendered questionable even in a war zone, one may wonder, what is its role in civilian spaces and in the absence of war?

Bodies, Emotions, and Fashion

Multiple social actors—states, organizations, institutions, individuals—have taken measures to address security concerns, especially those deemed a violent threat. How does the body, including embodied emotions and inequalities, figure in such security-oriented measures? After all, as Columba Peoples and Nick Vaughan-Williams note in their account of gender approaches to human security, "the physical body is very often the site of security/insecurity."[93] Bodies are protected, surveilled, armed, or disarmed as part of societal, governmental, and individual efforts to produce security. In that vein, it is important to consider who might be viewed as worthy of protection, as a member of the body politic, and who might be instead construed as a security threat.

Bodies matter to securitization. Studies show how, particularly after 9/11, states have deployed a number of security-oriented measures in which the body takes center stage: body scanning, biometrics, and gender and ethnoracial profiling at airports and border-crossings, for example.[94] In these cases, the body is treated as a site of information and surveillance that can bolster authorities' ability to identify potential threats. Clothing can also play a role in this context, whether in relation to the users' physical appearance or the materials incorporated in the garments. For instance, as airport security rituals became more invasive and time consuming, individual passengers have had reason to be concerned about additional scrutiny, delays, and potentially unpleasant interactions with security personnel. Post-9/11, some clothing businesses and designers started devising apparel that would help travelers go through checkpoints swiftly, replacing materials that could set off detectors.[95] Such initiatives implicitly illustrate the embodied contours of a political economy of fear and state control flourishing under the banner of national security. Indeed, fear, securitization, and business profits can go together as market sectors capitalize on a more expansive and sensitive security apparatus.

This book draws linkages between security and the body but from a different angle. While the fashion of fear relates to prevalent state and private efforts to achieve security regarding selected forms of violence, the focus here is not on bodies deemed potentially dangerous, but on what kinds of bodies are represented by different protection strategies and what narratives and meanings are associated with such bodies. That is, fashion of fear technologies are not designed to verify whether particular individuals constitute a threat but to secure individual bodies against potential threats. Still, this raises the question of how the construction of threat and danger is distributed, and who is seen as a legitimate or illegitimate wearer of bulletproof garments. The body can function as "evidence" of security or threat, and power relations shape the interpretation of such evidence.[96]

Returning to the idea of fortresses, and linking them to the body, we can think about the fashion of fear as a way of "forting up" the body—to render it strong and impenetrable.[97] Various types of insecurity are often addressed through borders, fences, and protective barriers, and the body is the last frontier. Enclosing or shielding the body in this way, while maintaining a sense of autonomy, is consistent with other individualistic strategies prevalent under neoliberalism, such as gated communities.[98] Yet whether such methods can provide security in a deeper sense might be questionable. Samira Kawash asks, "[D]oes enclosure endanger body precisely to the extent that it forecloses and denies the very connections and interdependencies that make it possible for there to be any body at all?"[99] The logic of the fortress body is not one of openness or connection but of separation and suspicion. In that sense, it is worth thinking about what kinds of subjectivities the fortress body fosters, and how they relate to broader social processes. In the context of neoliberalism and neoconservatism, Zeynep Gambetti and Marcial Godoy-Anativia considered "whether we are facing what might be called a global production of subjectivities of security."[100]

The fashion of fear adds to the creation of "subjectivities of security" and can also be thought of as a "technology of power" operating at the level of the body, in the Foucauldian sense.[101] This is the case to the extent that it fosters forms of embodiment and subjectivity that are compliant with a militarized social order, even outside the confines of the military. Through bulletproof fashion, the ways of the military—a powerful social institution—reach individual civilian bodies. Kenneth T. MacLeish points out that, in the military, armor and other technologies are meant to generate "subjects who, thanks to their insensitivity to pain and their immunity from danger, can reliably be sent to face bullets, bombs, and the other attendant threats of a war zone."[102] In her study of private armed response officers in South Africa, Tessa Diphoorn notes that the bulletproof vests that the officers wear come to be experienced as part of their bodies, integral to the "bodily capital" that enable them to assert masculinized power and authority in the face of danger.[103] Many civilians, beyond those in security sector occupations, experience or perceive everyday spaces as dangerous zones, and some decide to wear armor, mimicking the strategies of military and law enforcement. While certain kinds of gear are conspicuous—like the bulletproof vests, weaponry, and military-style camouflage donned by some pro-gun and "militia" type groups—other civilians seek armor that is hidden. The goal of such garments is to produce immunity to bullets for people engaged in business other than war or law enforcement activities, while also blending in with civilian society.

As feminists and other critical scholars have noted, militarization seeps through many aspects of everyday life, shaping political priorities, cultural events, governmental budgets, and also individual bodies. This is the case, for instance, through clothing choices.[104] While militarized fabrics and patterns—such as khaki and "camo" (camouflage)—are visible in many civilian items, they have no inbuilt protective features, except perhaps symbolically. Instead, bulletproof garments are designed to protect users from bullets, but this dimension may be hidden. The body is militarized inconspicuously, in this way keeping the secret both of ballistic protection and of inequality (especially if one considers the extra financial cost of armor). Militarized clothing, whether armored or not, is one example of how war-related rationality and technology become integrated into civilian life via the body.

References to the looks of ballistic apparel hint at the need to consider not only the *fear* aspect in "fashion of fear" but also the *fashion* component. A focus on fashion brings to the fore social and cultural dimensions such as distinction, style, performance, self-expression, and consumption. In this sense, clothing can also serve to demarcate boundaries based on class, race-ethnicity, gender, and other social hierarchies. Scholars studying the body sociologically have addressed the significance of clothing with respect to identity, beauty, work, culture, and power; however, linking these topics to the subjective and political experience of fear is rarer.[105] In this book, we can see how notions of distinction and conformity are mobilized through garments that are meant not only to dress the body but also to offer ballistic protection. And yet, even if this solution were the most desirable, it is not available to everyone. Some types of bulletproof clothing are tailored-made and have a high price attached, reinforcing privilege and elite status. Products displayed on company websites can range from hundreds to thousands of dollars. For instance, Talos Ballistics Woman's Falcon Leather Jacket was selling for $850.[106] Aspetto's Venezia Grey Brown Windowpane suit ascended to $3,825 once the armor with the highest protection was selected.[107] Bullet Blocker offered the Bulletproof Gucci Diaper Bag for $3,100 and the Bulletproof Saint Laurent Leather Moto Jacket for $6,450.[108] Other items geared toward the general public can be unaffordable to many. For example, Wonder Hoodie's Kid's Bulletproof Hoodie was offered at the discount price of $450, and the Denim jacket for $545 (originally $725).[109] Additionally, social disparities permeate certain representations of bulletproof clothing, making some bodies seem to be better suited than others for different kinds of protection.[110] Attending to various features related to bulletproof apparel—including costs, targeted clientele, and visual and textual representations—offers clues regarding the construction of vulnerability and protection across differences.[111]

Bulletproof fashion is part of a wider universe of garments connected with the goal of enhancing personal security. Not all of these products have ballistic components, but they often relate in one way or another to the presence of guns. In the United States, widespread gun ownership goes together with security-oriented garments and gadgets that combine functionality, comfort, and even style.[112] For instance, as the number of people with permits to carry concealed guns increased over the years, clothing companies such as Woolrich designed fashionable wear that can also hide guns "stylishly."[113] Although much of the gun world is masculinized, increasing numbers of women are also gun owners, seek firearms training, and have formed their own gun organizations, such as The Well Armed Woman (with chapters across the country).[114] Some companies offering security-oriented apparel specialize in women's gear specifically. For instance, Gun Goddess offers "feminine & functional concealed carry"[115] and Femme Fatale sells holster corsets and garters with embroidered lace—items described as the "sexiest undercover ever!"[116] Both concealed carry clothing and bulletproof fashion items are indicative of social milieus experienced as threatening, where some people decide that arming/armoring themselves is imperative to achieve security. At the same time, some of these clothing items patently underscore the value attached to bodies that conform to hegemonic notions of style and fashion, in turn overlaid with gender, racial, sexual, and class meanings.

In analyzing these dimensions, my research on bulletproof fashion draws from the interdisciplinary fields of feminist and body studies, which have paid attention to inequalities in relation to a wide array of bodily experiences and practices, from beauty, to health, sexuality, reproduction, sports, religion, and sexual violence.[117] However, the question of security and embodiment in relation to guns and gun violence is less frequent in this literature.[118] Through theorization and empirical analyses of the fashion of fear, this study explores the role of body representations and inequalities in security discourses. It also points to the need to account for embodied emotions since security matters are often experienced emotionally, and bulletproof fashion is steeped in emotions (including but not only fear). In his discussion of the sociology of emotions, Eduardo Bericat explains that "*emotions constitute the bodily manifestation of the importance that an event in the natural or social world has for a subject. Emotion is a bodily consciousness that signals and indicates this importance.*"[119] Bulletproof clothing and related body accessories emerge as a response to a problem that causes fear and anxiety, or at least an alert and "prepared" stance. While bulletproof products offer a practical solution (to keep the body safe and protect vital organs), these objects are also meant to operate at the level of feeling:

to provide peace of mind. Additionally, as it will be shown, the stylistic features and representations of some of these ballistic products appeal to varied social identities.

While bulletproof apparel is meant to shield the body from gun injuries, there are also garments and devices designed to address other bodily dangers, such as sexual violence. These items include anti-rape garments, vaginal inserts that would harm an unwelcomed penis, and nail polish with the ability to detect drugs poured in drinks to facilitate date rape.[120] In the case of these technologies, the body becomes the focal point of efforts to protect against personal security threats, but, as we shall see, it is not only pragmatic concerns that drive design. A number of these products seem to do additional, more intangible, affective work.

In that vein, D. Asher Ghertner, Hudson McFann, and Daniel Goldstein point out that security is "as much a sensibility as a calculative logic—something felt as much as thought."[121] In other words, the realm of security engages a range of emotions, diffused feelings, and sensibilities. Fear figures prominently in several security discourses and strategies: whether it is politicians instilling fear of immigrants depicted as "terrorists" and "rapists" to justify fortified borders,[122] companies selling home security devices to avert intruders and give peace of mind to property owners, or bulletproof garment companies that remind consumers of the fear and terror of mass shootings while also offering emotional relief through their products. Yet we might ask to what extent these strategies help prevent harm and for whom, and whether and how they might displace fear and insecurity onto people not deemed worthy of protection. These considerations apply at both the national and international levels.[123] As we shall see, emotions are central to the narratives, perceptions, and experiences of security addressed in this book, both in relation to bulletproof garments specifically and in terms of security more broadly conceived.

In her book *The Cultural Politics of Emotion*, Sara Ahmed notes that "[e]motions shape the very surfaces of bodies, which take shape through the repetition of actions over time, as well as through orientations towards and away from others."[124] Fear is an emotion that orients away from that which is perceived as threatening, and it is sometimes managed through several types of barriers and enclosures that separate self from other. Bulletproof fashion embodies this separation, literally shaping the contours of the body and crystallizing fear into armor. At the same time, the promise embedded in this commercialized object is to transform fear into peace of mind, through an alchemy of sorts. However, enclosure and armoring might not be the only way of dealing with fear or the conditions that generate fear in the first place. Other strategies and emotional orientations—for example, based on care and mutuality—can produce other forms of security. In that sense, this project encourages us to consider security beyond that offered by arming and armoring strategies and to envision collective futures and social relationships that are not primarily based on fear and other aversive emotions. The concept of a fashion of fear, and the research stemming from it, provides a pathway toward theorizing and examining the emotions that permeate public life in relation to security; the gendered, classed, and racialized dimensions of security; and the centrality of "the body" to different security strategies.

Research Approach

In order to explore discourses, practices, and perceptions of security—and the role of bulletproof fashion within it—I adopted a dual research strategy that combined an "object-centered approach" focused on ballistic garments and a broader inquiry into different stakeholders' concerns and ideas about security.[125] In this way, the project relied on a narrow and wide lens simultaneously, which allowed me to examine a specific type of security object as well as to widen the angle through an examination of the meanings of security from multiple perspectives.

The book builds upon my longstanding interest and research on body politics and diverse forms of violence. In particular, I extend two previous studies on bulletproof fashion. In the first one, conducted in 2012, I performed a content analysis of Miguel Caballero (MC)'s website, supplemented by media reports, focusing on bulletproof clothing for adults.[126] I found that women and men were differently addressed by the company, and I analyzed the class and ethnoracial representations in the marketing of the products. My second study, conducted with Kate Paarlberg-Kvam in 2014, examined company content and media coverage of the Miguel Caballero Kids line, consisting of armored backpacks and clothing.[127] Here, too, we found that social inequalities played a significant role, not only in terms of the products' price tag but in how they seem to protect more than the vulnerable bodies of children. Through colorful patterns and designs, these garments' aesthetics also worked to preserve a sense of innocence for relatively privileged kids. Themes related to militarization, neoliberal globalization, and the social construction of vulnerability appear in both projects.

The present study incorporates these findings and expands the scope of inquiry to additional companies and products, as well as includes the viewpoints of various stakeholders. I had initially researched the Miguel Caballero company, given that it is well-established in the bulletproof fashion industry, has transnational reach, and has attracted extensive media coverage over the years.[128] Yet other companies also compete for a share of the civilian market, including relative newcomers. Overall, these companies produce a range of security-oriented garments and accessories tailored for specific populations. Drawing on my previous studies, and as I expanded my research, the following questions guided my inquiry: What kinds of bodies are foregrounded and purportedly protected through bulletproof products? How do ideas of femininity and masculinity, childhood innocence, ethnoracial and national difference, and class-infused identities play out in public discourse about these products? How do key stakeholders perceive and talk about these products and what are their broader perspectives on security? As I proceeded through my research, one dimension that was embedded in my concept of "fashion of fear," but that I had not focused on, became particularly salient: emotions. The significance of emotions—including but transcending fear—was more readily apparent in the analysis stage of this project and ended up being a central aspect addressed in this book.

I conducted my inquiry through a multimethod design that included content analysis, focus groups, and individual semi-structured interviews. The study features content analysis of online materials pertaining to bulletproof fashion, including the websites of companies, corporate videos, media reports, and other available company information and news coverage.[129] I selected companies that were producing and/or selling bulletproof garments and accessories to private citizens (though some businesses additionally catered to militaries and law enforcement), and that were either based in the United States or had logistics centers or branches in the country. The companies include the following: ArmorMe, Aspetto, AVS Active Violence Solutions, Bac-Tactical, Bullet Blocker, Bulletproof Everyone, Bulletproof Zone, Guard Dog Security, Innocent Armor, Leatherback Gear, MC Armor/Miguel Caballero, Safeguard Clothing, Talos Ballistic, Thyk Skynn, TuffyPacks, Wonder Hoodie and an apparently no longer active business, M30 Bullet Proof Apparel (Given the changing nature of websites and the evolution of businesses, it is important to note that the information presented and analyzed here is based on what was available at the time of data collection/access).[130] I also gathered the perspectives of corporate representatives of several of these companies through publicly available media interviews, and I additionally conducted two semi-structured interviews with members of this industry, whose names are kept confidential.

While my earlier work on the fashion of fear was solely based upon already available company materials and media reports regarding Miguel Caballero products, for this book, I not only expanded the number of companies examined but also enriched and deepened my analysis by talking with different stakeholders regarding their notions of security and views about the products. In order to explore different perspectives, I conducted eight targeted focus groups (4–6 participants each) with members of strategic constituencies: gun violence prevention advocates, gun rights supporters, law enforcement officers, activists in organizations addressing police violence, members of organizations addressing sexual/gender violence, health care workers, teachers, and mothers of school-age children.[131] The focus groups as a whole amounted to 37 participants (see the following note for demographic information).[132]

To form the focus groups, I reached out to diverse individuals and members of organizations and institutions in New York State, where my university is located. In addition to the possibility of accessing pre-existing networks based on my knowledge of and ties to the area, I was able to identify many groups and organizations that are relevant to the study, while still covering a region ruled by the same federal and state-level laws and policies. The research started in 2020 during the COVID-19 pandemic, and at the time, all interactive activities with participants had to take place online. I held focus group discussions via Zoom, one of the video-conference platforms that many people became familiar with in the context of the pandemic. This facilitated the inclusion of participants from across the state, including urban, suburban, and rural areas. The focus group meetings lasted approximately one hour to an hour and a half, and the discussion was guided by my questions in the role of moderator. While at times we had to deal with technological difficulties, these were rapidly resolved, and the meetings generally proceeded smoothly. The discussions were recorded, transcribed, and analyzed, and the real names of participants changed to pseudonyms for confidentiality purposes. In terms of the issues discussed, I asked participants to reflect on the meanings of security, the strategies they believe would promote security, and the roles different social actors might play. Within that general framework, focus groups also discussed issues related to gun violence, gun rights, and/or experiences with guns—topics that sometimes emerged spontaneously or through my questions regarding the place of guns in U.S. society. Relatedly, I asked participants to share their perspectives on bulletproof fashion, and as a prompt to the discussion, I supplemented my questions with images of assorted products that appeared on company websites and media coverage.[133]

As with any study, my work was influenced by the specific historical moment in which it unfolded, but with a force I could not have anticipated. The period of my research—which started in September 2020, with prior preparations during the summer—was characterized by economic crisis, upended work and family routines, the spread of illness and loss of life, and myriad everyday challenges associated with the pandemic. The topic of violence and inequality became particularly salient, while also reflecting longtime forms of injustice. For instance, scholars and advocates pointed to how the isolation and tensions linked to the pandemic exacerbated the risk of gender violence in the home. Racial violence and police brutality also came to the fore in late May of 2020 as the public witnessed on camera the killing of George Floyd, an unarmed Black man suffocated under the knee of a white police officer (Derek Chauvin, later convicted for murder). While this case became emblematic, country-wide protests during the summer of 2020 denounced more generalized and ingrained patterns of racial injustice, marching under the banner "Black Lives Matter" (BLM). The ramifications of these events could still be felt as I initiated my research.

Additionally, this was a period of political turmoil surrounding the 2020 presidential election season in the United States, in which incumbent president Donald Trump and former vice-president Joseph Biden faced off. Around this time, armed right-wing and white nationalist groups became more visible in street protests and in self-appointed vigilante roles, including in spaces where Black Lives Matter demonstrations were taking place. In this context, there were also instances of organized armed Black people who showed up in some rallies to demand social change, particularly in relation to racial injustice and the killing of Black individuals by the police.[134] On January 6, 2021, shortly before the last two focus groups in this study took place, large numbers of Trump supporters stormed the nation's Capitol to contest the certification of the election that handed victory to Biden. Among other things, this was a historic breach of security. Notorious scenes of the day included chaos and violence as Trump supporters pushed to enter the Capitol building, the image of an armed standoff at the door of the House Chamber, the display of a noose and gallows structure outside the U.S. Capitol, and the sight of a white man carrying a large confederate flag inside the building. Not surprisingly, many of these social and political issues emerged in the focus groups as participants engaged in discussions about security.

As it could also be expected, I was not exempt from the effects of the tumultuous and emotional context of my study, trying to conduct research in seemingly cataclysmic times. Furthermore, as someone originally from Argentina who grew up during a military dictatorship, the challenges to democracy I was witnessing in the United States—however imperfect a system to begin with—sent all my internal alarms into high alert. I, too, was drawn into emotion-filled conversations about various aspects of "security," not just from a scholarly perspective but in my personal life. In my study, this meant approaching a difficult, multifaceted, and often "raw" topic, aiming to keep my mind open, checking my own assumptions, managing my emotions, and learning what different perspectives had to teach me. As someone who has lived and worked for a long time in the United States, but is still marked as an outsider, I sometimes struggled to find my footing in the project. I worried, "Am I getting it right?" Upon reflection, I realized that my life trajectory between Argentina and the United States has also provided me with a distinct vantage point, one that might have allowed me to ask certain questions and interrogate "common sense" assumptions animating life in the United States.

Overview

The following chapters present key research findings. To situate bulletproof fashion in context, I examine the role of emotions in relation to security concerns embedded in broader issues, including the pandemic, gun violence, social unrest, crime, policing, protest, and injustice (Chapter 2). This discussion not only illuminates contextual factors that were salient during the time of my research but also adds to understandings about the relationship between security and emotions. Following this analysis, I narrow the lens from security broadly defined to a focus on one specific security concern, also involving emotions: the possibility of being injured or killed with a firearm (whether as a result of a targeted attack or because of a mass shooting). I explore how such emotional events ignite and sustain a particular market-based approach to security: the commercialization of bulletproof fashion. I analyze the representations of bulletproof products, primarily in company materials, in relation to a range of emotions, including fear and anxiety, sadness and grief, anger and rage, love and care, and pride (Chapter 3). I then discuss the aesthetics of security reflected by different bulletproof garments and accessories, exploring the connection between emotions, bodies, and fashion in this particular security arena. In this analysis, I pay particular attention to gender, in intersection with other vectors of difference such as class and race-ethnicity, as well as the garments directed to different age groups (Chapter 4). Finally, I discuss the overlapping and distinct perspectives offered by different stakeholders about bulletproof products, once again revealing the emotional contours of this particular security strategy (Chapter 5). In the book's conclusion, I come back to the "big picture" of security, with an invitation to consider what security means to each of us, and what types of worlds might different visions of security prefigure.

Notes

1. In this book I use terms such as "bullet-resistant," "bulletproof," "ballistic," or "armored" interchangeably to refer to products designed to avert gunshot injury. While "bulletproof" may be the most frequent designation, companies sometimes note that these products do not make one invincible but that the materials they contain are "resistant" to different types of bullets (depending on the level of protection offered by specific products).
2. Kamala Harris (@KamalaHarris), "Parents Shouldn't Have to Buy a Bulletproof Backpack for Their Child Just to Keep Them Safe at School," *Twitter*, July 26, 2019, 3:30PM, https://twitter.com/KamalaHarris/status/1154836333531189255?ref_src=twsrc%5Etfw.
3. *Bulletproof Backpack* was directed by Kody C. Jones and written by the playwright Eric Coble. See A. A. Cristi, "Florida Rep's Conservatory Returns to the Arcade with World Premiere Bulletproof Backpack," July 21, 2021, www.broadwayworld.com/ft-myers-naples/article/Florida-Reps-Conservatory-Returns-To-The-Arcade-with-World-Premiere-BULLETPROOF-BACKPACK-20210721. The artist who created the *Back to School Shopping* art installation uses the nom de plume WhIsBe. See, Roselle Chen, "Tiny Bulletproof Vests Centerpiece of New York Art Exhibit on School Shootings," *Sojourners*, June 18, 2019, https://sojo.net/articles/tiny-bulletproof-vests-centerpiece-new-york-art-exhibit-school-shootings.
4. This school shooting in Newtown, Connecticut, resulted in the death of 20 children and six adults. The 20-year-old perpetrator killed himself afterward.
5. "The Need for Bulletproof Vests in Schools," *Safeguard Clothing*, accessed October 13, 2020, www.safeguardclothing.com/articles/ballistic-protection-for-teachers/.
6. Although Kevlar came to be associated with body armor, what prompted Stephanie Kwolek's research was the goal of developing "a replacement for the steel used in tires (DuPont wanted something lighter to improve gas mileage in anticipation of a fuel shortage)" (Dan Samorodnitsky, "You Can Thank Chemist Stephanie Kwolek for Bulletproof Vests and Yoga Pants," *Smithsonian Magazine*, August 21, 2019, www.smithsonianmag.com/innovation/you-can-thank-chemist-stephanie-kwolek-bulletproof-vests-and-yoga-pants-180972948/. See also, Kenneth R. Rosen, *Bulletproof Vest* [London: Bloomsbury, 2020]). Body armor may be hard or soft, and the exact materials vary, including ceramic or steel plates and different synthetic materials. See, for example, "Body Armor Materials," *Body Armor News*, accessed September 29, 2022, www.body-armornews.com/body-armor-materials/.
7. For information and updates on these standards, see National Institute of Justice, "Body Armor Performance Standards," *nij.ojp.gov*, February 22, 2018, https://nij.ojp.gov/topics/articles/body-armor-performance-standards.
8. The company Miguel Caballero was founded in the early 1990s (See "Trajectory," *Miguel Caballero*, accessed September 29, 2022, https://en.miguelcaballero.com/about-us/). However, bulletproof fashion for civilians predates this business. A 1981 article from the *New York Times*, for example, mentions that "a dozen makers of bulletproof clothing catered to civilian buyers" at the time, including Tim Zuffle's Solutions—based in New Orleans—that "specialize[d] in 'fashion conscious ballistic apparel'" (Michael de Courcy Hinds, "One Answer to Violence: Bulletproof Clothing," *New York Times*, May 16, 1981, ProQuest Historical Newspapers, 21).
9. "Bulletproof Clothing in Colombia," *Metropolis*, January 15, 2009, Video, www.youtube.com/watch?v=Tp0At-a-_TQ.
10. David Owen, "Survival of the Fitted," *New Yorker*, September 26, 2011, 69–73, 69.
11. Journeyman Pictures, "Bulletproof Fashion," Video, March 31, 2008, www.journeyman.tv/film/3893/bulletproof-fashion.
12. For instance, at the time of this research, bulletproof backpacks were reportedly available at Bed Bath & Beyond, Home Depot, and Kmart.
13. "Our Story," *Wonder Hoodie*, accessed September 30, 2020, https://wonderhoodie.com/pages/our-story.
14. See Enloe's groundbreaking and extensive feminist critique of militarization, for example, Cynthia H. Enloe, *Maneuvers: The International Politics of Militarizing Women's Lives*

(Berkeley: University of California Press, 2000) and Cynthia H. Enloe, *Globalization and Militarism: Feminists Make the Link*, 2nd ed. (Lanham: Rowman & Littlefield, 2016) as well as other feminist analyses connecting militarization to violence and responses to violence in civilian spaces—for example, Catherine Lutz, "Living Room Terrorists," pp. 223–7 in *Security Disarmed: Critical Perspectives on Gender, Race, and Militarization*, eds. Barbara Sutton, Sandra Morgen, and Julie Novkov (New Brunswick: Rutgers University Press, 2008); Jacqui True, *The Political Economy of Violence against Women* (New York: Oxford University Press, 2012); Alicia C. Decker, Summer Forester, and Eliot Blackburn, "Rethinking Everyday Militarism on Campus: Feminist Reflections on the Fatal Shooting at Purdue University," *Feminist Studies* 42, no. 1 (2016): 194–216.

15 Philip J. Cook and Kristin A. Goss, *The Gun Debate: What Everyone Needs to Know* (New York: Oxford University Press, 2014); Roxanne Dunbar-Ortiz, *Loaded: A Disarming History of the Second Amendment* (San Francisco: City Lights Books, 2018).

16 See sociologist David Yamane's account about the shift from what journalist Michael Bane called Gun Culture 1.0 (emphasizing hunting and recreation) to Gun Culture 2.0 (more focused on self-defense): David Yamane, "The Sociology of U.S. Gun Culture," *Sociological Compass* 11, no. 7 (2017), https://doi.org/10.1111/soc4.12497.

17 On concealed carry, see, for example, David Yamane, "'The First Rule of Gunfighting Is Have a Gun:' Technologies of Concealed Carry in Gun Culture 2.0," pp. 167–93 in *The Lives of Guns*, eds. Jonathan Obert, Andrew Poe, and Austin Sarat (New York: Oxford University Press, 2019). On broader "forting up" practices, see Ann Dupuis and David Thorns, "Gated Communities as Exemplars of 'Forting Up' Practices in a Risk Society," *Urban Policy & Research* 26, no. 2 (2008): 145–57.

18 See, for example, Alexandra Petri, "What We Know About How the Buffalo Shooting Unfolded," *New York Times*, May 14, 2022, www.nytimes.com/2022/05/14/nyregion/shooting-tops-timeline-buffalo.html; Lindsay Whitehurst, Gene Johnson, and James Anderson, "Buffalo Is Latest Mass Shooting by Gunman Wearing Body Armor," *The Associated Press*, May 26, 2022, https://apnews.com/article/mass-shootings-buffalo-body-armor-f7789ba97dee4d786ac24ec5c642b7ca.

19 Cynthia H. Enloe and Joni Seager, *The Real State of America Atlas Mapping the Myths and Truths of the United States* (New York: Penguin Books, 2011), 70.

20 Also, the same report notes: "Of the 857 million civilian-held firearms estimated in 2017, 393 million are in the United States—more than those held by civilians in the other top 25 countries combined" (*Small Arms Survey*, "Small Arms Survey Reveals: More than One Billion Firearms in the World," *Press Release*, June 18, 2018, www.smallarmssurvey.org/sites/default/files/resources/SAS-Press-release-global-firearms-holdings.pdf).

21 Sabrina Tavernise, "Gun Sales Surge in United States Torn by Distrust," *New York Times*, May 30, 2021, 1.

22 Barbara Sutton and Kate Paarlberg-Kvam, "Fashion of Fear for Kids," *InVisible Culture: An Electronic Journal for Visual Culture* 25 (2017), https://ivc.lib.rochester.edu/ready-fashion-of-fear-for-kids/, citing Sarah Parker, "Chapter 9: Balancing Act: Regulation of Civilian Firearm Possession," *Small Arms Survey 2011: States of Security*, July 11, 2011, 36, https://www.smallarmssurvey.org/resource/small-arms-survey-2011-states-security.

23 See Richard L. Legault, Nicole Hendrix, and Alan J. Lizotte, "Caught in a Crossfire: Legal and Illegal Gun Ownership in America," pp. 533–54 in *Handbook on Crime and Deviance. Handbooks of Sociology and Social Research*, eds. Marvin Krohn, Nicole Hendrix, Gina Penly Hall, and Alan J. Lizotte (Cham: Springer, 2019), https://doi.org/10.1007/978-3-030-20779-3_27; Kim Parker, Juliana Menasce Horowitz, Ruth Igielnik, J. Baxter Oliphant, and Anna Brown, "America's Complex Relationship with Guns," *Pew Research Center*, 2017, www.pewresearch.org/social-trends/2017/06/22/americas-complex-relationship-with-guns/; Terry L. Schell, Samuel Peterson, Brian G. Vegetabile, Adam Scherling, Rosanna Smart, and Andrew R. Morral, "State-Level Estimates of Household Firearm Ownership," *RAND Corporation*, 2020, www.rand.org/pubs/tools/TL354.html; State Firearms Laws, 2020, www.statefirearmlaws.org/.

24 Jonathan Obert, Andrew Poe, and Austin Sarat, *The Lives of Guns* (Oxford: Oxford University Press, 2019); Jennifer Carlson, "Gun Studies and the Politics of Evidence," *Annual Review of Law and Social Science* 16, no. 1 (2020): 183–202.
25 See, for example, Decker, Forester, and Blackburn, "Rethinking Everyday Militarism on Campus"; Andrew J. Baranauskas, "Public Opinion on Support for Arming Teachers with Guns in the United States," *Justice Quarterly* (November 2020): 1–21.
26 Kristin A. Goss, "Whatever Happened to the 'Missing Movement'?" pp. 136–50 in *Gun Studies: Interdisciplinary Approaches to Politics, Policy, and Practice*, eds. Jennifer Carlson, Kristin A. Goss, and Harel Shapira (London and New York: Routledge, 2019), 141; see also, Carlson, "Gun Studies and the Politics of Evidence."
27 For data on mass shootings over the years, see Mark Follman, Gavin Aronsen, and Deanna Pan, "US Mass Shootings, 1982–2020: Data from Mother Jones' Investigation," *Mother Jones* (blog), accessed September 15, 2020, www.motherjones.com/politics/2012/12/mass-shootings-mother-jones-full-data/; Gun Violence Archive, "Mass Shootings," accessed September 15, 2020, www.gunviolencearchive.org/mass-shooting.
28 Rosanna Smart and Terry L. Schell, "Mass Shootings in the United States," *RAND Corporation*, Updated April 15, 2021, www.rand.org/research/gun-policy/analysis/essays/mass-shootings.html. Definitions vary based on the number of fatal and/or non-fatal injuries taken as points of reference (e.g., 3 or 4 casualties excluding the shooter), the motivation of the perpetrator (e.g., indiscriminate versus connected to other crimes), and the spaces in which the event takes place (public versus any space) (Smart and Schell, "Mass Shootings in the United States"). The Federal Bureau of Investigation collects data on "active shooter" incidents defined as those in which individuals try to kill (or succeed in killing) others in populated areas, excluding cases such as shootings in the context of drug, gang, domestic, or other crime-related violence—See Advanced Law Enforcement Rapid Response Training (ALERRT) and the Federal Bureau of Investigation (FBI), *Active Shooter Incidents in the United States in 2019* (Washington, DC: U.S. Department of Justice, 2020), www.fbi.gov/file-repository/active-shooter-incidents-in-the-us-2019-042820.pdf/view. Between 2000 and 2019, 333 active shooter events took place in the United States, and 135 were "mass killings" under the definition of three or more fatalities, as recorded by the Federal Bureau of Investigation (FBI), "Active Shooter Incidents 20-Year Review, 2000–2019," May 2021, www.fbi.gov/file-repository/active-shooter-incidents-20-year-review-2000-2019-060121.pdf/view. In 2020, the number of recorded active shooter incidents rose with respect to previous years, adding 40 more shootings to the tally, a number that "represents a 33% increase since 2019 and a 100% increase from 2016" according to Federal Bureau of Investigation (FBI) and Advanced Law Enforcement Rapid Response Training (ALERRT), *Active Shooter Incidents in the United States in 2020* (Washington, DC: U.S. Department of Justice, 2021), 3, www.fbi.gov/file-repository/active-shooter-incidents-in-the-us-2020-070121.pdf/view.
29 Gun Violence Archive, "Past Summary Ledgers," November 12, 2022, www.gunviolencearchive.org/past-tolls.
30 Jill D. McLeigh, "The New Normal? Addressing Gun Violence in America," *American Journal of Orthopsychiatry* 85, no. 3 (2015): 201–2; Mary Bernstein, Jordan McMillan, and Elizabeth Charash, "Once in Parkland, a Year in Hartford, a Weekend in Chicago: Race and Resistance in the Gun Violence Prevention Movement," *Sociological Forum* 34, no. S1 (2019): 1153–73.
31 April M. Zeoli, Rebecca Malinski, and Brandon Turchan, "Risks and Targeted Interventions: Firearms in Intimate Partner Violence," *Epidemiologic Reviews* 38, no. 1 (2016): 125–39.
32 According to previous research, "[t]he US accounts for 31% of the population of the OECD [Organization for Economic Cooperation and Development] high-income countries, but in 2015, 92% of the women killed by guns, 96.7% of children aged 0–4 years and 92% of children aged 5–14 years killed by guns were from the US" (Erin Grinshteyn and David Hemenway, "Violent Death Rates in the US Compared to Those of the Other High-Income Countries, 2015," *Preventive Medicine* 123 [June 2019]: 20–6, 23).

33 See, for example, Sudernman and Rankin's report on a gun-rights demonstration (Alan Suderman and Sarah Rankin, "Virginia Gun-Rights Rally: Activists Plan Unprecedented Show of Force at Capitol," *Washington Times*, January 19, 2020, www.washingtontimes.com/news/2020/jan/19/virginia-gun-rights-rally-activists-plan-unprecede/); and Mahoney et al. on the presence of white armed men "patrolling" Black Lives Matters demonstrations related to the police shooting of Jacob Blake, a Black man, in Kenosha, Wisconsin (Adam Mahoney, Lois Beckett, Julia Carrie Wong, and Victoria Bekiempis, "Armed White Men Patrolling Kenosha Protests Organized on Facebook," *The Guardian*, August 26, 2020, www.theguardian.com/us-news/2020/aug/26/kenosha-militia-protest-shooting-facebook).

34 See, for example, Baker and Bogel-Burroughs's report on armed confrontations in Oregon (Mike Baker and Nicholas Bogel-Burroughs, "A City Prepares for Violent Showdowns," *New York Times*, September 25, 2020, www.nytimes.com/2020/09/25/us/portland-proud-boys-antifa-protests.html) and *BBC News* on the presence of armed demonstrators protesting in the Michigan Statehouse in opposition to health measures related to the COVID-19 pandemic (*BBC News*, "Coronavirus: Armed Protestors Enter Michigan Statehouse," May 1, 2020, www.bbc.com/news/world-us-canada-52496514).

35 For different interpretations on this matter, see, for example, Nelson Lund and Adam Winkler, "Second Amendment," *The Constitutional Center*, accessed May 27, 2022, https://constitutioncenter.org/interactive-constitution/interpretation/amendment-ii/interps/99. As summarized by Lund and Winkler, in 2008, the Supreme Court of the United States ruled by a 5–4 majority, in *District of Columbia v. Heller*, that the Second Amendment "protects a private right of individuals to have arms for their own defense, not a right of the states to maintain a militia" (Lund and Winkler, "Second Amendment").

36 See *New York State Rifle & Pistol Association Inc. v. Bruen*, www.supremecourt.gov/search.aspx?filename=/docket/docketfiles/html/public/20-843.html.

37 Didier Fassin, "Afterword: The Age of Security," pp. 271–5 in *Futureproof: Security Aesthetics and the Management of Life*, eds. D. Asher Ghertner, Hudson McFann, and Daniel Goldstein (Durham: Duke University Press, 2020), 271.

38 The role of the state has been questioned, however, by those who primarily point to state-perpetrated violence, particularly against marginalized communities, whether through military or police forces.

39 See, for example, the differential risks of hospitalization and death by race/ethnicity: Center for Disease Control, "Risk for COVID-19 Infection, Hospitalization, and Death by Race/Ethnicity," June 2, 2022, www.cdc.gov/coronavirus/2019-ncov/covid-data/investigations-discovery/hospitalization-death-by-race-ethnicity.html.

40 United Nations Development Programme (UNDP), *Human Development Report* (New York: Oxford University Press, 1994), 24–5. See also, Aili Tripp, Myra Marx Ferree, and Christina Ewig, eds., *Gender, Violence, and Human Security: Critical Feminist Perspectives* (New York: New York University Press, 2015).

41 Women for Genuine Security, "What Is Genuine Security?", accessed July 21, 2022, www.genuinesecurity.org/.

42 See, for example, Catherine Lutz, "Making War at Home in the United States: Militarization and the Current Crisis," *American Anthropologist* 104, no. 3 (2002): 723–35; Chandra Talpade Mohanty, Robin Riley, and Minnie Bruce Pratt, eds., *Feminism and War: Confronting US Imperialism* (London: Zed Books, 2008); Barbara Sutton, Sandra Morgen, and Julie Novkov, eds., *Security Disarmed: Critical Perspectives on Gender, Race, and Militarization* (New Brunswick: Rutgers University Press, 2008); and the National Priorities Project's "Cost of National Security" (www.nationalpriorities.org/cost-of/).

43 Scholars, advocates, and activists have pointed to the historical and contemporary links between the military and the police, including the transfer of equipment and tactics from the military to domestic security and law enforcement. This move has in turn negatively affected members of communities of color who are disproportionally policed, as well as political dissidents and protesters. See Jessica Katzenstein, "The Wars Are Here: How the United States' Post-9/11 Wars Helped Militarize U.S. Police," *Cost of War*,

September 16, 2020, https://watson.brown.edu/costsofwar/files/cow/imce/papers/2020/Police%20Militarization_Costs%20of%20War_Sept%2016%202020.pdf; Guillermina Seri, "A Borderless Police World," *International Politics Reviews* 8, no. 1 (2020): 21–31; Lindsay Koshgarian, Ashik Siddique, and Lorah Steichen, "State of Insecurity: The Cost of Militarization Since 9/11," *Institute for Policy Studies*, September 1, 2021, www.nationalpriorities.org/analysis/2021/state-insecurity-cost-militarization-911/.

44 Rob Nixon, *Slow Violence and the Environmentalism of the Poor* (Cambridge: Harvard University Press, 2011).

45 Judith Butler, *Notes Toward a Performative Theory of Assembly* (Cambridge: Harvard University Press, 2015), 149.

46 Butler, *Notes Toward a Performative Theory of Assembly*, 149.

47 Bryan S. Turner, *Vulnerability and Human Rights* (University Park: Pennsylvania State University Press, 2006), 28.

48 Deborah White and Lesley McMillan, "Innovating the Problem Away? A Critical Study of Anti-Rape Technologies," *Violence Against Women* 26, no. 10 (2020): 1120–40.

49 Mark Maguire and Ursula Rao, "Introduction: Bodies as Evidence," pp. 1–23 in *Bodies as Evidence: Security, Knowledge, and Power*, eds. Mark Maguire, Ursula Rao, and Nils Zurawski (Durham: Duke University Press, 2018), 9.

50 D. Asher Ghertner, Hudson McFann, and Daniel Goldstein, "Security Aesthetics of and Beyond the Biopolitical," pp. 1–32 in *Futureproof: Security Aesthetics and the Management of Life*, eds. D. Asher Ghertner, Hudson McFann, and Daniel Goldstein (Durham: Duke University Press, 2020).

51 Binational Migration Institute, "Migrant Deaths in Southern Arizona: Recovered Undocumented Border Crosser Remains Investigated by the Pima County Office of the Medical Examiner, 1990–2020," University of Arizona, April 2021, https://sbs.arizona.edu/sites/sbs.arizona.edu/files/BMI%20Report%202021%20ENGLISH_FINAL.pdf.

52 Austin Sarat, "Trump's Law-and-Order Campaign Relies on a Historic American Tradition of Racist and Anti-Immigrant Politics," *The Conversation*, September 8, 2020, https://theconversation.com/trumps-law-and-order-campaign-relies-on-a-historic-american-tradition-of-racist-and-anti-immigrant-politics-145366.

53 Iraq Body Count, "Iraq Body Count," 2021, www.iraqbodycount.org/; Watson Institute for International and Public Affairs, "Costs of War," August 2021, https://watson.brown.edu/costsofwar/figures/2021/human-and-budgetary-costs-date-us-war-afghanistan-2001-2022.

54 Barry Buzan, Ole Wæver, and Jaap De Wilde, *Security: A New Framework for Analysis* (Boulder: Lynne Rienner Publishers, 1998), 23–24.

55 See, for example, Harvey Molotch, *Against Security: How We Go Wrong at Airports, Subways, and Other Sites of Ambiguous Danger* (Princeton: Princeton University Press, 2012).

56 Elke Krahmann, ed., *New Threats and New Actors in International Security* (New York: Palgrave Macmillan, 2005); Monika Barthwal-Datta, *Understanding Security Practices in South Asia: Securitization Theory and the Role of Non-State Actors* (New York: Routledge, 2012); Maya Eichler, "Gender and the Privatization of Security: Neoliberal Transformation of the Militarized Gender Order," *Critical Studies on Security* 1, no. 3 (2013): 311–25.

57 Inderpal Grewal, *Saving the Security State: Exceptional Citizens in Twenty-First-Century America* (Durham: Duke University Press, 2017).

58 See, for example, Kenneth T. MacLeish, "Armor and Anesthesia: Exposure, Feeling, and the Soldier's Body," *Medical Anthropology Quarterly* 26, no. 1 (2012): 49–68; Rosen, *Bulletproof Vest*.

59 At the federal level, the U.S. federal law prohibits the "purchase, ownership, or possession" of body armor by individuals convicted of a violent felony, except when: "(A) the defendant obtained prior written certification from his or her employer that the defendant's purchase, use, or possession of body armor was necessary for the safe performance of lawful business activity; and (B) the use and possession by the defendant were limited to the course of such performance" (18 U.S.C.A. § 931). Additionally, individual states regulate the use of body armor, with restrictions such as banning their use by people convicted of certain crimes or enhancing sentences for the use of body armor during

the perpetration of a crime, or making it a crime to wear body armor while committing a crime (Janet Portman, "When It's Illegal to Own a Bullet-Proof Vest," accessed September 10, 2021, www.criminaldefenselawyer.com/resources/criminal-defense/criminal-offense/when-its-illegal-to-own-a-bullet-proof-vest).

60 In New York State—the region from which focus groups in this study were recruited—the "unlawful wearing of body armor" is considered a felony; it is against the law to wear body armor during the perpetration of a violent crime "while possessing a firearm, rifle or shotgun" (NY Penal § 270.20). In 2020 and 2021, when the focus groups were conducted, the law had a narrower definition of the type of gear covered, referred to as "body vests." During the summer 2022, more restrictions were added to the law and the language changed to "body armor." The NY Department of State summarized the regulations as follows: "Effective July 6, 2022, when not being engaged or employed in an eligible profession, the purchase, taking possession of, sale, exchange, giving or disposing of body armor is prohibited" (See "Body Armor," New York State Department of State, accessed September 1, 2022, https://dos.ny.gov/body-armor#:~:text=Effective%20July%206%2C%202022%2C%20when,of%20body%20armor%20is%20prohibited.)

61 See, for example, Jaclyn Diaz, "Sales of Body Armor Are on the Rise. Who's Buying and Why?" *NPR*, June 14, 2022, www.npr.org/2022/06/14/1103935711/body-armor-sales-increase-rise-mass-shootings-bans.

62 Teresa Caldeira, *City of Walls: Crime, Segregation, and Citizenship in São Paulo* (Berkeley: University of California Press, 2000); Ghertner, McFann, and Goldstein, "Security Aesthetics of and beyond the Biopolitical."

63 "Fortress Fleece Vest Closeout—Previous Model," *Bullet Blocker*, www.bulletblocker.com/men39s-fortress-fleece-vest-closeo39.html.

64 Drawing on Emily Martin's work, Lynda Birke referred to the notion of a "fortress body" in relation to Western and militarized ideas about the functioning of the biological body. See, Lynda I. A. Birke, *Feminism and the Biological Body* (New Brunswick: Rutgers University Press, 2000), 158; and also, Emily Martin, *Flexible Bodies: Tracking Immunity in American Culture from the Days of Polio to the Age of AIDS* (Boston: Beacon Press, 1994). Rather than focusing on biological functions and disease fighting, I draw on the metaphor of the fortress body to highlight how militarized notions of security shape bulletproof fashion and the aspiration of an impenetrable body that is ready to fend off bullets. At the same time, in the context of the COVID-19 pandemic, notions of fortressing got renewed salience as individuals and societies struggled to envision an effective defense against the novel coronavirus.

65 Elisabeth Anker, "Mobile Sovereignty: Guns in Public," pp. 21–42 in *The Lives of Guns*, eds. Jonathan Obert, Andrew Poe, and Austin Sarat (New York: Oxford University Press, 2019), 24 (emphasis in original), 22.

66 See, for example, Krahmann, *New Threats and New Actors in International Security*; Rita Abrahamsen and Michael C. Williams, "Securing the City: Private Security Companies and Non-State Authority in Global Governance," *International Relations* 21 (June 2007), 237–53; Barthwal-Datta, *Understanding Security Practices in South Asia*; Eichler, "Gender and the Privatization of Security."

67 David Harvey, *A Brief History of Neoliberalism* (Oxford: Oxford University Press, 2005).

68 Judith Butler, *Frames of War: When Is Life Grievable?* (London: Verso, 2009), 25.

69 National Priorities Project, "Federal Spending, Where Does the Money Go: Federal Budget 101," *National Priorities Project*, accessed July 1, 2022, www.nationalpriorities.org/budget-basics/federal-budget-101/spending/; Koshgarian, Siddique, and Steichen, "State of Insecurity: The Cost of Militarization Since 9/11."

70 For example, in 2019, the U.S. military spending constituted "a full 38% of global military spending. That's more than the next 10 countries combined," according to Ashik Siddique, "The U.S. Spends More on Its Military Than the Next 10 Countries Combined," *National Priorities Project*, April 30, 2020, www.nationalpriorities.org/blog/2020/04/30/us-spends-military-spending-next-10-countries-combined/).

71 "Bulletproof Clothing in Colombia," *Metropolis*.

72 *NTN24*, "Colombiano diseña prendas blindadas para proteger a niños de tiroteos en EE. UU. y Canadá," Video, January 1, 2013, www.youtube.com/watch?v=nmDN8iK-AQI; *CBS News*, "Designer Makes Bulletproof Clothing for Kids," June 23, 2013, Video, www.cbsnews.com/news/designer-makes-bulletproof-clothing-for-kids/.

73 "FAQ: Frequently Asked Questions," *ArmorMe*, accessed November 2, 2020, www.armorme.com/faq.

74 See Neptune Wellness Solutions Inc, "Neptune Appoints Joseph Buaron and Michael de Geus to Board of Directors," *Cision PR Newswire*, April 6, 2020, www.prnewswire.com/news-releases/neptune-appoints-joseph-buaron-and-michael-de-geus-to-board-of-directors-301035612.html.

75 "About BulletBlocker," *Bullet Blocker*, accessed November 2, 2020, www.bulletblocker.com/info.html.

76 I use the shorthand 9/11 to refer to the September 11, 2001, terrorist attacks in the United States, which marked a turning point in many aspects of life and politics, not only in the United States but around the world.

77 Cindi Katz, "Banal Terrorism: Spatial Fetishism and Everyday Insecurity," pp. 349–61 in *Violent Geographies: Fear, Terror, and Political Violence*, eds. Derek Gregory and Allan Pred (New York and London: Routledge, 2007).

78 Sutton and Paarlberg-Kvam, "Fashion of Fear for Kids."

79 Zygmunt Bauman, *Liquid Fear* (Cambridge: Polity Press, 2006); Molotch, *Against Security*; Ruth DeFoster, *Terrorizing the Masses: Identity, Mass Shootings, and the Media Construction of Terror* (New York: Peter Lang, 2017); Jaclyn Schildkraut, ed., *Mass Shootings in America: Understanding the Debates, Causes, and Responses* (Santa Barbara: ABC-CLIO, 2018).

80 Caroline E. Light, *Stand Your Ground: A History of America's Love Affair with Lethal Self-Defense* (Boston: Beacon Press, 2017), viii.

81 Light, *Stand Your Ground*, 8.

82 Goldstein Market Intelligence, "Global Bulletproof Clothing Industry Analysis: By Product Type, by End User & by Geography with COVID-19 Impact | Market Outlook 2019–2035," May 14, 2021, www.goldsteinresearch.com/report/global-bulletproof-vest-clothing-market.

83 Goldstein Market Intelligence, "Global Bulletproof Clothing Industry Analysis." See also, "Bulletproof Vests Market to cross USD 2 Bn by 2026: Global Market Insights, Inc," *Financial Services Monitor Worldwide*, August 27, 2020, http://bi.gale.com.libproxy.albany.edu/essentials/article/GALE%7CA633632725/698e2507455837900417237 45f712705?u=nysl_ca_dmvacces.

84 Goldstein Market Intelligence, "Global Bulletproof Clothing Industry Analysis."

85 For instance, this blurring between the military and the civilian occurs with regard to both functionality and aesthetics, particularly as some fashionable items or some civilian uses are overtly militarized (e.g., the use of "camo" [camouflage]).

86 See for example: "Global Bulletproof Clothes Market 2016–2024: Demand Accelerated with Government's Investing in Defense," Press Release, *Digital Journal*, accessed December 20, 2020, www.digitaljournal.com/pr/3732459; "Bulletproof Vest—Market Drivers and Forecasts from Technavio," *Business Wire*, November 29, 2016, www.businesswire.com/news/home/20161129005112/en/; "Bulletproof Vests Market to cross USD 2 Bn by 2026."

87 Rosen, *Bulletproof Vest*, 11.

88 See, for example, Safeguard Clothing's cautionary note in this regard: "How Effective Is a Bullet Proof Vest at Stopping a Gun Shot?" *Safeguard Clothing*, accessed September 28, 2022, www.safeguardclothing.com/articles/how-effective-are-bullet-proof-vests-at-stopping-a-gun-shot/.

89 See, for example, Nathan James, "Body Armor for Law Enforcement Officers: In Brief," *Congressional Research Service*, January 28, 2016, https://fas.org/sgp/crs/misc/R43544.pdf; Mark Greene, "Body Armor: Protecting Our Nation's Officers from Ballistic Threats," *National Institute of Justice*, 2018, https://nij.ojp.gov/topics/articles/body-armor-protecting-our-nations-officers-ballistic-threats.

90 Greene, "Body Armor."
91 A Congressional Research Service report mentions: "Data from the FBI indicate that 67% (338) of the 505 non-federal law enforcement officers feloniously killed in the line of duty between 2005 and 2014 were wearing body armor when they were killed" (James, "Body Armor for Law Enforcement Officers," 7).
92 Rosen, *Bulletproof Vest*, 66.
93 Columba Peoples, and Nick Vaughan Williams, *Critical Security Studies: An Introduction*, 2nd ed. (New York: Routledge, 2015), 165.
94 Michael Shapiro, "Every Move You Make: Bodies, Surveillance, and Media," *Social Text* 23, no. 2 (2005): 21–34; Peter Adey, "Facing Airport Security: Affect, Biopolitics, and the Preemptive Securitisation of the Mobile Body," *Environment & Planning D: Society & Space* 27, no. 2 (2009): 274–95; Paisley Currah and Tara Mulqueen, "Securitizing Gender: Identity, Biometrics, and Transgender Bodies at the Airport," *Social Research* 78, no. 2 (2011): 557–82; Laura J. Shepherd and Laura Sjoberg, "Trans-Bodies in/of War(s): Cisprivilege and Contemporary Security Strategy," *Feminist Review* 101, no. 1 (2012): 5–23.
95 Michael Quintanilla, "Fashion Security: Air Travelers Dress to Avoid the 'Buzz,'" *Orlando Sentinel*, February 23, 2003, http://articles.orlandosentinel.com/2003-02-23/travel/0302200375_1_airport-security-metal-sensors-detector.
96 Maguire, Rao, and Zurawski, *Bodies as Evidence*.
97 Edward J. Blakely and Mary Gail Snyder, *Fortress America: Gated Communities in the United States* (Washington, DC: Brookings Institution Press, 1997), 1; Dupuis and Thorns, "Gated Communities as Exemplars of 'Forting Up'," 145.
98 Caldeira, *City of Walls*.
99 Samira Kawash, "Safe House?: Body, Building, and the Question of Security," *Cultural Critique* 45 (2000): 185–221, 189.
100 Zeynep Gambetti and Marcial Godoy-Anativia, eds., *Rhetorics of Insecurity: Belonging and Violence in the Neoliberal Era* (New York: New York University Press, 2013), 2.
101 Michel Foucault, *Vigilar y Castigar: Nacimiento de la Prisión* (Buenos Aires: Siglo XXI, 1989), 198.
102 MacLeish, "Armor and Anesthesia," 49.
103 Tessa Diphoorn, "'It's All About the Body': The Bodily Capital of Armed Response Officers in South Africa," *Medical Anthropology* 34, no. 4 (2015): 336–52.
104 See, for example, Enloe, *Maneuvers*; Enloe, *Globalization and Militarism*; Women of Color Resource Center, *Fashion Resistance to Militarism*, Video DVD, directed and edited by Kimberly Alvarenga, Executive Producer Christine Ahn (Oakland, 2006); Sutton, Morgen, and Novkov, *Security Disarmed*; Suzy Kim, Gwyn Kirk, and M. Brinton Lykes, "Unsettling Debates: Women and Peace Making," Special Issue of *Social Justice: A Journal of Crime, Conflict & World Order* 46, no. 1 (2019).
105 Among sociological works on fashion and the body, see, for example, Erynn Masi de Casanova, *Buttoned Up: Clothing, Conformity, and White-Collar Masculinity* (Ithaca: Cornell University Press, 2015); Joanne Entwistle, *The Fashioned Body: Fashion, Dress and Modern Social Theory*, 2nd ed. (Hoboken: Wiley, 2015).
106 "Talos Ballistics NIJ IIIA Bulletproof Woman's Falcon Leather Jacket," *Talos Ballistics*, accessed May 28, 2021, https://talosballistics.com/product/bulletproof-womans-falcon-leather-jacket/.
107 "Venezia Grey Brown Windowpane," *Aspetto*, accessed May 27, 2020, https://apparel.aspetto.com/#/product/venezia-grey-brown-windowpane.
108 "Bulletproof Gucci Diaper Bag," *Bullet Blocker*, accessed May 27, 2020, www.bulletblocker.com/bulletblocker-nij-iiia-bulletproof-gucci-diaper.html; "Bulletproof Saint Laurent Leather Moto Jacket," *Bullet Blocker*, accessed May 27, 2020, www.bulletblocker.com/bullet-blocker-nij-3a-bulletproof-saint-laurent-moto-jacke3.html.
109 "Kid's Bulletproof Hoodie (NIJ-IIIA)," *Wonder Hoodie*, accessed May 28, 2020, https://wonderhoodie.com/collections/wonder-hoodie-bulletproof-clothing/products/kids-bullet-proof-hoodie?variant=13837983449143; "Bulletproof Jacket—Denim

(NIJ-IIIA)," *Wonder Hoodie*, accessed May 28, 2020, https://wonderhoodie.com/collections/wonder-hoodie-bulletproof-clothing/products/bullet-proof-denim-jacket?variant=13837982072887

110 Barbara Sutton, "Fashion of Fear: Securing the Body in an Unequal Global World," pp. 75–99 in *Bodies without Borders*, eds. Erynn Masi de Casanova and Afshan Jafar (New York: Palgrave, 2013); Sutton and Paarlberg-Kvam, "Fashion of Fear for Kids."

111 Turner, *Vulnerability and Human Rights*; Judith Butler, "Bodily Vulnerability, Coalitions, and Street Politics," pp. 99–119 in *Differences in Common: Gender, Vulnerability and Community*, eds. Joana Sabadell-Nieto and Marta Segarra (Amsterdam: Rodopi, 2014).

112 Yamane, "The First Rule of Gunfighting is Have a Gun."

113 Matt Richtel, "New Fashion Wrinkle: Stylishly Hiding the Gun," *New York Times*, April 23, 2012, www.nytimes.com/2012/04/24/us/fashion-statement-is-clear-the-gun-isnt.html.

114 See the organization's website: https://thewellarmedwoman.com/.

115 "Feminine & Functional Concealed Carry," *Gun Goddess*, accessed November 2, 2020, www.gungoddess.com/. While focused on the business of selling gun-related apparel, jewelry, purses and other accessories to women, in the context of the U.S. 2020 presidential election, Gun Goddess urged customers in its website: "Vote! Your gun rights depend on it!" hinting at the linkage between business profits, gun policy, and gun culture.

116 "Garter Holsters," *Femme Fatale*, accessed November 2, 2020, https://shop.femmefataleholsters.com/Garter-Holsters_c4.htm.

117 See, for example, Kathy Davis, *Embodied Practices: Feminist Perspectives on the Body* (London: Sage, 1997); Janet Price and Margrit Shildrick, *Feminist Theory and the Body* (Edinburgh: Edinburgh University Press, 1999); Judith Lorber and Lisa Jean Moore, *Gendered Bodies: Feminist Perspectives* (New York: Oxford University Press, 2011); Erynn Masi de Casanova and Afshan Jafar, *Bodies without Borders* (New York: Palgrave, 2013); Chris Bobel and Samantha Kwan, *Body Battlegrounds: Transgressions, Tensions, and Transformations* (Nashville: Vanderbilt University Press, 2019).

118 See Jennifer Carlson, "The Embodied Politics of Guns," *ASA Section on Body & Embodiment* (blog), 2015, http://sectionbodyembodiment.weebly.com/blog/the-embodied-politics-of-guns.

119 Eduardo Bericat, "The Sociology of Emotions: Four Decades of Progress," *Current Sociology* 64, no. 3 (2016): 491–513, 493 (emphasis in original).

120 Olivia Fleming, "Wall Your Body: Bulletproof Clothing and Anti-Rape Wear," project presented at the National Conference of Undergraduate Research, University of Central Oklahoma, April 4–7, 2018; Bridget Harris, "Anti-Rape Devices May Have Their Uses But They Don't Address the Problem," *The Conversation*, September 29, 2019, https://theconversation.com/anti-rape-devices-may-have-their-uses-but-they-dont-address-the-ultimate-problem-123011; Renee Marie Shelby, "Techno-Physical Feminism: Anti-Rape Technology, Gender, and Corporeal Surveillance," *Feminist Media Studies* (September 2019): 1–22; White and McMillan, "Innovating the Problem Away? A Critical Study of Anti-Rape Technologies."

121 Ghertner, McFann, and Goldstein, "Security Aesthetics of and beyond the Biopolitical," 2.

122 See, for example, the way that then presidential candidate Donald Trump talked about immigration: "Donald Trump Doubles Down on Calling Mexicans 'Rapists,'" *Cable News Network* (CNN), June 25, 2015, Video, www.cnn.com/videos/tv/2015/06/25/exp-presidential-candidate-donald-trump-immigration-intv-erin.cnn.

123 Neta C. Crawford, "Emotions and International Security: Cave! Hic Libido," *Critical Studies on Security* 1, no. 1 (2013): 121–3; Michelle Pace and Ali Bilgic, "Studying Emotions in Security and Diplomacy: Where We Are Now and Challenges Ahead," *Political Psychology* 40 (2019): 1407–17. More on this on Chapter 2.

124 Sara Ahmed, *The Cultural Politics of Emotion* (Edinburgh: Edinburgh University Press, 2014), 4.

125 I borrow the idea of an "object-centered approach" from Emilia Sanabria, *Plastic Bodies: Sex Hormones and Menstrual Suppression in Brazil* (Durham: Duke University Press, 2016), 5.
126 This first exploration of bulletproof fashion is based on content analysis of Miguel Caballero's main website (www.miguelcaballero.com/), conducted during June 1 to July 15, 2012. The company's website also contained links to media reports (videos and news articles), which presumably helped to bolster the message that the company wanted to deliver. I accessed and noted the information covered in 21 video clips and 30 news articles linked through the website. I also read 40 news reports that I accessed through Lexis-Nexis, EBSCO, and Google searches (see, Sutton, "Fashion of Fear").
127 This co-authored project analyzed the representations of Miguel Caballero's children-oriented products in the MC website, as well as that of Elite Sterling Security, a company that was selling these products in the United States. We also examined news coverage for the period between January 1, 2013 and June 30, 2014 (retrieved through Lexis-Nexis and Google News search, as well as the posted media content in the companies' websites, with a focus on the kids' items). In total, we examined 54 news items and 13 videos, in addition to the companies' websites (see, Sutton and Paarlberg-Kvam, "Fashion of Fear for Kids").
128 See also a newer study focused on this company: Jashim Uddin Ahmed, Tasnim Tarannum, Asma Ahmed, and Kazi Pushpita Mim, "Miguel Caballero: Marketing Strategy of Colombian Bulletproof Fashion Brand," *FIIB Business Review* 10, no. 2 (2021): 102–13.
129 I analyzed 102 news reports for the 2019–2020 period, which included coverage of the bulletproof product companies in this study. These sources were retrieved from the Lexis-Nexis database. Additionally, some companies also link news articles or videos in their websites, which I read or viewed while doing the content analysis of the websites.
130 A few notes regarding some of the businesses included in the study are in order: With respect to ArmorMe, its website indicated that the company "is based out of Hong Kong. The bags are developed and tested in Israel and orders are shipped out of [their] New Jersey Logistics Center" ("Frequently Asked Questions," *ArmorMe*, accessed June 25, 2022, www.armorme.com/faq). The company Aspetto gained visibility as a producer of stylish bulletproof clothing for men, and the website analyzed focused on civilian apparel (https://apparel.aspetto.com/). However, that page is no longer available and the company seems to have embraced more fully the defense and law enforcement realms (https://aspetto.com/#/tactical). Regarding MC Armor and Miguel Caballero, MC Armor has offices in the United States and specializes in bulletproof garments by Miguel Caballero, a company headquartered in Colombia. Given the relationship between these two linked entities—also apparent in the combined names of MC Armor and Miguel Caballero in some of the logos—I analyzed both of their websites: https://mc-armor.com/and https://miguelcaballero.com/). Finally, toward the beginning of the study, a business website for M30 Bullet Proof Apparel was offering bulletproof garments online, and this brand's apparel was also advertised in at least one other vendor's website (Bulletproof Zone). Yet, information about company owners/representatives could not be tracked and the website (https://m30bulletproof.com/) was no longer available later on.
131 While I reached out to "parents," only mothers responded to my call for participation in the parents focus group. Nevertheless, I also heard perspectives from both fathers and mothers who joined other focus groups organized around different criteria (i.e., not by parental status).
132 Focus group members included 22 women, 13 men, and 2 participants whose gender identities did not fit the male/female binary (genderqueer and gender nonconforming). The majority of participants identified as white, sometimes in combination with specific ethnicities, such as white/Hispanic (1) and white/Jewish (1). The sample also included participants who identified as Indian (1), mixed-race Latino (1), Black/Native (1), Black (Latina "infused") (1), Black (4), and white/Black (1). In terms

of their occupations, besides the participants who were invited based on their jobs (i.e., teachers, law enforcement officers, and health care workers), other occupations included the following: stay-at-home mother, university professor, attorney, pastor, community organizer, chief of staff of an arts organization, non-profit business owner, city worker, self-employed, IT consultant, systems analyst, and personnel in organizations working to prevent violence and/or support victims of violence. All participants had post-secondary education, including those with some college and others who earned Associate or Bachelor's degrees, RN diplomas, graduate certificates, Master's, JD, PhD, and EdD degrees.

133 Focus group discussions as well as the information collected from media sources and company websites were analyzed through qualitative research approaches, including inductive coding (derived from the data at hand), deductive coding (defined based on previous studies), thematic memos, and concept maps. News sources, market reports, and scholarly literature were used to contextualize the findings. This approach allowed me to see patterns and themes in the public discourse disseminated through the media, representations by industry representatives, and how different stakeholders define security and construct meaning about bulletproof products through group interaction.

134 See, for example, Nicole Chavez, Ryan Young, and Angela Barajas, "An All-Black Group Is Arming Itself and Demanding Change, They are the NFAC," *CNN*, last modified October 25, 2020, www.cnn.com/2020/10/25/us/nfac-black-armed-group/index.html.

2
EMOTIONS AND SECURITY

Fear. Anger. Sadness. Disgust. Compassion. Relief. What do these and other emotions have to do with security? How are security matters experienced and narrated through the language of emotions? Why is it important to pay attention to emotions when considering security issues? Although security-oriented policies and measures may appear devoid of evident emotional components, they often rest upon emotion-laden experiences and can trigger significant emotional reactions. After all, whether we think of the September 11, 2001, terrorist attacks in the United States, the violent right-wing assault on the U.S. Capitol on January 6, 2021, or the various mass shootings perpetrated across the country in recent times, we can see that these types of security breaches have a strong emotional impact. These emotions can in turn help propel policy makers and civil society to various courses of action, public demands, and political discussions.

Emotions help signal what is at stake with particular security issues as well as rally people in support of one or another response, such as decisions to heighten surveillance, bolster the armed forces, implement active shooter drills, or enact gun safety regulations. Political speech regarding security may appeal to emotions, for instance, encouraging us to *care* about salient security problems, to *fear* or *hate* individuals or groups presented as threatening, to have *compassion* for or *grieve* certain victims of violence, to *feel loyalty* toward leaders who promise to protect us, and to *love* one's country, including to the point of being willing to die for it.

During the past two decades, there has been increasing academic interest in the role that emotions play in security, world politics, and international relations.[1] Scholars who pay attention to emotions in these and other related fields have challenged the assumed primacy of rationality in politics, rejecting the binary between (unemotional) reason and (irrational) "passions." Instead, they have analyzed how cognitive and emotional processes are entwined in political decision-making, how emotions matter in security discourses, and how emotions are mobilized in relation

DOI:10.4324/9781003326854-2

to national identity. Relatedly, scholars of social movements have also shown the significance of emotions in political participation,[2] including events that have security implications (for instance, in the case of violent demonstrations or state repression). Others have shed light on how government leaders and diplomats with a stake in national security "make sense of feelings that have both individual and state-level implications,"[3] how insecurities associated with war are "felt" in gendered ways,[4] and how emotions are racialized, influencing the construction of ethnoracial "others" represented as security threats.[5]

Fear is one of the most recognized emotions relevant to security, though Neta Crawford noted that it has not always been critically examined in security studies but taken for granted.[6] Examples of how fear matters to security can be found in political responses to terrorist attacks, in the motivations of countries to go to war, or in deterrence strategies among the parties in conflict.[7] It is also inbuilt in the political notion of "terror" itself, whether in reference to attacks on civilians by militant groups or by state forces. Roland Bleiker and Emma Hutchison considered the impact of fear on collective responses to terrorism, noting

> how the fear engendered by terror can create moral certainty and lead otherwise diverse and disagreeing constituencies to swift, universal agreements on basic principles and actions. As a result, though, the foundations of our morals are articulated mostly in negative ways, based on fear and closure, rather than on open discussions of difficult issues and a willingness to ground political positions in a positive affirmation of basic values and principles.[8]

These observations raise important questions about how ordinary citizens and government officials navigate the disturbing emotions associated with security breaches—not only at a personal level but also at the level of institutions, governments, and international organizations—and how those emotions influence political decisions and social responses.

While it is often expected for politics and policy to be driven by rationality—as in the figure of the "rationally acting and emotionally abstinent" bureaucrat[9]—the separation between reason and emotions may be unattainable in practice. Thus, acknowledging the presence of emotions in those realms is an important first step toward understanding their workings, and perhaps toward helping orient politics in directions that may serve the greater good. In other words, emotions might not be realistically extracted from politics, and some might question whether it is desirable to do so, depending on the kinds of emotions at issue and their concrete effects. Rather, it is important to consider which emotions might be at play in specific realms or situations, how they become embedded in political decisions and policy, and to what extent they might influence distinct political outcomes or guide different courses of action. For instance, emotional responses such as empathy might be entwined with particular sets of policies, while those based on anger or fear might lead to different paths, including in unexpected ways.

Scholars of emotions warn against easy assumptions about emotions as good or bad in themselves, or as uniformly leading to positive or negative outcomes. For example, even emotions deemed "positive," such as love, may be invoked to justify hateful attitudes or behavior, as in white nationalist narratives that couple "love for the nation" with hatred toward migrants and people of color who purportedly threaten the nation's integrity.[10] Or consider the role that some versions of love toward political leaders might play when said leaders stoke hatred, authoritarianism, and violence. On the other hand, emotions that some may classify as "negative," such as anger, can turn into moral indignation, prompting social movements to challenge injustice, including through political protest.[11] In her work regarding international development workers in Canada, Sophia Boutilier examined how unpleasant emotions such as frustration may lead to burn out but also to critical reflection and the impetus to press for change in some situations.[12] When it comes to security, we might consider how emotions commonly defined as "negative" may appear in tandem with those seen as "positive." What role might these juxtapositions play in security discourses, practices, and perceptions? How might the subject, object, and direction of the emotion matter?

In my previous work on security-oriented clothing, fear was at the center of the concept I used to describe the use and commercialization of such garments: "fashion of fear." I hypothesized that discourses and experiences of fear regarding certain forms of gun violence—particularly "spectacular" and highly publicized events such as mass shootings—were important to the commercialization of these products. The specter of fear does appear in company messaging about bulletproof apparel and accessories, and a bulletproof garments industry representative I interviewed situated such products in the context of fear: "the more we can provide security and safety for people, I think the better off. I mean, there's a lot of people who are scared right now. It's kind of sad." In focus group discussions with different stakeholders, fear was also one of the emotions that figured prominently, though not always explicitly stated. Variations of the terms "fear," "scared," or "afraid" appear in all but the gun rights supporters focus group. Yet even in that group, notions of security based on avoidance, alertness, and being ready for potential attacks can be interpreted as a way of managing or preempting fear. Furthermore, in reflecting on self-protective strategies such as bulletproof products, one participant in the group alluded to an especially intense form of fear—paranoia—noting that "it's possible to work yourself up into a state where you're more paranoid than you really have to be."

In analyzing news media and online company materials regarding bulletproof products, in conjunction with different stakeholders' discussion of security broadly defined, I detected a wide universe of emotions surrounding the topic. Most of these were what are often considered unpleasant emotions, including anxiety, worry, sadness, fear, and anger. However, love, compassion, and other non-aversive emotions also emerged. In some of the focus group conversations, memories and feelings associated with breaches to international security (e.g., the 9/11 attacks) were juxtaposed with other issues at the domestic level (e.g., mass shootings in schools and armed political demonstrations). Given the significant presence of emotions in these narratives, I explored how perspectives and strategies of security are linked with emotional dimensions. Furthermore, following Sara Ahmed, one may ask, what do these emotions "do" when it comes to security?[13]

Public Feelings, Politics, and Security

In this study, discussions about security among different stakeholders were embedded in the more general and emotionally saturated context of the pandemic, mass protests against racialized police violence, the visibility of civilian armed demonstrators in the public sphere, and a contentious 2020 elections season filled with confrontation at various levels of society. Furthermore, two of the stakeholder focus groups—gun rights supporters and members of law enforcement—took place shortly after Trump supporters stormed the nation's Capitol, when Congress members met to certify the electoral result.

Not surprisingly, the emotions associated with the tumultuous events at the time of this research, which some participants connected with longer-standing issues, filtered into the conversation about security. These emotions were sometimes named, sometimes implied in the actions described, and sometimes expressed through tone of voice or body language. In fact, it is hard to talk about security and its various meanings without considering the significance of "public feelings": the pervasive presence of emotions in public and political life.[14] Public events, such as social and economic crises, shape individual and shared emotions, and emotions in turn influence political action and reflection.[15] Conversely, modes of political action, and their consequences or lack thereof, may produce their own sets of emotions.[16] Ann Cvetkovich, for example, describes the notion of "political depression"—conceptualized by the Feel Tank Chicago—as "the sense that customary forms of political response, including direct action and critical analysis, are no longer working either to change the world or to make us feel better."[17] In that vein, ideas and experiences about security are also politically imbued and steeped in emotional worlds that are both personal and political.

This chapter explores the connections between security, politics, and emotions based on the events and concerns discussed in focus groups with different stakeholders (mothers, teachers, health care workers, law enforcement officers, gun rights supporters, and members of organizations addressing police violence, gun violence, and sexual/gender violence). The discussion of the broad contexts of security addressed in this chapter forms the backdrop for the in-depth analysis of a specific security-oriented strategy—bulletproof gear—in subsequent chapters. After all, the decision to fit oneself or one's children in ballistic apparel happens in a particular social and historical context, even as it carries the lingering effects of previous times.

Political Polarization and Volatile Encounters

The climate of political and social polarization that marked the years of the Trump administration, and particularly the 2020 elections season, shaped the discourse and emotions surrounding security. For instance, President Trump's condemnatory "law and order" stance toward Black Lives Matter demonstrators contrasted with his more sympathetic attitude toward far-right groups such as Proud Boys, whom he instructed to "stand back and stand by."[18] A few months later, members of Proud Boys would be among the Trump supporters who stormed the Capitol, part of a breach of security of historic proportions.

This research can be read, in some ways, as a chronicle of the political events that were unfolding at the time. In that sense, the first focus group that was conducted—composed of mothers of school-aged children—shed light on public feelings surrounding visible political developments and their potential for violence, including armed violence. This conversation took place a couple of days after the first debate between presidential candidates Donald Trump and Joseph Biden. When asked about what comes to mind when thinking about security, Suzanne, a member of the mothers group responded:

> Right now, hearing that term for me makes me think of the debate and Black Lives Matter and Proud Boys—which I'd never heard of until the debate—and our President's incendiary words about security and just where our country is.

Members of this focus group connected the political context during the presidential election season to security matters broadly defined, commenting on pervasive anger in the political realm and expressing feelings of sadness, fear, and hopelessness. In Monica's words,

> there has been a lot of anger popping up that it was probably always there, but it is. . . . I guess it has been eye-opening, this . . . that anger in the country that's now. I feel like every . . . there's a lot of instances where people will say things and people will go from 0 to 60 very quickly. [. . .] You could see, yes, some real issues bubbling up, and it makes me sad, you know. I want to have a Black Lives Matter sign out [. . .] and I want to put something on it where it says, and 'If you disagree, let's talk.'

Monica's impetus to invite dialogue through her sign was partly related to security concerns, namely, that the sign would be forcefully removed by people who disagreed with her political position, or might prompt more severe repercussions (She also recalled that someone had recently put rusty nails in a neighbor's driveway, and she suspected it was due to a political sign). While in disagreement, Monica still tried to understand: "Because anybody who's like taking the sign, you must feel very strongly, and let's have a discussion about it." She then established a connection between these political experiences at the neighborhood level in a relatively affluent and largely white suburb, and the wider realm of national politics, specifically the presidential debate:

> Because I feel like this, like the anger of the debate was, you know, was not talking. It's just so much anger. And I think it was very symptomatic of what the whole country is, the state we're in right now.

Media sources had also noted the particularly acrimonious nature of this debate; for instance, the *BBC* described it as "one of the most chaotic and bitter White House debates in years. Mr. Trump frequently interrupted, prompting Mr. Biden to tell him to 'shut up' as the two fought over the pandemic, health care and the economy."[19] Reflecting on the times, Suzanne added,

> it's just name calling and take a position and fight to the death for it and pivot anytime your opponent says something contrary. There's no trying to reach any kind of consensus for the greater good. I feel hopeless about it right now. I do.

Although the narrated conversation about the political climate may be interpreted as mostly relevant to politics and emotions, this group of mothers of school-aged children were also linking it to what security meant to them. One dimension of security in this case related to a desire for peaceful coexistence despite political differences. From the perspective of participants, that kind of security could no longer be assured in the political climate they were living in. Another participant in this group, Kate, noticed fewer political signs than usual in the public space during the lead-up to the elections, and she speculated that "people don't want to spark up conversation or incite somebody to get angry and take their sign, or damage their property or their car." In other words, the possibility of an open democratic sphere seemed undermined by certain types of public feelings that had political consequences, for instance, as some citizens may have refrained from peacefully expressing their views due to security concerns. In hindsight, a more extreme example may be the case of U.S. legislators who reportedly supported objections to the results of the presidential election won by Joseph Biden partly because they feared for their family's safety.[20]

Suzanne and Linda, in the mothers focus group, echoed concerns about the divisive and volatile political environment, expressing a yearning for a more "civilized" time, when neighbors across the political spectrum were able to coexist in relative peace. This focus group—composed of all-white women in a suburban area—decried the lack of security embedded in the political milieu, in this case, fear of being targeted because of one's political beliefs. At the same time, the group also recognized that the sense of security that they yearned for revealed itself as a form of privilege not traditionally afforded to the population as a whole in the context of multiple injustices. Monica and Linda spoke explicitly about a kind of security "privilege." Monica commented:

> A year ago, I was aware of systemic racism, but this idea, it's become much more apparent that I was feeling secure. But that idea of, you know, the police injustice, and just that, you know, people of color. A lot of people are saying COVID has caused people of privilege to now realize how people of color are feeling all the time, in terms of the systems not working. Like what do you mean my child can't go to school all the time? Like, this is what one does. What do you mean I'm on furlough, or I'm laid off?

The conversation in the group went from noticing the anger and polarization embedded in contemporary U.S. politics to the systemic forms of violence and injustice encountered by marginalized groups, particularly based on race and class.

The unfair treatment of people of color is one of the injustices that became more visible to many, as Monica noted. Indeed, Black Lives Matter protesters denounced ongoing racialized police violence as well as other injustices that span a longer period. As the other mothers in the group, Linda reflected on her own life, and the emotions associated with security/insecurity, in this broader context:

> I am not worried about something blowing up down my street, but I do feel, in the last several months, like I am living with a thing that is there as soon as I wake up and stays all day and affects my sleep and starts again the next day, a security, a lack of security either in my neighborhood, not really, but sort of, because you never know where the anger is popping up and coming from. [. . .] And in the middle of the Black Lives Matter thing, what I find myself thinking about is, again, I have a significant amount of privilege. Right? Significant. And so, if I feel that lack of security in my privilege, can I even get my head wrapped around what [. . .] that lack of security feels like to someone who does not have privilege?

In this passage, we can see how the insecurities experienced by many people of color, for instance when interacting with law enforcement, can be unfathomable for those with racial privilege and other sorts of advantages, even when trying to put themselves in their shoes. And yet the public reckoning with police violence and racial injustice during the summer of 2020, as well as the malaise that Linda associated with the possibility of random "anger popping up" during emotionally charged political times, prompted her reflection about the disparity of feelings and experiences related to security. The conversation pointed to the fact that many people have not traditionally experienced the type of security that relatively affluent white people in the United States might take for granted. Indeed, multiple forms of insecurity can be traced to the intersections of racism, hetero- and cis-sexism, ableism, xenophobia, gender inequality, economic disparities, and other forms of marginalization in specific contexts.

This broad political context constitutes the ground of certain security concerns, shaping behaviors and perceptions. As we shall see, the connection between emotions, politics, and security emerged in the discussions among other focus group participants—including in relation to protest, policing, and gun violence—revealing some of the fault lines in U.S. society.

Politics, Protest, and Policing

Some of the ways in which emotions, politics, and security were connected in stakeholders' conversations highlighted the role of policing and authorities' handling of political protest and expression. In the focus group with activists in organizations addressing police violence, the political climate—and the emotions that surrounded it—emerged pointedly in the discussion of security. Santiago, a young Latino, told an anecdote about an activist initiative in his organization, which was geared toward protecting the elections results in the context of President Trump having cast doubt about their legitimacy (Santiago's organization tackles multiple social justice issues and political matters). He narrated the experience of another organizer who was making phone calls ahead of the rally event, and in one case, was initially receiving no answer:

> They didn't pick up. And then they called her back, and then just asking her about it, what was going on, and then started like getting really angry and defensive, saying like, "You shouldn't do that. All the Biden people, they're the ones who are going to cause trouble if Trump wins. If Biden wins, Trump people are just going to go home, and they're going to accept it like adults. And, you know, you better not go out there and cause . . . be causing trouble. Never reach out to us again. By the way, I'm a police officer," and all that kind of stuff. And mentioned that he's conservative, and most police officers are conservative, so like just making it very clear that [. . .] we do not have friends in them if it were to come out to counter-protesters with guns start attacking us. They might simply just not do their job.

Santiago's narrative highlights both the emotional component (anger and defensiveness) of political interactions in the inflamed climate of the elections season and how these public feelings, compounded by the power of firearms can generate a sense of insecurity—in this case for activists engaged in legitimate political activities.

Maya, a Black social justice activist, agreed with Santiago and built upon his point as she described her experience during a street protest. She recalled that at that demonstration there were also counter-protesters who were acting in intimidating ways, while the police seemed to be more concerned about the activists on her side:

> And we were saying to officers, "Why are you facing us? We're standing here. We got nothing but a bullhorn. They've got motorcycles. They're threatening us. Why are you not turning around? Why are you not looking at them? Why you . . ." And they didn't move. They didn't assess whether or not the people behind them were a security risk to the area. They kept looking at the teachers, the parents, the grandparents. There was a woman in a motorized wheelchair. And the officers stood there with their batons and their shields and their full like face masks while those other folks are screaming all kinds of epithets at us, saying horrible, disgusting things that any individual would think, "Wow, that sounds threatening." The officers never turned around, didn't look at them, didn't, like they're not there to protect us. Those guns are not aimed outside of our direction.

Emotions and Security **39**

In addition to underscoring disparities in law enforcement, this passage implicitly points to connections between politics, security, and emotions. The political expression of activists in Maya's group was laced with a sense of insecurity: Emotions ran high, and they were confronted with threatening counter-protesters and a police force that seemed to locate danger primarily on unarmed activists. This lack of security in the context of political expression is a far cry from the yearning for peaceful coexistence mentioned earlier, and not a new situation for many people of color.

Perhaps what was noteworthy in the recent political context was the resurgence and increased visibility of far-right groups who showed up at protests with their guns. This posed another level of security concern for social justice activists, also manifested in the emotional terms of fear. This is how David, a white man with years of political experience, put it:

> So, you went from situations in which you had, you know, police heavily armed, which is like really intimidating as a deterrent effect to individuals attempting to exercise their right of free speech. And now that's been amplified or magnified by areas in which there's now armed white supremacists who are sort of vigilantes who have been given license to carry lethal weapons and to intimidate protesters in a very similar way. So, it's a scary dynamic out there.

Words like "intimidating" and "scary" are emotional markers of certain experiences of protest, heightened by the presence of guns—artifacts designed to harm and that can be perceived as especially threatening in volatile situations. Here insecurity is closely linked to the emotion of fear, which can potentially operate as a mechanism of political silencing. While the use of fear as a repressive tactic is often associated with non-democratic political regimes, the presence of fear can also serve as an indicator of authoritarian threads emerging in the context of electoral democracies.[21]

This sense of fear in relation to political participation might not only be experienced by protesters but also circulate more broadly. Greg, a white anti-racist activist, talked about the reaction of his conservative-leaning family members in an increasingly perilous political environment:

> My parents, when I tell them I'm going out to protest or I'm organizing or whatever, they've started saying things like, "be careful." And I know that they would never explicitly say to me, "be careful because a white supremacist might shoot up this rally that you're at." But there's like a subtext there that even they kind of recognize, you know. So, I think there is a historical precedent that this has been happening forever. But like the fact that even my parents are saying, "be careful" to me when I go out to rallies is like, that maybe means something. Something feels different now.

While fear is not explicitly mentioned in this passage, the thing that "feels different now" causes parents to express their concern as their son exercises a basic right of freedom of expression in a liberal democracy. Part of what made this issue salient for Greg was that his parents, who are on the conservative side of the political spectrum, seemed to be worried, or perhaps afraid, about the increasingly risky conditions of protest. In this way, we can see how politically inflected feelings circulate laterally, moving among people beyond the most direct targets. Sara Ahmed notes that emotions can "move sideways (through 'sticky' associations between signs, figures, and objects) as well as backward ([. . .] 'what sticks' is also bound up with the 'absent presence' of historicity)."[22] In Greg's narrative, the "backward" movement relates to the "historical precedent that this has been happening forever." That is, it is tied to the precedent of white supremacist violence against anti-racist protesters, particularly people of color. Additionally, for members of this focus group, this sense of danger was heightened by feeling threatened rather than protected by the police. These activists were highly critical of law enforcement as an institution. In fact, Greg called for "abolishing the police and prisons," a proposition that found agreement in this group and that also echoed the increasingly visible critiques by abolitionist scholars and activists.[23]

On the other hand, for members of law enforcement, those types of abolitionist demands can stir strong emotions as well, not only due to possible implications to their job security but also in terms of discrepant visions of how to promote security in the sense of public safety. Although not the central part of the conversation, this issue came up in the focus group with members of law enforcement (four white men and a Black/Latina woman). Fear, anger, and frustration could be detected in some of their statements, entwined with interpretations about the impact of politics on law enforcement. For instance, Walter, a police officer, commented:

> Security in our jobs seems like the one thing they're trying to take from us these days, the legislature, and doing everything they can to take our security away and make us feel uncomfortable. So that's fresh on my mind right now.

These issues were salient in the midst of heightened social scrutiny of law enforcement practices as well as activist demands to "defund the police" and invest in other areas of social need, such as housing, health care, and marginalized communities.

Participants in the law enforcement focus group critiqued what they saw as knee-jerk and opportunistic responses from politicians to societal demands, for example, to defund the police, or in the wake of specific incidents of violence. In some of these exchanges, the public was depicted as largely uninformed and in need of being educated. According to Rosalie, a member of the police force in a large city:

> When you defund us, when you make all these . . . you say to the public, we're going to make all these concessions for you, you're not telling them that you're trying, in this hand, you're feeding them, but in this hand, you're trying to feed me, you know.

In this narrative, politicians appear as duplicitous, and in another part of the conversation, Rosalie commented that a "politician is going to say whatever you want him to say because he wants to get those votes." She additionally noted how public feelings might influence political debates on crime and violence that are then converted into legislation:

> And so what happens is when the bell gets wrung by that Joe Public or Jane Public, who's just been gone through a . . . and in our case, it would be something where my child, while they were playing in the schoolyard, they were shot, and all they were doing was swinging, and they caught a bullet in the head. The public outcry, the sorrow, that's their fodder. And they come in there and say, "Well, this is why. Bob, here's the bill." That bill has been sitting on your desk for ten years. And all of a sudden, today, you remembered it? You remembered because they play it so they can push stuff through when the emotion is at its height.

These types of statements convey frustration and a certain mistrust about the political adjudication of priorities, including conflicting notions of security. For instance, while abolitionist activists and scholars aim to end the U.S. system of mass incarceration, pointing to the array of injustices that it perpetuates and its failure to create safe communities,[24] members of the law enforcement focus group conveyed frustration with policies that would prevent or reduce detention/incarceration time, which they described as creating further security problems.

References to serial killers, child molesters, and perpetrators of domestic violence were wielded in ways that provided emotional weight to these officers' points, raising the specter of harm connected to especially scary and egregious actions. For instance, Phillip, a longtime member of the police force in a rural area, commented:

> I think bail reform has really affected safety and security when you want to come about that. We have a hard time keeping people safe now. I mean, when you get people, say you got a domestic [violence complaint] and the guy breaks the girl's nose. We arraign them, and they can't go to jail anymore. So that's a real issue, too. And I believe that's why you see crime gone up everywhere in the state, even in our community. Our felonies were way up last year. We have no accountability, and you've got a victim here who's crying, and we basically can't. . . . How do we really help her, you know?

The emotions described in this account, and the gendered vulnerability of the victim, fuel the view that safety and security equal detention or incarceration. The image of a crying young woman with a broken nose carries emotional weight. It can elicit concern and a desire to protect, particularly if she already fits social definitions of a victim who deserves sympathy and support (a construction mediated by intersecting social statuses such as race and class). The type of protection envisioned in this case is jail time for the perpetrator. Yet, feminists concerned with violence against women have engaged in vigorous debates on whether the criminal justice system is a good solution to gender violence, particularly violence against women of color who are less likely to be regarded as "proper" victims and whose communities have disproportionately experienced state violence. Many intersectional feminist scholars and activists have challenged carceral solutions to social problems, and groups and organizations critical of societal reliance on incarceration have experimented with and proposed alternative forms of accountability.[25]

Still, the view that security and safety are connected with keeping people locked up as long as possible is compelling to many. In the focus group discussion with law enforcement members, the emphasis was on holding crime perpetrators accountable in the ways the criminal justice system defines accountability, that is, largely through punitive measures. For example, Arthur, another police officer in the focus group, shared his emotional response to news he heard about a proposed bill to lower the time of incarceration by easing parole:

> I literally got angry and shook my head and like stopped reading it because I was like, you've got to be kidding me [. . .] it's like no longer is anyone going to be held accountable. I work court for overtime, and I sit there every day just shaking my head. Every felony gets reduced to a misdemeanor, and then they get to plea to a violation because they're worried about something being on their record. Oh, I'm sorry, you committed a felony.

The emotional tone of this statement is one of frustration and sarcasm, consistent with the disagreement that members of this focus group expressed regarding policy proposals and reforms interpreted as soft on crime. Absent from these considerations were aspects brought up in other focus groups, such as critiques of the class and racial inequalities that the criminal justice system reproduces, or the social contexts and forms of marginalization that may lead to crime and violence.

Accountability for criminal behavior emerged as a key concern in the law enforcement group, connected with how participants envisioned security. This demand seemed to apply especially to the individuals being policed. Less salient was the accountability of police officers accused of undue use of force and disproportionate violence against people of color, including with fatal consequences. While Rosalie did mention specific measures such as "choke hold" bans and the "diaphragm law" in New York—reforms aimed at curbing police violence and holding officers accountable—these references were in the context of describing how members of the police force are sometimes sought to comment on and give validation to certain policy initiatives.

Regardless of whether members of the group supported the described police reform efforts or not, one can see how a conversation about security can become entwined with emotionally laden issues that have a personal stake for police officers, such as job security or critiques of their conduct. Not surprisingly, the emphasis of their analysis differs from those of activists aiming to end police violence and hold officers accountable. Policing and protest had moved to the center of emotionally contentious political debates, into the wider realm of public feelings, particularly as the killing of Black people by police officers continued and as a flurry of legislative proposals to restrict and criminalize protest proliferated in the aftermath of racial justice demonstrations.[26] The emotions emerging in conversations on policing, protests, and politics reflect and signal a range of meanings and analyses of security. Some of these discussions also reveal varied understandings regarding the presence of guns in U.S. society and the possibility of being harmed by someone with a firearm.

Guns and Social Unrest in Pandemic Times

During the challenging times that surrounded this research, emotions also served as an index of multiple and compounded crises, including the pandemic, heightened racial injustice, economic devastation, and attacks on the basic functioning of electoral democracy. The ongoing environmental crisis also manifested in dramatic and destructive ways in parts of the country, for example, through the massive force of raging fires across the West Coast during the Fall of 2020. These mounting crises also had security implications and involved different sectors of society in both overlapping and distinct ways. Emotions are often intertwined with those kinds of experiences and are also shaped by ideological frameworks, whether it is grief for the loss of life and homes to wildfires, worry and anxiety for loved ones held in prison amid the pandemic, outrage at the sight of racialized police violence, fear of social breakdown, or concern about the erosion of democratic institutions.

In discussions about security/insecurity with different stakeholders, anger, for example, emerged in varied ways in relation to security issues and events of public significance. Monica, from the focus group of mothers, pointed to the combustible combination of anger and guns in the context of armed white vigilantism during racial justice protests. She mentioned the Second Amendment and the associated "right to guns" and related it to the presence of guns in the political sphere: "like I saw a video of the police passing out water to these militia people who had guns—this idea that there's sort of this alternate . . . we can deputize anybody who has a gun, and the anger." From the event description in this and other parts of the conversation, Monica was referring to the confrontations that occurred during an August 25, 2020, demonstration against police violence in Kenosha, Wisconsin, in response to the police shooting of Jacob Blake, a Black man. In addition to the police, this protest was met by armed white civilians, including 17-year-old Kyle Rittenhouse, who showed up carrying a military-style semi-automatic rifle and who was later charged (though ultimately acquitted) for the fatal shooting of two people and injuring a third during the event.[27] Monica's narrative about this case associates insecurity with an emotionally volatile political situation, permeated by anger and aggravated by the presence of private citizens with firearms, who additionally seemed to have the support of law enforcement. Monica characterized the situation as "terrible," "scary," and a "powder keg."

A different way in which anger emerged in focus group discussions about security—beyond noting the anger of political leaders or of clashing groups in the public space—involved participants' own feelings about the social and political events they were witnessing. For instance, this was the case of one participant in the focus group with members of organizations addressing gun violence (two Black men, one Black woman, and one Black/Native woman). As we shall see, in this group, Donna expressed a sense of indignation with respect to the state of affairs in the country, but this emotional thread started with Byron's observation about the rise in demand for guns and toilet paper during the pandemic:

BYRON: [. . .] I've never seen toilet paper and guns being almost in the same headlines, you know, when the pandemic hit. Like all the guns going off the shelf, and all the toilet paper are going off the shelf. I said, I've never seen these things being mentioned in the same. . . . I never knew toilet paper could be the headline, man.
MARK: I heard there's a shortage coming back again, so go as soon as you can.
DONNA: Yep, trust me, I have, I mean, I've packed up a little bit, not too much, but, yeah, you need to run back to the stores and get this toilet because we're getting crazy. But, yes, it's so true. I mean, the environment is just crazy right now. And a lot of people is blaming it on the pandemic, but I think the pandemic is just zeroing in on all these hidden issues that we had all this time. And it's just coming out, and people are paying more attention to it. I've never thought, in my entire life, to see where we are as a nation right now. This is the most ridiculous thing I've ever seen in my damn life. And I've been angry for four years, and now I'm not as angry.

The focus group took place shortly after the presidential election resulting in Joseph Biden's victory, and Donna expressed a "sense of relief," presumably in relation to the prospect of change. She commented: "And I'm just hoping that we could just come to a more civilized thing, you know." Although she did not explicitly mention the end of the Trump presidency, the alluded "four years" coincided with that administration's period.

Rose, a woman in the focus group addressing sexual/gender violence who identified as white/Black, also referred to the previous "four years," mentioning security issues in relation to the political environment of recent times:

> [W]e have had an interesting last four years politically in our country, and what that has—you know, I'm trying to be politically correct here—like what that has incited over time. Right? So I think that we can all admit that there definitely were levels of violence that we had not so openly and blatantly seen and experienced from many large groups of people—not that they didn't exist, and not that they weren't who they were prior to all this—but just people feeling different levels of safety of their own ability to kind of express that in ways that they felt that they could do that, and that causing safety issues for other people.

Like Donna, Rose also suggested that the issues that were surfacing were not necessarily new but found fertile ground for overt expression under recent conditions.

She further referred to the pandemic, the protests against racialized police violence, and the political campaign during the election year as a "trifecta." From her perspective, the piling up of these and other problems not only was difficult to cope with emotionally but also entailed security issues. She summarized: "[A]s a society, I think that we have like safety and security and fear and danger overload. And it's not panning out well." Similarly to how Byron pointed to the intensified demand for guns and toilet paper, Rose mentioned the soaring sales of alcoholic beverages during the pandemic—a trend that was also noted in the media and emerging studies.[28] Some analysts expressed concern that the use of alcohol as way to cope with disturbing emotions might outlive the pandemic, with public health implications.[29] Consistent with Rose's observation, an NPR piece reported: "According to Nielsen's market data, total alcohol sales outside of bars and restaurants have surged roughly 24% during the pandemic [in 2020]. They found sales of spirits with higher alcohol content rose even faster, a more than 27% increase" as compared with the previous year.[30]

Guns, alcoholic beverages, and toilet paper are consumer products that can serve as indicators of public feelings in a fraught social and political environment, with specific security dimensions in the United States, such as the presence of guns and heightened racial tensions. Fear, anger, and trauma are among the emotional responses that different objects may help to soothe or express amid uncertainty and insecurity. The recourse to these types of objects constitutes individualized and market-mediated approaches to dealing with various types of insecurity: whether social unrest in a charged political environment, the inability to satisfy basic needs due to unemployment or underemployment, or other disruptions associated with the public health crisis. Reflecting on the coupled demand for guns and toilet paper, author Debbie Millman pointed to the emotional contours of this phenomenon during the pandemic, arguing that these artifacts

> fulfill both our most primal physiological needs and the need for security and safety. These things provide us with immediate gratification as we search for something tangible to assuage our anxiety. The coronavirus has incited an unparalleled level of uncertainty not only into our individual lives but also the broader culture we are a part of; it has tapped into our deepest fears about the future.[31]

In a similar vein, media outlets reported that bulletproof vests were also increasingly sought in the context of the pandemic, police violence, and political turmoil, including after the storming of the U.S. Capitol by Trump supporters. Company and news reports described an increase in demand for body armor—among other "tactical gear"—by not only security personnel but also the more general citizenry.[32] The company Bulletproof Zone made the link between body armor, violence, and the coronavirus, noting that

> the increased risk of violence and chaos plus the decline in available resources raised the pressure in the public at a striking level. While you hope that the need for one does not come, it is better to be safe than sorry.[33]

This company's cautionary note appeals to emotions such as fear and anxiety, which were in large supply during much of the pandemic. Additionally, bulletproof apparel company Thyk Skynn—which seemed to cater especially to the Black community—reportedly saw a "nearly 400 percent increase in sales" around August 2020 "as Americans continue to grow concerned about their protection from police shootings and other random acts of violence."[34] This increase in sales did not materialize for everyone: A representative of a different company told me the pandemic had a negative effect on his business: Sales were "trickling because no one [was] buying anything except for ammo, ammunition." Still, he alluded to the relationship he perceived between "ammo" and bulletproof garments: "[Y]ou would think that since you can't get ammunition, what's the next best thing to protect yourself? Body armor." Some focus group participants also noted the presence of body armor in the public scene, worn by members of different political factions—from white supremacists to anti-racist protesters.

Focus group members alluded to fear or concern about various situations involving guns, for instance, school shootings, gun violence in urban communities, armed white supremacist groups, or heavily armed police. While guns can be scary and gun injury is something that body armor is meant to protect against, guns can also provide a sense of security and peace of mind to people who believe this is a valid and effective means of protection. At the same time, the presence of guns itself can be a source of fear or worry for others. This was the case for Sam—a participant in the teachers focus group—who expressed being "nervous" when he learned that his school "campus service officer had an AR-15 in a safe in his office." AR-15 style rifles are a particularly lethal and destructive type of firearm, which were used in several highly publicized mass shootings, including at the Marjory Stoneman Douglas High School in Parkland, Florida (2018) and the Sandy Hook Elementary School in Newtown, Connecticut (2012).[35] Its presence at school, even if under the control of security personnel, was not reassuring to Sam.

Anxieties, fears, and concerns were implicit and explicit in various media descriptions of recent developments in the gun world, for instance, an increase in firearms trainings.[36] This trend was mentioned in the focus group with gun rights supporters, which was composed of two white women and two white men. Katherine, who teaches various gun-related skills, linked this growing interest in gun training to the pandemic, saying: "I think, within the last year or so, especially since the COVID hit, that more people are stepping up to get the training that they need, get the defense, especially in the women field." Eleanor, who identified as a firearms educator, agreed and added another dimension: "social unrest." She elaborated on this trend based on her own experience as an instructor:

> Yeah. I absolutely concur with everything that everyone else has said. You know, being, in a normal year, I'll teach about five to six women on target clinics. This year, it's been 14. In a normal year, I'll teach these clinics spread out amongst like four different gun clubs. This year, it was six. And in a

normal year, I'll teach about 90 women just in these clinics alone, 1-day clinics, and this year it was 232. And my phone started exploding with all of these women calling for training in about [. . .] the May–June timeframe, when the social unrest exploded. You know, and, again, here again, they were not interested one iota in getting into the fight. That's not what they were about. They were all about, what happens if it comes on to my doorstep?

Consistent with the experiences of the two women in the gun rights supporters focus group, the organization A Girl & A Gun Women's Shooting League (AG & AG), which has chapters across the country, "saw an influx of new memberships. In July 2020, memberships were up 150% over the previous year."[37] The organization surveyed its members and found that "personal protection is the primary reason why women are seeking firearms training."[38] When new shooters were asked "What prompted you to learn about firearms?," among the top reasons given among 13 possibilities were the social and political contexts: "Riots/fear of mobs and civil unrest" (14%) and "Upcoming elections/concern of bans" (12%).[39] The large majority of respondents to the New Shooter Survey by AG & AG were white (77%), while 9% were Hispanic/Latinx, 7% were Black/African American, and 2% were multiracial (3% preferred not to respond to this demographic question and 2% were categorized within "other entries").[40]

While the specifics of the year 2020 apparently influenced an uptick in women's interest in firearms, scholar Caroline E. Light points to longer-term developments that resulted in increasing opportunities and appeals to women to arm themselves for self-defense, including from organizations such as the National Rifle Association.[41] Yet Light argues that in actuality "the invitation to armed empowerment isn't for *all* women."[42] She also points out that the people from which women have been called to protect themselves "aren't just *any* perpetrators; the trope is rooted in white nationalist assumptions of gender and sexual violence, which depend upon the juxtaposition of white women's vulnerability with implicitly racialized and classed figures of predatory masculinity."[43] One may wonder how these tropes might inflect fear, anxiety, and perceptions of danger in contexts of social unrest, such as those that emerged in 2020.

The period of social unrest that Eleanor referred to—May–June, 2020—coincides with the massive multiracial demonstrations against police violence and for racial justice in the United States, though this was not explicitly stated in the discussion (neither were terms like "race," "racism," or "Black Lives Matter" mentioned).[44] The vast majority of these remarkably widespread protests were peaceful, but some devolved into confrontations with the police, vandalism, and looting by a minority of people in different parts of the country (including violence that was reportedly instigated by "*agent provocateurs*" in some cases)[45]—which in turn convoked focused media attention. While "social unrest"—as part of the impetus for women to seek gun training—was discussed in racial neutral terms in the focus group, racial injustices and racial politics were at the core of the many demonstrations during the mentioned period.

The motivations and emotions associated with the surge in gun purchases and training need to be understood not only in relation to the specific events at hand but also in the context of group histories and individual location in the social structure.[46] White men are the most likely gun owners in the United States, and research such as Angela Stroud's suggests that, for some groups, upholding "patriarchal authority" and "defense against racialized others" is implicated in gun ownership.[47] Jennifer Carlson refers to scholarship that analyzes the "overrepresentation of white, conservative men among gun owners, gun carriers, and gun rights advocates" pointing to "fear of crime, racial resentment, status anxiety, and socioeconomic insecurity as key factors shaping the appeal of guns."[48] Interestingly, around the time of this research, several reports noted a growing trend of gun purchases among other demographic groups—such as women, Black, and Hispanic people—including as first-time gun owners. Among the reasons cited were the need for personal protection in the context of fear of social breakdown connected to the pandemic, heightened racial tensions, and social and political unrest.[49] These concerns should be placed within a larger social and political context. According to Carlson's review, scholarly analyses of

> progun attitudes and practices among women, racial minorities, and sexual minorities show that guns are not simply a reflection of conservative ideology but also embedded in relations of inequality and domination that shape the constraining contexts in which guns become appealing objects of self-preservation and self-defense.[50]

For instance, in the case of Black people, the impetus for armed self-defense may be understood within the context of historical and contemporary manifestations of violence against Black communities, by both civilians and the police.[51]

Black communities have been particularly affected by and concerned about gun violence, and stakeholders interested in preventing this violence have spoken about the need to situate it within multiple forms of trauma related to racism, systematic disinvestment in communities of color, and law enforcement approaches that fail to keep communities safe.[52] Beverly, from the focus group of gun violence prevention advocates, highlighted distinct group experiences as she discussed fear of gun violence. She said that

> gun violence does stem from also trauma and mental health issues. But in the Black community, you also have systemic oppression layered on top of that that heightens it and creates it to be a bigger issue. So I think that it's just different levels and dynamics of what gun violence looks like, depending on what community you are in.

According to a nationally representative survey by the Pew Research Center:

> Concerns about gun violence, particularly in local communities, vary greatly by race. Nearly half (49%) of blacks and 29% of Hispanics say gun violence

is a very big problem in their local community; just 11% of whites rate this as a very big problem.[53]

The same study shows that a large majority of Black people (73%) also expressed concern about gun violence in the country as a whole versus 62% of Hispanics and 44% of whites. Additionally, the report points to a "racial gap" in terms of the experience of having been threatened by guns, something more likely for Black people:

> Roughly a third of blacks (32%) say someone has used a gun to threaten or intimidate them or their family, compared with 20% of whites. About a quarter of Hispanics (24%) say this has happened to them or their family members.[54]

These statistics reveal both a racially inflected incidence of armed aggression, especially likely to be experienced by people of color, and a concerning level of incidence even in the case of white people who experience it at lower rates.

Whether due to mass shootings in schools or more frequent forms of gun violence, the loss of family and community members is a cause of grief, no matter the group. Still, Beverly underscored how there are group-specific dimensions to these types of events in the context of broader trauma and oppression. From the standpoint of emotions, we can see how the question of security is enmeshed with emotional responses such as sadness and grief, and yet Judith Butler's question about whose lives are "grievable" is pertinent here. Indeed, not all lives are given the same importance socially when it comes to grieving, mourning, caring, and addressing problems that disproportionally affect marginalized communities.[55] According to an analysis based on data from the Center for Disease Control:

> Fifty-three % of all firearm homicide victims (63% of male victims) in 2019 were Black males. Across all ages, Black men were nearly 8 times more likely to die by firearm homicide than the general population (all sexes) and 14 times more likely to die by firearm homicide than White men. Black males were followed by (in order of decreasing risk): American Indian/Alaska Native, Latino/Hispanic, White, and Asian/Pacific Islander males.[56]

In the case of the loss of life of Black people at the hands of police officers, a whole movement had to emerge to powerfully assert that "Black Lives Matter." Participants in the gun violence prevention movement also pointed to the deadly impact of gun violence in communities of color, not only by law enforcement but also by ordinary citizens, which has cut short the lives of so many youths.[57] Activists and advocates of color often have to take an extra step to assert the value of those lives against the backdrop of a "broader cultural/societal narrative of black criminality" by which "black and brown victims are not presumed innocent, stripping them of their worthiness to be mourned."[58] Which kinds of gun violence receive public attention is also influenced by the politics of race and the types of communities affected.

50 Emotions and Security

In that vein, gun violence prevention advocate, Byron, contrasted the proliferation of active shooter drills in schools (often evoking the specter of mass shootings in predominantly white, suburban schools[59]) with the need to also attend to everyday gun violence in marginalized communities, beyond school settings. He asked:

> But what about when a youth got to walk home, what's the drills that you're showing the youth when they walk home? We have all these makeshift memorials that the youth walk by every day, mothers walking by with their kids by these makeshift memorials every day. And they got to have that discussion. But we need to have that discussion as a whole.

In the face of state, institutional, and societal failures to prevent gun violence, it is as though affected communities are only left to grieve and mourn the dead. And yet, activists and advocates of gun violence prevention, such as those who joined the focus group with related participants, are mobilizing for change. They are creating multiple structures of support, including education programs and community outreach, as well as appealing to government officials and other authorities to enact meaningful change. Still, public mourning rituals—which include the expression of emotions such as grief, anger, and moral indignation—are integral to denouncing injustice, connecting with the public, and inspiring political action to prevent gun violence.[60] In other words, in efforts to tackle the insecurities associated with gun violence, emotions can help amplify circles of concern, enlist solidarity, and make the case for social change.

Feeling and Envisioning "Genuine Security"

Most of the emotions that emerged in stakeholders' conversations about security were those often categorized as "negative" (e.g., fear, worry, anger, and sadness). Yet other emotional responses that are generally seen as "positive" (e.g., compassion and empathy) were also discussed or expressed by some of the focus group participants, including by way of pointing to their absence. Monica—from the mothers focus group—invoked the need for empathy. She mentioned empathy as she reflected on the various forms of insecurity that surfaced in 2020 with particular force, including the insecurities stemming from systemic racism, unemployment or underemployment, and uneven access to education. She commented:

> I think it has been really eye-opening in terms of [. . .] the privilege, and just trying to have a greater empathy for the lack of security that we all have, and then work with the solution. What are we going to do about it?

While referring to "all," Monica did not equate the forms of insecurity that different groups faced but did encourage a more empathic and holistic approach that recognizes each situation. She said, "[Y]ou can have security, but you need to be thinking about the other, and how we all can have security—to think about that."

Similarly, Claire—a nurses' union representative who participated in the health care workers focus group—invoked related emotions that she saw as necessary to improve the current state of society. She asked: "Where is our compassion?" In her view, "we'd have to just treat each other with more respect and compassion."

These calls for empathy, compassion, and respect toward other people are in contrast with emotions such as fear, anger, and anxiety, which have flourished in the polarized political environment of recent times. The defensive and alert stances that sometimes surround such emotional states also echo atomistic views of society as a collection of separate and self-reliant individuals. Still, these views do not necessarily prevent tender emotions toward those in the "in-group" (close family or community members). Rather, they might not be extended to those who are seen as too different, construed as undeserving, or viewed as potential threats (e.g., based on race-ethnicity, nationality, religion, and social class). In that context, appeals to empathy and compassion are also about building bridges and recognizing a sense of shared humanity, interdependency, and need for connection—for both basic survival and resolution of common problems. Sociologist Arlie Hochschild speaks of the need for empathy to "go global, perhaps even harder, it has to go local—three zip codes down the street, up or down the class ladder. It must cross the barriers of class, race, and gender."[61] Aware that people have different "empathy maps"—which include some fellow human beings but exclude others, she also advocates for crossing the "empathy walls" that hinder dialogue and understanding among people on different sides of ideological and political divides.[62] From that perspective, empathy would be required to cooperatively tackle some of the central problems the world faces, such as catastrophic environmental degradation. In that sense, it is important to ask who we empathize with, which experiences tend to elicit our compassion, and which stories meet our indifference, or perhaps callousness and contempt.

Scholars have also cast empathy and compassion in a critical light. For instance, compassion often implies a hierarchical relation between the subject of the emotion and those toward whom it is extended (e.g., between the "haves" and the "have-nots").[63] Further, compassion that leads to charity, humanitarianism, and "rescue" of those deemed worthy is not the same as organizing society in ways that guarantee human rights across the board or that fosters solidarity based on a vision of social justice. With respect to empathy, this emotional stance often involves processes of identification and it can entail other sorts of biases, which can leave out those who are construed as too different or too undeserving to be extended that emotion.[64] Empathy may also result in appropriation of the experience of others[65] in ways that center the individual who is extending empathy rather than those to whom the emotion is directed. In a commentary regarding societal responses to racial injustice in the United States in the aftermath of the killing of George Floyd, historian Robin D.G. Kelley warns: "Empathy can reinforce racism, ethnocentrism, sexism, ableism, etc., because we look for ourselves in others rather than take the time to understand the social, historical, and cultural contexts of people's lives."[66] As part of the same dialogue, memory studies scholar Marianne

Hirsch similarly advocates for "eschewing identification and even empathy, in favor of accompaniment, solidarity and co-resistance in the political fight for systemic change."[67] And Kate Schick proposes a "greater emphasis on listening, and vulnerable interrogation of the self as well as the other."[68]

Activist and scholarly observations about the systemic dimensions of social problems, which nevertheless are experienced at a personal and often emotional level, remind us that having the "right" emotions may not be sufficient. Furthermore, while emotions such as love, interest, hope, and gratitude can have positive social and personal impacts, emotions that are often deemed negative are sometimes warranted responses to entrenched injustices or to the insecurities generated by the failures of social systems. This is illustrated in one of the exchanges in the health care workers focus groups, which addressed long-term problems in the health care system in connection to various dimensions of security.[69] Following Claire's call for compassion and "to be nice and respectful to each other," Sophia, who was working as a case manager in a health care facility, followed up pointing out the limitations of individual kindness amid a failing system. She contextualized the anger that sometimes erupts in health care settings, an emotion easily directed to frontline workers:

> I think one of the ways that I see people being angry, at least as a case manager, is that they are pushed up against a wall a lot of times in terms of they have a loved one in the hospital, and the system in place is not good. And they are mad, because they are not able to . . . they're overwhelmed with their situations. And then on top of that, the way that people are billed, and the way that the hospital has to get people out as soon as possible, and the way that nurses . . . have too many patients and can't take the time to make sure pain is managed. And so people are feeling very out of control of their lives, unable to help their loved ones. And so I agree. We need to be kind, but I think it goes when people feel trapped and don't have agency in their lives to make their lives better, they're going to feel angry. And I think right now a lot of the way that health care is set up is just not for people. It is . . . we need, it needs to be economical, but I think that the system is just not, is not for caring, and it's not for healing, and it's not set up to do those things right now.

Drew, a younger nurse in the health care workers group, concurred with Sophia and pointed out that nurses are often the face of the institution and, as such, the target of anger and frustration in the context described. According to Drew, "patients are going to become frustrated and patients are going to become angry at the care that they're not getting. [. . .] So that does lead to violence, that does lead to insecurity for patients and for nurses." In other parts of the conversation, the group discussed the eruption of physical forms of violence in health care settings, even with firearms in some cases. Drew and Sophia's reflections point to more than the need of individual changes in behavior or emotion but structural transformations.

Marie, a nurse with a long trajectory in the field, called for a "huge system change" to address the insecurities discussed and the barriers to provide needed care.

In the discussions about security, particularly amid the pandemic and other crises, we can see how care may be linked to certain dimensions of security, particularly in its "human security" version. Care has also been explicitly included in antimilitaristic and feminist activist calls for "genuine security," which build on the notion of human security and link its absence to systemic oppression.[70] While the importance of care may be more obvious in the case of health security, the connection between care and security is important in other settings as well, and there too is entangled with various emotions. Amelia, an experienced teacher, recalled her desire to create a sense of security for her students in the context of the pandemic and the aftermath of racialized police violence that was in the media spotlight:

> [W]hen we're on remote [instruction] last spring, my partner and I had just finished teaching *All American Boys*, which is a very racially charged book [addressing police brutality]. And George Floyd was murdered while we were like still in the throes of that book, and we had just finished, and we struggled, as teachers, with how to respond to our students. And, you know, in the shower that morning, I wrote this letter in my head of what I would say if I were in person to them, because then security took on a different feeling to me. It took on a feeling from a mother, and I wanted to grab those kids, all of them, and hug them tight and make them feel safe, not only physically, but safe emotionally and safe like I work really, really hard to make my classroom a safe place for them. One that they feel they can come to.

Amelia's caring approach was evident in her efforts to create a safe environment for her students during a socially and politically tumultuous time. She strove to deal with a hard situation while providing nurturance and a welcoming place. Her emotional investment and yearning for physical closeness were also gendered to the extent that she associated the type of security she wanted to provide with motherly feelings and practices. This raises questions about the role of (gendered) emotions with respect to different conceptualization of security. Consider the contrast between Amelia's narrative of connection and care as a form of security with the emotions associated with other security practices and discourses, exalting fences, surveillance, and militarization. In school settings, for example, a different meaning of security is embedded in the installation of metal detectors and active shooter drills[71]—approaches that can be associated with disturbing emotions such as fear, rather than a "safe place" in the sense that Amelia envisioned. Additionally, a nurturing approach is not characteristic of male-dominated occupations involved in implementing notions of security focused on crime prevention, border control, and militarized prowess.

While care can be thought of as paramount to achieving "genuine security,"[72] it is often associated with feminized activities and subjectivities. A caring and empathic disposition is a central component of various occupations in which workers tend to other people's needs, strive for their well-being, and help them cope with multiple types of insecurity. Many of these occupations are populated by women (e.g., teachers, nurses, social workers, and childcare and eldercare providers) and share in some of the feminized expectations—including emotional—applied to unpaid care work at home. Much of this work is devalued or undervalued, particularly when performed by women of color, and at the same time expected to be a "labor of love."[73] While this labor addresses essential needs, its "romanticization" in its emotional dimensions can easily morph into an "excuse for oppression."[74] In light of these considerations, we might ask, who cares for the carers? What about their security?—including their physical and economic security and the sense of security derived from feeling valued and respected.

Around the time of the focus group with health care workers, unionized nurses in Albany, New York, participated in a 24-hour strike to protest, among other things, practices they saw as endangering both patients and personnel during the pandemic. The CEO of the medical facility responded to this labor measure in emotional terms, opining that for the striking "nurses to walk away from their patients during this global health crisis is irresponsible and, quite frankly, heartbreaking" (in the meantime temporary workers were hired to fill the gap).[75] One of the nurses commented in emotional terms too but with a different analysis:

> It's sad. [. . .] This is a facility that has so much access to wealth and knowledge, and its nurses have to stand out here and strike to get safe staffing, PPE [Personal Protective Equipment] and a fair wage?[76]

The mobilization of emotion by management could serve to pit patients against nurses, reinforce a sacrificial demand on the latter, and downplay workers' rights to be safe at their workplaces (which in the context of a contagious disease is also entangled with patients' safety). In the case of the nurse, the emotion of sadness seems to stem from feeling forced into a last-resort measure due to institutional failure to properly address the various dimensions of security she expected. In the conflict surrounding different aspects of security, emotions are sometimes mobilized to put those who denounce prevailing arrangements "in their place." Emotional displays and statements sometimes individualize the conflict with moralizing tones while leaving the social structures that create insecurity intact. This begs the question of how to organize institutions and society in ways that mind for everyone's security, broadly defined.

Drew, a queer-identified nurse who works in a different facility, spoke about other dimensions of security, this time in relation to how people react to one's "personal identity," including in the area of nursing. Drew specifically referred to interactions in health care settings and the nursing field: "I think all of those people aren't necessarily kind and accepting of who I am at my core." Lack of acceptance of diverse sexual/gender identities has taken diverse forms in society, including violent ones, creating insecurity for those who do not fit hetero- and gendernormative scripts. Drew also narrated other work-related experiences in which emotion, identity, inequality, and security matters were interlinked, in this case in the context of racism:

> One of my nursing colleagues was speaking to me about all of the micro aggression she feels as a Black woman in nursing, and just about the recent, all the recent turmoil in the country about police brutality and Black Lives Matter, and how she just feels like she doesn't matter, and her voice doesn't matter.

These examples contain many layers of meaning related to inequality. They throw into relief how members of feminized occupations—in intersection with other vectors of inequality such as race-ethnicity—are often expected to care for others, even sacrifice themselves for others, but might not feel that they are cared for, valued, or offered basic levels of security. How might notions of security shift when considered from the perspective of care?

In imagining "genuine security," social arrangements based on the recognition of the human need for care, support, and connection—as opposed to those based on fear, mistrust, and separation—might lead to more sustainable and broader forms of security than those premised on circles of enclosure, surveillance, and gun proliferation. It is important to note that while care and the emotions expected in care-oriented occupations have been associated with the feminine, care as an emotional disposition, practice, and principle of social organization does not need to be attached to any particular gender. Instead, structures of care could be valued and spread throughout society as essential for individual, community, and societal survival and security.

Conclusion

No matter how one defines security—whether as protection against the threat of violence or in more expansive ways—emotions are entwined with ideas, experiences, and approaches to security. This is the case not only in international relations but also at the level of domestic politics and local communities. The emotions surrounding experiences of security/insecurity by different groups do not happen in a vacuum but are connected to existing relations of power as well as concrete social and political events that spark emotions. Debates about gun violence and gun rights, harm and accountability, political protest and the quality of democracy, policing practices and racism, economic inequalities and health disparities, and gender and sexual identities are all relevant to conceptions and experiences of security/insecurity in which emotions play an important role.

Cognitive assessments are enmeshed with emotions that matter to interpretations of security. Emotions influence interpretation of political events, ways of coping with crises of insecurity, and the articulation of favored security strategies by individuals and communities—whether they entail accumulating guns, buying body armor, pushing for policy reforms, or organizing mutual aid. In that sense, we might ask what emotions have been invited to or excluded from the political realm at different historical moments and how they affect conceptualizations and practices of security at the macro level of political systems and micro level of individual experience. What is the role of expanded circles of love, care, grief, and solidarity? In which ways have the emotions associated with misogyny, white supremacy, economic dominance, and exclusionary practices bolstered multiple and intersecting forms of insecurity? Which emotions respond to injustice and how are they mobilized against dominant notions of security? As we have seen, during the period of this study, various sets of emotions were visible in the public sphere as the country grappled with mounting crises and layers of insecurity. Many of these emotions related to what the state—its political actors, policies, and institutions—was or was not doing, though it also involved other social arrangements, cultural norms, and interpersonal relations.

This broad panorama of security and emotions helps situate gun-related concerns and ballistic products in proper context. The following chapter narrows the lens to focus on one particular security strategy to protect against gun-related injury or death: bulletproof fashion. As we shall see, armored garments appeal to different groups of people—and social context matters. While some security strategies rely on the state, private security guards, or community organizations, bulletproof fashion consists of consumer products. They are part of the expansion of certain security modalities across civilian society, through commodification mechanisms that are also heavily reliant on emotions.

Notes

1 See Neta C. Crawford, "The Passion of World Politics: Propositions on Emotion and Emotional Relationships," *International Security* 24, no. 4 (2020): 116–56; Roland Bleiker and Emma Hutchison, "Fear No More: Emotions and World Politics," *Review of International Studies* 34, no. S1 (2008): 115–35; Linda Åhäll and Thomas A. Gregory, "Security, Emotions, Affect," *Critical Studies on Security* 1, no. 1 (2013): 117–20; Simon Koschut, Todd H. Hall, Reinhard Wolf, Ty Solomon, Emma Hutchison, and Roland Bleiker, "Discourse and Emotions in International Relations," *International Studies Review* 19, no. 3 (2017): 481–508; Michelle Pace and Ali Bilgic, "Studying Emotions in Security and Diplomacy: Where We Are Now and Challenges Ahead," *Political Psychology* 40, no. 6 (2019): 1407–17; Simon Koschut, "Emotion, Discourse, and Power in World Politics," pp. 3–26 in *The Power of Emotions in World Politics,* ed. Simon Koschut (New York: Routledge, 2020).
2 Jeff Goodwin, James M. Jasper, and Francesca Polletta, *Passionate Politics: Emotions and Social Movements* (Chicago: University of Chicago Press, 2001); James M. Jasper, *The Emotions of Protest* (Chicago: The University of Chicago Press, 2018).
3 Barbara Keys and Claire Yorke, "Personal and Political Emotions in the Mind of the Diplomat," *Political Psychology* 40, no. 6 (2019): 1235–49, 1235.
4 Laura Sjoberg, "Centering Security Studies Around Felt, Gendered Insecurities," *Journal of Global Security Studies* 1, no. 1 (2016): 51–63.
5 Sara Ahmed, *The Cultural Politics of Emotion* (Edinburgh: Edinburgh University Press, 2014); Eduardo Bonilla-Silva, "Feeling Race: Theorizing the Racial Economy of Emotions," *American Sociological Review* 84, no. 1 (2019): 1–25.
6 Crawford, "The Passion of World Politics."
7 Crawford, "The Passion of World Politics."

8 Bleiker and Hutchison, "Fear No More," 119.
9 Peter Collin, Robert Garot, and Timon De Groot, "Bureaucracy and Emotions—Perspectives across Disciplines," *Administory* 3, no. 1 (2018): 5–19, 5.
10 Ahmed, *The Cultural Politics of Emotion*, 43.
11 Jasper, *The Emotions of Protest*.
12 Sophia Boutilier, "Feeling Privilege: How Frustration and Reward Reveal Solidarity Commitments among Development Workers," paper presented at the Sociologists for Women in Society Winter Meeting, Online, January 2021, 27–31.
13 Ahmed, *The Cultural Politics of Emotion*, 191.
14 Ann Cvetkovich, "Public Feelings," *South Atlantic Quarterly* 106, no. 3 (2007): 459–68.
15 See, for example, the embodied emotions associated with public and political events in the context of the economic crisis of late 2001 in Argentina: Barbara Sutton, *Bodies in Crisis: Culture, Violence, and Women's Resistance in Neoliberal Argentina* (New Brunswick: Rutgers University Press, 2010).
16 Jasper, *The Emotions of Protest*.
17 Cvetkovich, "Public Feelings," 460.
18 See a video of the exchange posted by the Associated Press, "Trump Tells Proud Boys: 'Stand Back and Stand By,'" Video, September 30, 2020, www.youtube.com/watch?v=qIHhB1ZMV_o.
19 "Presidential Debate: Trump and Biden Trade Insults in Chaotic Debate," *BBC*, September 30, 2020, www.bbc.com/news/election-us-2020-54350538.
20 John Bowden, "GOP Representative: Some Republicans Voted to Challenge Election Results Due to Safety Concerns," *The Hill*, January 10, 2021, https://thehill.com/homenews/house/533548-gop-representative-some-republicans-voted-to-challenge-election-results-due-to.
21 See, for example, Barbara Sutton and Kari Marie Norgaard, "Cultures of Denial: Avoiding Knowledge of State Violations of Human Rights in Argentina and the United States," *Sociological Forum* 28, no. 3 (2013): 495–524.
22 Sara Ahmed, "Affective Economies," *Social Text* 22, no. 2 (2004): 117–39, 120.
23 See, for example, Sean Illing, "The 'Abolish the Police' Movement, Explained by 7 Scholars and Activists," *Vox*, June 12, 2020, www.vox.com/policy-and-politics/2020/6/12/21283813/george-floyd-blm-abolish-the-police-8cantwait-minneapolis.
24 Angela Y. Davis, "Deepening the Debate over Mass Incarceration," *Socialism and Democracy* 28, no. 3 (2014): 15–23; Michelle Alexander, *The New Jim Crow: Mass Incarceration in the Age of Colorblindness* (New York: The New Press, 2020).
25 INCITE! Women of Color against Violence, ed., *Color of Violence: The Incite! Anthology* (Cambridge: South End Press, 2006); Danielle Sered, *Until We Reckon: Violence, Mass Incarceration, and a Road to Repair* (New York: The New Press, 2019); Beth E. Richie, Valli Kalei Kanuha, and Kayla Marie Martensen, "Colluding with and Resisting the State: Organizing against Gender Violence in the U.S," *Feminist Criminology* 16, no. 3 (2021): 247–65.
26 See, for example, Reid J. Epstein and Patricia Mazzei, "G.O.P. Bills Target Protesters (and Absolve Motorists Who Hit Them)," *New York Times*, April 21, 2021, Updated June 16, 2021, www.nytimes.com/2021/04/21/us/politics/republican-anti-protest-laws.html.
27 See, for example, the following journalistic narrative of the event: Haley Willis, Muyi Xiao, Christiaan Triebert, Christoph Koettl, Stella Cooper, David Botti, John Ismay, and Ainara Tiefenthäler, "Tracking the Suspect in the Fatal Kenosha Shootings," *New York Times*, August 27, 2020, updated April 22, 2021, www.nytimes.com/2020/08/27/us/kyle-rittenhouse-kenosha-shooting-video.html. The names of the two white men killed are Joseph Rosenbaum and Anthony Huber. Gaige Grosskreutz, also a white man, was injured but survived. In a much-debated trial, Rittenhouse—who claimed self-defense—was acquitted of all charges (see, e.g., Julie Bosman, "What to Know About the Trial of Kyle Rittenhouse," *New York Times*, November 19, 2021, www.nytimes.com/article/kyle-rittenhouse-trial.html.)

28 See, for example, Elyse R. Grossman, Sara E. Benjamin-Neelon, and Susan Sonnenschein, "Alcohol Consumption during the COVID-19 Pandemic: A Cross-Sectional Survey of US Adults," *International Journal of Environmental Research and Public Health*, 17, no. 24 (2020): 9189; Michael S. Pollard, Joan S. Tucker, and Harold D. Green, "Changes in Adult Alcohol Use and Consequences During the COVID-19 Pandemic in the US," *JAMA Network Open* 3, no. 9 (2020): e2022942.
29 Brian Mann, "Hangover from Alcohol Boom Could Last Long After Pandemic Ends," *NPR,* September 11, 2020, www.npr.org/2020/09/11/908773533/hangover-from-alcohol-boom-could-last-long-after-pandemic-ends.
30 Mann, "Hangover from Alcohol Boom Could Last Long After Pandemic Ends."
31 Debbie Millman, "The Real Reason People Are Hoarding Toilet Paper and Guns," *Fast Company*, April 20, 2020, www.fastcompany.com/90491828/the-real-reason-people-are-hoarding-toilet-paper-and-guns.
32 See, for example, Anna M. Phillips and Brian Contreras, "After a Year of Civil Unrest, the U.S. Is Running Low on Body Armor and Gas Masks," *Los Angeles Times*, January 15, 2021, www.latimes.com/politics/story/2021-01-15/after-a-year-of-civil-unrest-the-u-s-is-running-low-on-body-armor-and-gas-masks; Bloomberg, "Americans Are Frantically Buying Military Gear before the Election," *Fortune*, October 24, 2020, https://fortune.com/2020/10/24/military-gear-gas-masks-protests/; Ryan Broderick, "It's Not Just Food and Hand Sanitizer—Panicked Coronavirus Shoppers Are Stocking Up On Guns and Body Armor," *BuzzFeed News*, March 12, 2020, www.buzzfeednews.com/article/ryanhatesthis/its-not-just-food-and-hand-sanitizer-panicked-coronavirus.
33 Nicolette Erestain, "What Does Body Armor Have to Do with the Coronavirus (COVID-19)?" *Bulletproof Zone*, March 24, 2020, https://bulletproofzone.com/blogs/bullet-proof-blog/what-does-body-armor-have-to-do-with-the-coronavirus.
34 "Black-Owned Line of Bulletproof Vests for Adults and Children Sees 400% Increase in Sales," *Blackbusinees.com*, August 31, 2020, www.blackbusiness.com/2020/08/thyk-skynn-black-owned-bulletproof-vests-increase-in-sales-demand.html.
35 For the characteristics and types of injuries caused by this weapon, see, for example, Heather Sher, "What I Saw Treating the Victims from Parkland Should Change the Debate on Guns," *The Atlantic*, February 22, 2018, www.theatlantic.com/politics/archive/2018/02/what-i-saw-treating-the-victims-from-parkland-should-change-the-debate-on-guns/553937/. Reported mass shootings with AR-15 style rifles are listed by Bayliss Wagner, "Fact Check: AR-15 Style Rifles Used in 11 Mass Shootings since 2012," *USA Today*, April 23, 2021, www.usatoday.com/story/news/factcheck/2021/04/22/fact-check-post-missing-context-ar-15-rifles-and-mass-shootings/7039204002/.
36 See, for example, Monica Ortiz, "Local Firearm Training Facilities Sees Increased Demand for Classes During Pandemic," *CBS19*, July 23, 2020, www.cbs19.tv/article/life/local-firearm-training-facility-sees-increased-demand-for-classes-during-pandemic/501-638adc54-13d8-4342-b0ce-e46284a85edf; Tim McLaughlin and Melissa Fares, "U.S. Gun Sales Soar Amid Pandemic, Social Unrest, Election Fears," *Reuters*, October 15, 2020, www.reuters.com/article/usa-guns-insight/u-s-gun-sales-soar-amid-pandemic-social-unrest-election-fears-idUSKBN2701HP.
37 Robyn Sandoval, "Why Are Women Buying Guns?" *A Girl and A Gun* (blog), August 20, 2020, www.agirlandagun.org/why-are-women-buying-guns/.
38 Sandoval, "Why Are Women Buying Guns?"
39 The latter was virtually tied with having been "Urged by family member/friend" (12%).
40 Sandoval, "Why Are Women Buying Guns?"
41 Caroline E. Light, " 'What Real Empowerment Looks Like': White Rage and the Necropolitics of Armed Womanhood," *Signs: Journal of Women in Culture and Society* 46, no. 4 (2021): 911–37.
42 Light, "What Real Empowerment Looks Like," 911.
43 Light, "What Real Empowerment Looks Like," 911.
44 See, for example, "In Pictures: A Racial Reckoning in America," *Cable News Network (CNN)*, July 9, 2020, www.cnn.com/2020/05/27/us/gallery/george-floyd-demonstrations/index.html; Derrick Bryson Taylor, "George Floyd Protests: A

Timeline," *New York Times*, March 28, 2021, www.nytimes.com/article/george-floyd-protests-timeline.html.
45 Armed Conflict Location & Event Data Project (ACLED), "Demonstrations & Political Violence in America: New Data for Summer 2020," 2020, https://acleddata.com/acleddatanew/wp-content/uploads/2020/09/ACLED_USDataReview_Sum2020_SeptWebPDF_HiRes.pdf.
46 Regarding firearm sales, June 2020 had seen "the highest on record (since data collection began in 1998), with 3.9 million firearms sold" (Philip Levine and Robin McKnight, "Three Million More Guns: The Spring 2020 Spike in Firearm Sales," *Brookings*, July 13, 2020, www.brookings.edu/blog/up-front/2020/07/13/three-million-more-guns-the-spring-2020-spike-in-firearm-sales/). Also, the *New York Times* reported: "Americans bought 15.1 million guns [. . .] from March through September [2020], a 91 percent leap from the same period in 2019 [. . . .] The F.B.I. has also processed more background checks for gun purchases in just the first nine months of 2020 than it has for any previous full year" (Dionee Searcey and Richard A. Oppel Jr., "A Divided Nation Agrees on One Thing: Many People Want a Gun," *New York Times*, November 30, 2020, www.nytimes.com/2020/10/27/us/guns-2020-election.html).
47 Angela Stroud, "Guns Don't Kill People . . . : Good Guys and the Legitimization of Gun Violence," *Humanities and Social Sciences Communications* 7, no. 169 (2020), https://doi.org/10.1057/s41599-020-00673-x, 2.
48 Jennifer Carlson, "Gun Studies and the Politics of Evidence," *Annual Review of Law and Social Science* 16, no. 1 (2020): 183–202, 194.
49 See, for example, Chauncey Alcorn, "First-Time Buyers Fuel Pandemic-Related Surge in Gun Sales," *CNN*, October 24, 2020, www.cnn.com/2020/10/24/business/gun-sales-surge-black-americans-women/index.html; Melissa Chan, "Racial Tension Is Behind a Rise in Black Gun Ownership," *Time*, November 17, 2020, https://time.com/5912612/black-gun-owners/; Maya King, "'It's My Constitutional Freaking Right': Black Americans Arm Themselves in Response to Pandemic, Protests," *Politico*, July 26, 2020, www.politico.com/news/2020/07/26/black-americans-gun-owners-380162; Sandoval, "Why Are Women Buying Guns?"; Christianna Silva, "Some Black Americans Buying Guns: 'I'd Rather Go to Trial Than Go to the Cemetery,'" *NPR*, September 27, 2020, www.npr.org/2020/09/27/911649891/some-black-americans-buying-guns-i-d-rather-go-to-trial-than-go-to-the-cemetery; Sabrina Tavernise, "An Arms Race in America: Gun Buying Spiked During the Pandemic. It's Still Up," *New York Times*, May 29, 2021, www.nytimes.com/2021/05/29/us/gun-purchases-ownership-pandemic.html.
50 Carlson, "Gun Studies and the Politics of Evidence," 194–5.
51 Sandra Ellen Weissinger, Dwayne Mack, and Elwood Watson, *Violence against Black Bodies: An Intersectional Analysis of How Black Lives Continue to Matter* (New York: Routledge, 2017), www.nytimes.com/2020/08/27/us/kyle-rittenhouse-kenosha-shooting-video.html.
52 See, for example, the intervention of Rev. Ciera Bates-Chamberlain during the "Clergy For Safe Cities National Gun Violence Summit," Video, February 16, 2021, www.youtube.com/watch?v=c5-DzFfsy-c.
53 Pew Research Center, "America's Complex Relationship with Guns," 2017, www.pewresearch.org/social-trends/wp-content/uploads/sites/3/2017/06/Guns-Report-FOR-WEBSITE-PDF-6-21.pdf, 54-55.
54 Pew Research Center, "America's Complex Relationship with Guns," 43.
55 Judith Butler, *Precarious Life: The Powers of Mourning and Violence* (New York: Verso, 2004).
56 Educational Fund to Stop Gun Violence and Coalition to Stop Gun Violence, "A Public Health Crisis Decades in the Making: A Review of 2019 CDC Gun Mortality Data," https://efsgv.org/wp-content/uploads/2019CDCdata.pdf, 14.
57 According to analyses of gun violence incidence: "Young Black males (15–34) are especially disproportionately impacted, making up 2% of the population but accounting for 37% of all gun homicide fatalities in 2019. Their rate of firearm homicide was more than 20 times higher than White males of the same age group" (Educational Fund to Stop Gun Violence and Coalition to Stop Gun Violence, "A Public Health Crisis Decades in the Making," 14).

58 Mary Bernstein, Jordan McMillan, and Elizabeth Charash, "Once in Parkland, a Year in Hartford, a Weekend in Chicago: Race and Resistance in the Gun Violence Prevention Movement," *Sociological Forum* 34, no. S1 (2019): 1153–73, 1165.
59 For an analysis of shootings in K-12 schools during the 2009–2018 period, see "10 years. 180 School Shootings. 356 Victims," *Cable News Network (CNN)*, 2019, www.cnn.com/interactive/2019/07/us/ten-years-of-school-shootings-trnd/.
60 Bernstein, McMillan, and Charash, "Once in Parkland, a Year in Hartford, a Weekend in Chicago."
61 Arlie Russell Hochschild, *So How's the Family?: And Other Essays* (Berkeley: University of California Press, 2013), 33.
62 Arlie Russell Hochschild, *Strangers in their Own Land: Anger and Mourning on the American Right* (New York: The New Press, 2018).
63 Lauren Berlant, "Introduction: Compassion (and Withholding)," pp. 1–14 in *Compassion: The Culture and Politics of an Emotion* (New York: Routledge, 2004).
64 Paul Bloom, "Empathy and Its Discontents," *Trends in Cognitive Sciences* 21, no. 1 (2017): 24–31.
65 Marianne Hirsch, "Presidential Address 2014—Connective Histories in Vulnerable Times," *PMLA* 129, no. 3 (2014): 330–48.
66 David Myers, "Knowing the Victim? Reflections on Empathy, Analogy, and Voice from the Shoah to the Present," Katz Center, University of Pennsylvania, June 25, 2020, https://katz.sas.upenn.edu/resources/blog/knowing-victim-reflections-empathy-analogy-and-voice-shoah-present.
67 Myers, "Knowing the Victim?"
68 Kate Schick, "Emotions and the Everyday: Ambivalence, Power and Resistance," *Journal of International Political Theory* 15, no. 2 (2019): 261–8, 262.
69 Incidentally, we need to keep mind how the health system also became a deeply politicized issue in public discourse as different politicians in office and political candidates debated their health care models.
70 See, for example, the activism and conceptualizations of security by Women for Genuine Security, "What Is Genuine Security?" accessed July 21, 2022, www.genuinesecurity.org/aboutus/whatisGS.html.
71 Billie Gastic, "Metal Detectors and Feeling Safe at School," *Education and Urban Society* 43, no. 4 (2011): 486–98; N'dea Moore-Petinak, Marika Waselewski, Blaire Alma Patterson, and Tammy Chang, "Active Shooter Drills in the United States: A National Study of Youth Experiences and Perceptions," *Journal of Adolescent Health* 67, no. 4 (2020): 509–13; Keith J. Zullig, "Active Shooter Drills: A Closer Look at Next Steps," *Journal of Adolescent Health* 67, no. 4 (2020): 465–6.
72 I borrow this framework from Women for Genuine Security, "What Is Genuine Security?"
73 Premilla Nadasen, "Rethinking Care: Arlie Hochschild and the Global Care Chain," *Women's Studies Quarterly* 45, no. 3/4 (2017): 124–8, 126. See feminist analyses of the connections between gender, care work, and emotions, particularly as pertaining to women (e.g., Zuhal Yeşilyurt Gündüz, "The Feminization of Migration: Care and the New Emotional Imperialism," *Monthly Review* (blog), December 1, 2013, https://monthlyreview.org/2013/12/01/the-feminization-of-migration/; Hochschild, *So How's the Family?*; Mariela Solana and Nayla Luz Vacarezza, "Sentimientos Feministas," *Estudos Feministas* 28, no. 2 (2020): e72445.
74 Seminario Sobre Género, Afectos y Política (SEGAP), "Afectos, actividad esencial," *Cuadernos materialistas* 6 (2020): 17–21, 17.
75 Bethany Bump, "Albany Med Nurses Strike, CEO Calls it 'Heartbreaking'," *Times Union*, December 1, 2020, www.timesunion.com/news/article/Albany-Med-nurses-strike-CEO-calls-it-15765304.php.
76 Bump, "Albany Med Nurses Strike, CEO Calls it 'Heartbreaking'."

3
EMOTIONS AND THE COMMERCIALIZATION OF BULLETPROOF FASHION

As with other aspects of security, bulletproof garments and accessories are steeped in emotions. On the one hand, emotions play an important role in the perceived need for and commercialization of such products: Anxiety about random attacks and concerns about being individually targeted are part of the emotional contexts that give rise to ballistic apparel. Relatedly, fear of mass shootings increased in recent years in the United States; and nearly half of the respondents to a Gallup survey in 2019 worried about whether they or their family members would be victimized in that way.[1] On the other hand, the existence of bulletproof apparel *per se* can also produce a variety of emotional responses—from sadness, surprise, disgust, and frustration to relief, curiosity, and enthusiasm. Companies mobilize emotions when they promote bulletproof gear, for instance, through reminders of violent events that are likely to activate fear. Also, customers sometimes share their experiences in emotional terms, as shown in testimonials and online reviews of the products.

Emotions are integral to discourses and practices of security that aim to protect against the threat of violent attacks, whether international or domestic. Bulletproof fashion is no exception. One noteworthy aspect of this response is that it is a market-based approach, and as such, the role that emotions play is consistent with that of more general processes of commodification under capitalism. Sociologist Eva Illouz observes that "consumer acts and emotional life have become closely and inseparably intertwined with each other, each one defining and enabling the other; commodities facilitate the expression and experience of emotions; emotions are converted into commodities."[2] In the case of bulletproof products, fear and related emotions such as anxiety are central to the commodification of security, and acquiring the products can become a way for consumers to relieve or preempt disturbing emotions. At the same time, what is sold as part of the bulletproof product package is "peace of mind," an emotional state that *itself* has become a valuable commodity available to those who can buy it. However, other emotions—for example, those elicited by aesthetic features—are also entwined with bulletproof fashion, helping to motivate purchases or becoming commodities themselves.

In a consumer society such as the United States, the commercialization of bulletproof apparel through emotional appeals fits broader patterns, including the notion that systemic problems that generate fear and anxiety can be effectively addressed by individual behaviors, namely through the purchase of specific products and services. Zygmunt Bauman notes

> a nearly 'perfect fit' between the characteristics of commodities the consumer market offers, the fashion in which it offers them, and the kind of anxieties and expectations which prompt individuals to live their lives as a string of shopping expeditions.[3]

The market promises to provide relief from a host of disturbing social issues, including those that may be among the scariest: the demise of the people we love, or our own, at the hand of an armed attacker. Whether "integral" or "incidental" to the products advertised, emotions play a role in the marketing of products—in this case bulletproof fashion—and can have an effect in decision-making.[4] In that sense, bulletproof garments and accessories join a plethora of consumer products enmeshed with emotional appeals. Attending to emotional dimensions reveals some of the ways in which particular conceptions of security disseminate through society, and how security becomes another commodity available for consumption.

Bulletproof products are invested with meanings and emotions that exceed their practical protective function, though the promise of security remains at their core. Ballistic garments are imbued with the gravity of a life-threatening situation—they are supposed to save lives—and in selling bulletproof products, companies also promise the alleviation of fear or worry. Yet the representations of many of these products offer more than that. They also appeal to feelings, moods, and desires associated with a sense of style, leisure, beauty, fun, or adventure. Others connect emotionally to patriotic ideals, notions of childhood, gender expectations, and ethnoracial and cultural identities. In this sense, bulletproof fashion inserts itself in an already existing social milieu that encourages, glorifies, and reproduces particular kinds of bodies, femininities, masculinities, and affective relationships. Security turned-into-commodity overlaps with other processes of commodification in which emotions are center stage, engaging individuals through emotion-filled, market-based, mechanisms.

Paying attention to the range of emotions surrounding bulletproof fashion is important because it helps illuminate how certain security discourses and practices percolate among the civilian population. Emotions are key pathways through which corporate discourse and interests sediment in society, creating needs and inciting desires, in this case, related to security. Bulletproof fashion is propelled through the market, beyond the realm of the state, and the emotional resonances of different products contribute to amplify the securitization of society. It is partly through the work of emotions that the security state is legitimized and corporate security solutions are normalized. More generally, emotions influence how we make sense of social problems, including matters related to security. Kari Marie Norgaard and Ron Reed point out that "[a]s the link between individuals and power structure, emotions matter in part for their role in cognition."[5] When thinking about security, the ways in which individuals interpret this issue are not merely intellectual or ideological. Cognitive assessments are permeated by emotions, which in turn can help normalize or disrupt prevailing social arrangements and power structures. In the case of bulletproof products in corporate promotional materials, emotions help legitimize and stabilize market-based, militarized, and individually oriented security solutions. Through the analysis of news media, company websites, and promotional materials, this chapter shows some of the emotional contours of bulletproof fashion as evidenced in public discourse and representations.

Emotions, Bulletproof Fashion, and Media Representations

A range of emotions appears in news media coverage about bulletproof garments and accessories. Among the news articles analyzed, most of the emotions that emerged can be characterized as unpleasant, disturbing, or at least not relaxing. They include horror, panic, sadness, trauma, pain, nervousness, anxiety, stress, worry, helplessness, anger, discouragement, fear, and alertness. These emotional states were largely related to the issues that are the *raison d'être* for the bulletproof products industry, that is, gun violence and the failures of state and society to effectively address this problem. In that context, bulletproof products are presented as promising not only physical protection but also psychological relief. Yet questions regarding whether bulletproof garments and accessories are effective in the face of an actual gun violence scenario—or instead provide a false sense of security—also arose in some of the media coverage. In some cases, questions were additionally raised regarding the potentially negative emotional effects of wearing the products, particularly on children.

A number of news reports, including press releases, conveyed the information and perspectives offered by bulletproof company representatives. Not surprisingly, such statements advance the idea that in our current world bulletproof products are increasingly necessary. In some cases, this perspective prevails, and in others it is countervailed by critiques. Some of the commentary provided in news reports help normalize bulletproof fashion, and implicitly naturalize a society awash in guns, as when information on where to buy the products is given in a matter-of-fact way. For instance, in reference to bullet-resistant backpacks, a *Dayton Daily News* article stated: "Parents who are worried about the safety of their children while at school now have a new line of defense easily available at their local stores."[6] Similarly, a *Fox 35 Orlando* report announced in 2019: "Bulletproof backpacks can now be found in stores around Orlando, as back-to-school shopping begins. For some parents, safety is on the brain when checking off their back-to-school list."[7] Company representatives are sometimes quoted making the point that though it is unfortunate that their products are needed, they are offering a helpful response in the face of a regrettable state of affairs. Steve Naremore, from TuffyPacks, is cited in a *Hollywood Reporter* article saying, "It's a sad, sad, sad world that this has to exist,"[8] and Yasir Sheik, from Guard Dog Security, asserted, "Times have changed [. . . .] Our product is in response to that. It's a sad reality."[9]

Among the people interviewed for the news stories or commenting on the products, there are those who saw this trend with unease or expressed outright condemnation. Various critiques were emotionally charged, particularly in relation to bulletproof products for children. For instance, consider an opinion piece by columnist Shawn Vestal in the *Spokesman-Review*, a newspaper based in Spokane, Washington. Commenting on bulletproof and other security products for kids, Vestal pondered:

> This is . . . what? Absurd? Tragic? Sickening?
> All of these. But it's also something else: old hat. Ho-hum. Unsurprising. We are so deeply enmeshed in the gears of a machine that supplies and supports massacres that outrage itself feels stale and impotent. Huge majorities of Americans support stronger background checks, magazine limits and an assault weapons ban—and that's been true for a long time, as the NRA [National Rifle Association] checks clear and nothing is done.
> A child might ask how in the world decent adults let this happen. Our answer is to have that child prepare for being shot at.[10]

Emotions figure prominently in Vestal's condemnation of bulletproof products as evidenced by explicit emotional references such as "sickening" and "outrage," and the rhetorical tone of the commentary. Also alluding to emotions, a *New York Times* article quotes Shannon Watts, founder of Moms Demand Action for Gun Sense in America, saying, "We're asking children to stand up to gunmen because lawmakers are too afraid to stand up to the gun lobby [. . . .] There isn't a parent in this country that isn't terrified. These companies are capitalizing on that."[11] The article also quotes Igor Volsky, director of Guns Down America: "It's incredibly depressing [. . . .] The market is trying to solve for a problem that our politicians have refused to solve."[12] These and other statements for and against the use of bulletproof products highlight the emotional stakes of the problem of gun violence and of the solutions available in contemporary United States.

Following Sara Ahmed, it can be argued that as bulletproof objects are produced, advertised, purchased, and discussed, they become "saturated with affect, as sites of personal and social tension."[13] The analysis of news stories and company promotional materials, including corporate discourse and customer comments, shows a variety of emotions that are attached to and prompted by these objects. In *Feeling Things*, a book exploring the relationship between objects and emotions historically, Stephanie Downes, Sally Holloway, and Sarah Randles explain that *feeling* "is a reference both to the tactility of the object—its shape, form, substance, and size—and to the reciprocal ways in which contact with an object conditions feelings in human subjects."[14] They add that "objects shape emotions, and emotions shape objects."[15] The examination of narratives and visuals regarding bulletproof fashion shed light onto how emotions become entwined with these security-oriented objects: how their emergence is shaped by emotions and how these objects' existence itself also appeals to and generates a variety of emotional states.

Emotions appear at various stages of bulletproof garments' production and consumption. For example, emotions are visible in the testing of the products, particularly when tested on live human beings as a promotional strategy (as entrepreneur Miguel Caballero has done on employees, his own wife, celebrities, and others). Nervousness, apprehension, surprise, relief, and amusement are among the emotional states that can be read on the expressions of different people who have undergone or witnessed the experience of those tests, and who appear in different videos. At times, these demonstrations seem to test not only the product but the temperament of those who dare undergo the test. Even when not tried on living persons, there can still be a sense of excitement or expectation regarding the effectiveness of the product. In a DemolitionRanch demonstration of body armor, a mannequin dressed in a bulletproof hoodie is endowed with personhood and emotions, as the tester jokingly asks the mannequin after shooting at it, "Bud, how did it feel? You OK? You making it?"[16] While the spectacle in recorded demonstrations with media personalities or "influencers" sometimes includes jokes or lighthearted feelings, a bulletproof product company representative I interviewed underscored the seriousness that surrounds behind-the-scenes tests, which customers do not see: "[I]t's a security measure. And we're talking about potentially life and death. Right? So the standard and the guidelines have to be extremely stringent."

How do emotions figure in promotional materials and consumer commentary visible to the general public? The remainder of this chapter explores key themes centered on the emotions present on bulletproof product companies' websites. The discussion is based on the analysis of company narratives, product descriptions and images, and posted materials such as videos and customer reviews and testimonials. Regarding the customers' comments, a word of caution is in order, given that authorship cannot be independently confirmed. Some websites include the "verified" label for the reviews and others do not (regardless of whether the comments are favorable or otherwise). These comments are still worth analyzing for they form part of the discourse of security disseminated through the websites, and because they may indeed reflect the opinions of a variety of consumers. The texts, pictures, and audiovisual materials on the websites reveal the significant role that emotions such as fear, anxiety, sadness, anger, love, and pride play in relation to bulletproof products. Additionally, the aesthetic features of the products appeal to various emotions, an aspect further elaborated in the following chapter.

Fear, Anxiety, and the Promise of Peace of Mind

Against the backdrop of an ominous soundtrack, a video posted on the AVS (Active Violence Solutions) website presents an office building where a mock active shooter situation unfolds. The people on the premises enact different survival tactics as a man wielding a long firearm proceeds to kill in cold blood those who cross his path. The video illustrates the "Run. Hide. Fight" strategy that can be implemented in the event of an active shooter incident.[17] This approach consists of escaping the scene of danger as a first option; hiding if running away is not possible; and as a last resort, forcefully and physically confronting the shooter, including through a group effort. These materials recommend how to behave in an extremely scary situation and, at the same time, remind viewers of fear and terror—indeed, watching the video is more than a reminder but an embodied emotional experience. The video is posted on a website that also sells a particular security solution: bulletproof products.

With some overlaps and variations, companies' materials draw on and elicit different types of emotions as they make the case for armored products. References to mass shootings, for example, prompt fear and anxiety, but ballistic protection can purportedly address that. In other words, one particular manifestation of what Barry Glassner called a "culture of fear" is, in this case, a security-oriented product that cannot really solve the social problem of gun violence.[18] The association of bulletproof garments and accessories with "peace of mind" appears repeatedly in company materials, as bulletproof products are presented as a buffer against pervasive threats in an uncertain world. In reference to one of its bulletproof garments, Wonder Hoodie noted that it "was designed to protect vital organs against a .44 magnum, for habitual wear and, most importantly, for peace of mind."[19] About its Denali Daypack, Bullet Blocker said that "this bag enhances your safety and gives peace of mind."[20] And Talos Ballistics stated that its protective panels and inserts "are ideal for public safety personnel, government and business professionals, and family members young and old who want a little more peace of mind."[21] Bulletproof Zone concluded that "[t]he greatest benefit of purchasing a bulletproof backpack or bulletproof plates for an existing backpack is for 'Peace of Mind.'"[22] The evocation of peaceful feelings was powerfully depicted on the main page of Thyk Skynn, with the picture of a woman of color sitting against the backdrop of a waterfall, eyes closed and a blissful smile, her face tilted upwards, and her joint hands elevated and wrapped around by a string of prayer beads. While the spiritual connotations and articulation of bulletproof products as a "symbol for peace" are unique to this Black-owned business,[23] the association of bulletproof products with some level of tranquility is shared across companies. Nevertheless, one may wonder about the racialized meanings of "peace of mind," given the differential vulnerabilities to violence faced by different sectors of the population, including the disproportionate exposure of Black communities to gun violence and state violence.[24]

The promise of "peace of mind" is the counterpart to reminders of events that elicit altogether opposite emotions, such as fear in the face of mass shootings, violent crime in "dangerous" neighborhoods, targeted attacks during otherwise happy holidays, and societal disintegration amid widespread calamities. Indeed, the activation of unpleasant emotions may be needed for customers to consider purchasing these products in the first place. In the context of the pandemic, Bulletproof Zone alluded to "individual customers who fear that the Coronavirus pandemic will eventually create a scenario where people will have to defend themselves for survival."[25] Hence, the company pointed to various products that can become handy under such conditions. Similarly, MC Armor reminded potential customers of danger but offered its way to assuage negative emotions:

> Safety is a priority, especially in these unprecedented and uncertain times with the rise of school shootings, violence, and crime. Living in 2020 means preparing well in advance for possible threats to your life, or the lives of others. It is important to invest in high-quality personal protective gear in the form of bulletproof vests or tactical jackets to put your mind at ease and prepare for any extreme conditions that you or a loved one might be faced with.[26]

In another post, we learn that the company "understands these valid fears and concerns [about school shootings and violence], which is why the collection is fully stocked with personal protective gear options that alleviate the stress associated with worrying about potential dangers."[27] As we can see, the company identifies a series of problems and the emotions that may accompany them, while also offering a remedy. Worry or anxiety is also implicit in some of the customer review comments on the websites, such as when they express the hope to never have to report having survived or test the quality of the bulletproof items purchased.

Speaking directly to the set of customers perhaps most keenly attuned to the possibility of impending catastrophe—"preppers," individuals especially focused on disaster preparation—an article in the Bulletproof Zone blog stated:

> What if you wake up one morning to find an epidemic had broken out while you were sleeping?
> What if you suddenly find yourself with the world falling apart around you because of nuclear war or if the government fails and anarchy breaks loose, with neighbors attacking one another and everyone hoarding vital resources to themselves?
> How would you survive scenarios such as these? This is when the survivalist or "prepper" in you comes into play, and as far as survival gear is concerned, body armor, such as bullet proof vests, is among the many things that you should definitely have with you.[28]

The picture that accompanied the article depicted a bearded white man wearing a backpack, wielding a long firearm with one hand, and holding an infant dressed in pink with the other. He was standing behind a chain link fence, looking intently into the distance, apparently ready to act forcefully, if necessary, while keeping the child safe. He embodied the protector role socially assigned to men, as well as a valorized type of rugged white masculinity. The narrative and picture presented seem straight out of a dystopian movie script, and its very vividness might help engage both fear and pleasure, in the sense that it may give certain customers the opportunity to identify with the hero. Needless to say, scenarios in which our own lives and our loved ones' survival are at stake—and in which fellow human beings are turned into sources of threat rather than assistance—are surely scary. But the fantasy portrayed in this scene is that its protagonist, the one who buys the bulletproof products, gets to save the day. The imagery also taps into prevalent cultural notions of individualism in U.S. society, in this case, through the figure of what sociologist Allison Ford calls the "self-sufficient citizen." In a study that included "preppers," Ford describes the self-sufficient citizen as "independent, individualistic, and fully responsible for their own health and wellbeing, and that of their family"[29]—a disposition that is partly an emotional management response to risk.[30] Although preparedness for a generalized catastrophe might not be what motivates all or most bulletproof product customers, the media-reported increases in demand for these garments, and the stocking of other products to ensure survival during the pandemic, might suggest more people tuning into the emotional mentality of a "prepper."

Allusions to a different type of scenario—school shootings, mass shootings, or active shooter situations—appear more commonly in the online materials of companies selling bulletproof products. These types of gun violence incidents are prominent as a public source of fear and concern, and they are an opportunity for companies to advertise an array of armored products. One of the company representatives I interviewed mentioned that when a shooting incident is publicized in the news, "you see an increase in the engagement" by the public in the company's social media. Reminders of school shootings specifically appeal to the emotions of parents and others who care for children. In a promotional video of ArmorMe, a teenage boy and girl in a public setting—apparently a schoolyard—start running when they hear screams in the background and adopt protective stances using their bulletproof bags. The soundtrack reinforces a feeling of dread as the voiceover points to the utility of the products "should the unthinkable happen."[31] The specter of a school shooting is key to convey the value of the product. Similarly, under the heading "Everyday Civilian Protection," Innocent Armor presents the screen shots of TV news coverage of noted mass shootings such as those in San Bernardino (California) and Parkland (Florida), among others. The company then asks:

> How can you take control of your own fate in a world where the simple act of going out in public puts you at risk? When the fear that we may be injured or killed doing everyday things is real, we need to change how we think about being safe.[32]

Tips about how to use bulletproof backpacks or what approaches to take in school shooting situations also appeal to emotions, for instance, by describing terrible events such as the emblematic Columbine High School shooting in Colorado, in which two teenagers killed 12 students and a teacher in 1999. On the TuffyPacks website, one such reference appeared under a section titled "Training Our Kids for the Next School Shooter."[33] There is an air of inevitability in that statement, and the sense of doom elicited might help direct parents to the protection offered by the company. ArmorMe, in turn, entertained the possibility of various scenarios: "Many attacks do have some level of warning, whether it be gunshots coming from another location, the sound of panic, or even seeing the assailant approaching."[34] In the face of such dire situations, the company announced: "The ArmorMe backpack: Protection for your child, peace-of-mind for yourself."[35] Sometimes information about mass shootings not only is used as a reminder of the purported need for bulletproof products but is paired with advertisement of courses such as the "Active Attacker Response Training"[36] on the AVS website and/or videos representing mock active shooter situations, such as the emotional video described earlier illustrating the "Run. Hide. Fight" strategy.

In addition to specific images and descriptions that evoke fear and terror, some company materials also solicit emotions such as anxiety through references to more unspecified threats. For instance, Talos Ballistics stated that its "bulletproof inserts and panels are intended to help protect you and your loved ones from unforeseen danger."[37] This type of comment taps anxiety by suggesting the omnipresence of threat. Everyone and anyone might be an "unforeseen danger," thereby justifying the use of body armor in multiple situations and in everyday life. The kinds of events described on the companies' websites, including in their more ambiguous versions of possible danger, work to undermine trust in fellow human beings and the idea that one is safe in the world. Of course, various forms of security are not afforded to large swaths of the population, especially those most marginalized. Yet different companies promote the point that even, or particularly, privileged individuals are at constant risk, including due to both unspecified and specified risks. In an Innocent Armor piece titled "How Much Is Your Life Worth," we are confronted with the following questions and anxiety-provoking scenarios, also reminiscent of the prepper trope:

> When disaster strikes, will you be prepared?
> Having a response is important but having a plan of protection is imperative!
> You never know when you're going to need a shield of protection to defend you against the most dangerous threats. The world has changed. Simple tasks like going to the store require that you cover your face to safeguard you against the threat of viruses like Covid-19.
> In this new world environment, it also makes sense to defend yourself from being shot![38]

Here the narrative goes from an ambiguous "disaster" to unspecified "dangerous threats," to a world changed by the pandemic, to being shot. It moves from a sense of generalized anxiety about lurking chaos to fear linked to a specific threat, encouraging readers to question whatever basic sense of security they may have. While the allusions to danger point to threats against the security of the body, it can also be argued that other forms of security are also cast in doubt, including the "ontological security" derived from a certain level of predictability regarding everyday life expectancies and the relations of trust and interdependence on which they are founded.[39] Although threats to security can lead to different types of responses, companies point especially to one main strategy: Buy a bulletproof product. In other words, resort to the market to confront both the threat of gun-related harm and the feelings associated with it.

"A Sad Reality": Managing Sadness, Preempting Grief

"It's a sad reality"—this notion encapsulates another key emotion that sometimes appears in bulletproof product companies' materials and media interviews with company representatives. In addition to the promise to alleviate anxiety and fear, companies simultaneously normalize the problem of gun violence and implicitly offer protection from the sadness and grief of losing a loved one. As we shall see, sadness also punctuates commentary about the state of the world and the demise of certain ideals, for instance, about childhood or the nation. Whereas intense sadness such as grief can propel people to collective action against injustices or to address social problems, including gun violence, sadness can also lead to withdrawal or resignation.[40] When it comes to the responses offered by bulletproof garments companies, sad feelings serve to maintain the status quo and to normalize the violence. The strategy is simply to adjust to the unpleasant situation by seeking personal protection.

Sadness is repeatedly invoked in reference to the violent "reality" to which individuals must adapt through the use of bulletproof products. The Safeguard Clothing website refers to the "sad fact" behind the need for ballistic vests: "Body armor is not always seen as necessary for those working in the Emergency Medical Services, and yet the sad fact is that these individuals may need protection against attacks that can cause physical and psychological harm."[41] On the consumer side, a customer review comment by Edward K. conveyed sadness regarding a Bulletproof Zone bullet-resistant backpack: "Things being what they are in America today I'm saddened by feeling the need to have purchased this item for my grandson."[42] These comments illustrate how these emotions operate as a mechanism of tacit acceptance of the status quo; sadness in this case does not prompt collective action toward social change but individual, market-based, adaptations to an undesirable reality.

In commentary by company representatives, customers, and media coverage, sadness accompanies the references to the social conditions that purportedly justify the need for bulletproof gear. In an interview with *ABC Action News*, Yasir Sheikh from Guard Dog Security, was asked: "What do you think it says about our society that we are resorting to items like this?" He responded that "it's a sad reality, it's become a new normal."[43] This type of response—simultaneously lamenting and normalizing gun violence, and by extension bulletproof products—was also echoed by some customer reviews. Wade F., a Leatherback Gear customer, commented: "Sadly we live in a different world now and I highly recommend that every student should have one! In fact everyone period!"[44] Similarly, Leslie S., commenting on a backpack acquired through Bulletproof Zone said:

> Would love to purchase enough for my child's classroom if not the backpack just the panel so everybody is safe. Sad world that we have to think about back to school purchasing with something like this but I'm very grateful that it is on the market and available. What happened to crayons and water colors.[45]

As we can see, Leslie's lamentation includes a sense of loss regarding the ideal of childhood associated with more traditional school supplies. Individuals, then, have to cope with the feelings of living in a violent world and the concomitant sadness associated with a palliative measure that is nevertheless perceived as necessary.

Sadness also emerges in the narrative of one corporate representative I interviewed in 2021, who referred to the violence and unrest in U.S. society at the time, while additionally conveying a sense of loss regarding his image of the country:

> The more we can provide security and safety for people, I think the better off. I mean, people, a lot of people are scared right now. It's kind of sad. It's kind of a sad time here in the U.S. You know, it doesn't feel like the U.S. right now to me. So, yeah, hopefully things are going to change in the future, and I think they will. But, you know, there's a lot of civil unrest. There's a lot of random violence. And it's kind of sad, but, you know, we're trying to do our part. We're trying to provide a little bit more of a safety net, security for people.

In this passage, sadness is referenced repeatedly, and the hope for change is wishful—not connected to any specified action from social actors to address the underlying issues fueling "violence" or "unrest." Furthermore, since the business of bulletproof fashion rests on the very existence of gun-related violence, there is a tension between this entrepreneur's sad feelings about violence vis-à-vis the pragmatic business interests that require it. The tension seems to dissolve, however, when bulletproof fashion is framed in altruistic terms, as a sad but necessary intervention to partly offset the issues described. The market emerges as a central strategy to address the problem of gun violence as well as the sadness associated with it.

Sadness and grief are also thrown into sharp relief when survivors, friends, and relatives of victims of gun violence are brought into view. This was the case in Guard Dog Security's references to its donation program for Make Our Schools Safe—an organization described as "[b]orn out of the Marjory Stoneman Douglas High School massacre on Valentine's Day 2018, when their founders lost their 14-year-old daughter, Alyssa Alhadeff."[46] The description continued explaining that

> Make Our Schools Safe is here to strengthen the weaknesses in school security and they are here to take action, protecting schools so it never happens again. Children should thrive in classrooms, not fear for their lives. The time has come to make schools safe![47]

This narrative was published along with the picture of a group formed by an adult woman and six female youths—largely white-appearing—forming hearts with their hands. In addition to the textual reference to children's fear, the image evokes sadness entwined with love. Valentine's Day is juxtaposed with a horrifying event that no doubt caused unbearable sorrow to the survivors and relatives of those killed in the Parkland school shooting. The desire to help save lives and avoid such pain is stirred with the pledge, "Buy One & We Give," explaining that part of the proceeds from bulletproof backpack sales would go to Make Our Schools Safe.

Another example of a depiction of grief connected to gun violence incidents in schools appeared in online materials by Wonder Hoodie, a company that also has a donation program. In this case, the initiative focuses on teachers, promising: "Every 10 bulletproof hoodies we sell, we donate one bulletproof product to a public-school teacher."[48] The picture that accompanies this initiative's description is one of a candlelight vigil assembling a crowd, presumably mourning victims of gun violence. In these and other ways that Kate Paarlberg-Kvam and I previously noted, companies position themselves as socially minded benefactors "in service to the betterment of society."[49] At the same time, they implicitly offer customers the potential to be spared from the grief of senselessly losing those closest to their hearts, particularly children and youths.

Through the sale of ballistic products, companies promise to help avert the loss of life and concomitant sadness that come with mass shootings. When people directly affected by gun violence are mentioned—such as the case of the Marjory Stoneman Douglas High School mass shooting in Parkland, Florida—they become associated with security-oriented products via corporate philanthropy. In fact, grieving relatives and survivors of gun violence have organized collectively to demand policy changes and other societal-level interventions.[50] A number of student survivors of the Parkland mass shooting channeled grief into activism.[51] They have engaged public debates about guns, stirred mass mobilization, lobbied legislators, and demanded systemic cultural changes. In other words, their responses represent the very opposite of accepting or adapting to the "sad reality" comprised by gun violence in U.S. society.

Shields Against Anger and Rage

When it comes to emotions, the "peace of mind" that bulletproof product companies offer is a promise not only to alleviate consumers' own unpleasant emotions, such as fear, but to simultaneously protect against the disturbing emotions of others, such as the anger and rage of perpetrators of violence. Although anger has been found to be associated with many mass shooting incidents,[52] anger does not always lead to violence and aggression, and it can also be mobilized to challenge injustice.[53] However, in the context of security-oriented products and the possibility of being harmed by an attack, anger is coupled with danger. Furthermore, on some companies' websites, anger is linked to deviance or mental health issues, whether in reference to adults, youths, or children.

The goal of guarding against the angry emotions of other people is illustrated by the comments of James W., a Bulletproof Zone customer who extolled his purchase while saying,

> Great extra protection, I carry the shield in my car to protect myself from all the crazy people with road rage. With all the shooting on the road these days, you got to have extra protection. This is a must have in your car to protect you and your family![54]

Here, shooters are represented as angry "crazy people" who happen to be armed. Their "rage" is implicitly denounced, and while the reference to craziness is perhaps just a figure of speech, it still draws on stereotypes about people with mental health issues as a menace. What is left intact in these references is the naturalized proliferation of guns in the United States, making the purchase of a ballistic shield appear as just an appropriate pragmatic solution.

In some portrayals, dangerous anger is not limited to adults. While companies generally depict children as needing protection, in exceptional instances, young members of society are shown as potential sources of threat. The underlying emotion in this case is anger. A closeup picture of a young white boy with an angry facial expression and his arm extended against another child's body accompanies the advertisement of "Bite Resistant Arm Guards/Sleeves" sold by Bac-Tactical (a vendor that offers a variety of security-oriented products in addition to bulletproof gear). The company explained that the product has been "designed to help professionals who interact with children who bite, scratch and pinch be better protected."[55] Here, the angry child emerges as a personal security threat, becoming the face for a product that is advertised as especially suited for those working in fields ranging from corrections and security to mental health care and special education. That is, these are occupations dealing with people who carry different forms of stigma, associated here with disturbed or unruly emotions. Negative emotional expressiveness serves to draw attention to the product, reminding the viewers that the emotions of others can be a threat.

Teens or youths are also at times presented as vectors of problematic emotions and as potential sources of danger, namely, as school mass shooters. For instance, TuffyPacks referred to the Columbine High School shooting saying: "On that horrific day, 52 teens and four staffers huddled under tables in the library as two students roamed the hallways brandishing shotguns, a carbine, a semiautomatic handgun, and pipe bombs."[56] The age of the shooters is not specified in the article, but their student status implies their youth in this context. Later in the article, in speaking about shooters more generally, it is recommended that victims do not plead for their lives, given "the lack of empathy of most shooters." In the cases mentioned, security-oriented products are geared to protect against the violent expression of negative emotions that not only adults but children and youths may display—from anger to lack of empathy.

Relatedly, instances of disturbing emotions, including anger, appear in connection to perpetrators of active shooter incidents in AVS's depiction of "Active Attackers."[57] The portraits of the attackers are closeups of their faces largely with serious expressions, and sometimes seemingly troubled or angry. Two of the images show young men with hostile expressions, screaming or gesticulating toward the camera. Most of those portrayed in the 17 pictures appear to be male, comprising a mix of race-ethnicities. Among the two women depicted, one is Black and one is wearing a hijab. In light of this collection of pictures, it is worth noting that most perpetrators of mass shooting in the United States—the kinds of gun violence episodes that raise the most alarm—have been white and male.[58] The images presented on the AVS website remind viewers of danger and deviance, reinforced with the statement that the goal of these types of attackers is "to bring maximum chaos and predictable devastation to your world."[59] AVS then encourages readers to "Get Trained," selecting a training course in "Active Attacker Response" offered on the same website in which bulletproof products are sold.[60]

Lastly, a more idiosyncratic instance of how anger figures in relation to the sale of bulletproof products appeared in a Wonder Hoodie blog entry, this time in reference to the anger of people turned against a utility company's employees in the context of environmental disaster:

> Last week Pacific Gas and Electric (PG&E) announced an unprecedented decision to cut power to up to 2 million people over the course of multiple days. The decision was made to limit the possibility of wildfires in Northern California due to the state's windy conditions in the aftermath of last year's deadly fires. The company's announcement sparked an outrage from citizens on social media, while others took their anger and frustration much farther.
>
> As reported by ABC7 News, the PG&E office in Oroville was egged. Several PG&E field personnel were cursed at and even had rocks thrown at them. One unfortunate PG&E employee was shot at while driving a company marked vehicle down the interstate.[61]

To protect from angry behavior in this type of situations, Wonder Hoodie offered a line of Kevlar products "designed specifically for field personnel and corporate campus environments."[62] The vending of products for these groups implicitly suggests that people in the "corporate" world, or workers having to implement its plans, may need protection against the anger associated with corporate decisions. In this case, those decisions relate to weather events and other "natural" disasters predicted to be more common in the era of climate change and the unbridled capitalism that helps fuel it.

The connection between macro-level events, personal security threats, and the emotions that surround them is met with the individualized responses that the purchase of consumer products represents. The message is that anger and rage, translated into violent armed behaviors, may be shielded through ballistic apparel.

Tokens of Love and Care

"There is no price on the safety of you and your loved ones," announced Bulletproof Zone on its website.[63] Love also appeared in Guard Dog Security's online information, in reference to its partnership with Make Our Schools Safe, through images of youths and an adult woman forming hearts with their hands, as mentioned earlier. These are reminders of the importance of love and care as part of the emotions mobilized through company messaging. In other words, the discourse in companies' materials includes not only explicit or implicit references to unpleasant emotions such as fear, anger, and sadness but also those that have a positive valence, such as love and care for family members. Bulletproof products can also serve as vehicles for the circulation of socially encouraged feelings, via the connection between love and the desire to protect loved ones from harm. Commentary and posts particularly tap into notions of parental love, and the vigilance associated with parental roles.[64] In the customer review and testimonials sections, one can see the display of valued emotions such as love for family members as well gratitude toward companies for products deemed helpful. Some users have apparently lived through traumatic situations or experienced deep fear while doing mundane activities and found a sense of protection in bulletproof products. Maureen A., a Wonder Hoodie customer, related:

> The hoodie really helped with his PTSD from the event. You never know WHY someone is ordering your product. I just wanted to let you know that it made a big difference to an 18 year old young man who is also a husband and father.[65]

Maureen's comment reflects gratitude toward the company and also shows she cares for the young man who uses the product.

Other comments revealing care toward loved ones simultaneously cast some doubt on the wisdom of fitting them with bulletproof products. Mike, a Bullet Blocker customer, offered a meta reflection on his own emotions: "Maybe I'm just paranoid, but it gives me a bit more peace of mind knowing they have a little extra protection."[66] Although it is not clear exactly who Mike was referring to, "they" are apparently people he cares about, and the underlying question is whether acquiring these types of products might indicate too much fear. Similarly, Andy, another Bullet Blocker customer, said:

> My three daughters are at college and I purchased a bullet blocker for each of their back packs. [. . .] I hope not to be a paranoid father, but my daughters are worth the effort, that is why they carry a bullet blocker in their backpack as well as a rubber door stop. It does not hurt to be prepared.[67]

Here, the possibility that fitting people in ballistic gear for mundane activities might not be "normal" is offset by the love of a father for his precious children (they are "worth the effort"). Love, in this case, helps justify a possibly excessive fear and to normalize bulletproof fashion.

Testimonials and reviews in different company sites reveal signs of care, as husbands, wives, parents, and grandparents report on their acquisition of bulletproof products for their loved ones. In such cases, those objects function as tokens of positive emotions and connection. Shay, a Bullet Blocker customer commented:

> We bought the Bullet Blocker backpack for our grandson who is now in junior high. We bought the camo one and he really liked it. Of course, we hope it is never put to use, but we are more assured by having purchased it.[68]

Lynn R., a Bulletproof Zone customer reporting on the purchase of two bulletproof products (with the subheading "high school safety"), commented: "This is a MUST for kids in these crazy times. Keeping my babies safe."[69] And Mike L., a Bulletproof Everyone customer, gave his enthusiastic endorsement regarding an armored jacket for women: "Perfect!!! My wife is so happy!!!!"[70] As we can see, the content and form of the remarks also reveal Mike's own glee at his wife's happiness. In all of these examples, bulletproof fashion functions as a vehicle to not only quell fear but affirm loving bonds between people.

These comments, then, illustrate how bulletproof apparel enters into an economy of love and care—one that trades in gifts of security, or at least the promise of it. These types of affective ties are also emphasized through some of the companies, imagery and exhortations, such as a picture banner depicting a white woman wrapping her arms around two children (TuffyPacks),[71] a picture of two bulletproof backpacks with the legend "There IS something you can do for your children" (AVS),[72] and a "Happy Holidays" picture with pine leaves and mistletoe berries framing the following statement: "Bulletproof items can significantly add to your usual level of protection. The best part? These items can also be great tactical gift ideas for your relatives and friends during Christmas!" (Bulletproof Zone).[73] The implicit message in some of these statements and visuals is that if one truly cares about family members—and is mindful of their security—then acquiring bulletproof apparel would be the logical decision. In some of the websites' statements and images, bulletproof products equal love.

Children constitute a market of users that wholly depend on the adults who care about them to access consumer products, including bulletproof garments and backpacks. In that sense, companies need to appeal to parental love and concern to sell their apparel. At the same time, companies strive not only to offer security through ballistic protection but to make the products kid-friendly through aesthetic features, in ways that may reduce reminders of fear (a point to which I return in the following chapter). The social and political milieu during times of crisis can exacerbate parental concerns and desire to protect their loved ones, as Mick's testimonial on Innocent Armor's website shows:

> Sending my kids back to school this year with everything going on (pandemic, social unrest, climate) and realizing that a sense of protection and actually having

my kids with something they can use as a last resort would be a good idea. The panels easily slipped into my 13-year-old's backpack, and it's just one way I feel a little better as a parent, especially during these very crazy times.[74]

The affective tone of the passage links concern and care to the decision to fit a child with bulletproof gear during a period of social and political turbulence. Securitizing the child in this way seems to also be invested with the emotionally loaded expectation of being a good parent. "As parents, it is our responsibility to keep our children safe in this unstable unpredictable world," declared Lucia C. in her Bulletproof Zone customer review.[75]

More generally, concerned parents, grandparents, spouses, and others who bought bulletproof products for their loved ones are given the opportunity to "*do something*," a common expectation in the face of potential security threats.[76] The desire to do something may be particularly pronounced when the lives of those whom we love are at stake. Regardless of whether these products would effectively save lives in an actual gun violence situation, they function as tokens of love and care while also promising to alleviate fear.

Bolstering Pride

Visuals of the American Flag, school mascots, and assertions of patriotism pointed to pride as another emotion that may promote a positive appraisal of ballistic apparel and accessories. In circulating these emotions, some companies also encourage or bolster certain forms of social identification. On the spectrum of subjectively pleasant emotions, pride is associated with a sense of self-worth, whether in relation to individual- or group-related achievement.[77] Pride has also been mobilized by marginalized groups as an antidote to stigma; for instance, "Pride" events have served to celebrate queer-identified individuals and communities in resistance to discrimination and stigmatization. In a different register, pride in belonging to a group with high social status can be a way of associating the self with the "winners." Pride in collectivities such as the nation is part of the socialization of children and integral to commemorative events in many parts of the world. Yet pride can also hide inequalities and injustice under the mantle of a unified and successful "we." In the case of bulletproof product online materials, pride is not a way of countering stigma but functions to highlight socially valorized, or even dominant, social positions and symbols.

On bulletproof products websites, references to pride appear in relation to the quality of the products, the country they are associated with, and attachment to specific groups or institutions. As we shall see, some forms of pride are linked to the nation, but they can also be connected to groups or entities smaller than the nation, such as clubs or schools. In that sense, TuffyPacks noted:

We can design our ballistic insert labels to include your school mascot with our care and use instructions. This is an opportunity to not only *show your school pride* but provide students with a personal defensive product to supplement the security protocols every school has in place. (emphasis mine)[78]

In this passage, the value of security-oriented products for children and teens is enhanced through its connection to the pride of belonging to a particular educational institution assumed to be good (from the moment that a child can take pride for belonging to such a school).

As an emotion, pride attaches to having a good reputation, belonging to a valued social group, or accomplishing something that meets particular ideals.[79] Thus, emphasizing group belonging, attachment to the nation, or association with countries that purportedly have expertise in security fields can help with the marketization of the products. For instance, Bulletproof Zone described its products with assertions of pride: "[W]e're proud to say nearly all of our gear is manufactured within the United States."[80] Similarly, Bullet Blocker advertised "Ballistics proudly 100% made in the United States of America";[81] and the name of the company on the website banner is followed by the phrase, "An American Company." In different companies' materials, visuals featuring the U.S. flag reinforce pride in the nation/company/product. As a global superpower, and a country in which demonstrations of patriotic pride are ubiquitous (from the reciting of the Pledge of Allegiance in public schools to everyday displays of the national flag—not only by institutions but also by private citizens), resorting to the nation as a seal of virtue and positive qualities likely resonates with many U.S. consumers. Declarations of American pride appeal to users to whom association with the nation matters, as illustrated by a customer who signed a review of a Bullet Blocker vest under the pseudonym "Proud American."[82] In that vein, one of the corporate representatives I interviewed mentioned that "in terms of the U.S. population, people like to see things U.S.-made, especially now. People are becoming more nationalistic."

While the clothing lines directed to civilians are generally meant to blend in—downplaying the "tactical" (overtly militarized) components—one of the mechanisms through which pride is sometimes fostered is via associations with institutions strongly identified or charged with the defense of the nation, such as the military. Some companies' products are apt for both civilian and security personnel use, and references to military-inspired or military-like characteristics are invoked as positive features. For instance, Talos Ballistic described its Bulletproof Bravo Flight Jacket in connection to the military: "Inspired by the MA-1 Navy fighter pilot jacket it was the first military flight jacket to cross over into civilian fashion and it has stood the test of time."[83] Institutions like the military and law enforcement usually promote pride for the country they serve, and in the case of bulletproof products, even civilian customers can find items with names that appeal to patriotic pride, such as Bullet Blocker's "Patriot Vest" or products with the United States flag.[84]

Pride about the products is also associated with the companies' projection of confidence that the ballistics work as intended, that their quality is sound. In some cases, this can be asserted via connection to nations known for extensive experience dealing with security issues and/or through linkages to security-oriented institutions such as the military. ArmorMe, for instance, highlighted its connection with Israel, given the country's reputation in the area of security, saying: "We are proud to have worked with a top Israeli defense contractor for design and testing of our bags."[85] The line between tactical and civilian products starts to blur—the bags are designed for civilians but with input of defense contractors—and the invocation of a highly militarized nation is a point of pride regarding the quality of the products.

As mentioned earlier, to instill confidence in the products companies also run tests of various sorts, including public demonstrations, fitting the ballistic apparel onto mannequins or, in some cases, testing them on live individuals. Miguel Caballero has received significant media attention for shooting various people wearing bulletproof garments—in this way showing that he stands by the quality of his products. The company also instills pride in those who go through these tests, as they can boast "I was shot by Miguel Caballero" and join the club bearing the slogan.[86] While this type of demonstration can be nerve racking to individuals undergoing the test, the videos show that they not only survived but seem unscathed after being shot. Another version of that kind of test is recorded in a video posted on Bulletproof Everyone's website: Company representative Dallas Jolley, who asserted "I believe in our products,"[87] shot himself on camera while wearing a sports bulletproof jacket. He survived the demonstration, but the shot left a large bruise in his belly area. Jolley appeared to be in physical pain after the shot, having some difficulty composing himself, yet he proudly affirmed the effectiveness of the garment noting that he was "still here." In this case, pride about the product is entwined with markers associated with hegemonic masculine ideals, such as courage and the expectation for men to stoically withstand pain. The bruise becomes a badge of honor, akin to a brave warrior's scar.

Some of the themes described, including pride in the nation and warrior-like masculinity, also blend in one of the videos posted on the Active Violence Solutions website. In a section about the AR500 Armor first-aid kits, a white man describes the features of the product and additionally recommends the armored plates, ending with the exhortation, "Be strong. Be of good courage. God Bless America. Long live the Republic."[88] The soundtrack at that point resembles that of an action movie, and images of the product are interspersed with visuals and sounds of men firing at targets in a shooting range (among other images). Here, pride is implicit in the exaltation of the nation and footage that connects masculinity, nationalism, militarization, and gunmanship, including symbols with phrases such as "Armed Citizens" "True Advocates of the 2nd Amendment" and "Minuteman." While bulletproof products exist for a broader swath of the citizenry, some are meant to appeal to a segment of the population interested in guns, tactical gear, and military themes.

All in all, pride can help instill confidence in bulletproof products as well as enhance a sense of positive identification in relation to particular institutions and social groups: the nation, schools, gun owners, men of courage, and so on. Through the mobilization of emotions that feel good, such as pride, companies appeal to consumers with discourses and imagery that may include but transcend fear and dread. In other words, security as self-defense against certain types of violence may become associated with pride, courage, and a sense of belonging. As the following chapter shows, the aesthetics of security-oriented products can also appeal to subjectively pleasant feelings and sensibilities. These "positive" emotions might make bulletproof fashion palatable, not only to those already receptive to guns, armor, ammunition, and related accessories but to a broader sector of the population.

Conclusion

Emotions inform meaning-making about security, including bulletproof fashion. These emotions may flow through multiple channels, such as the state, the media, education systems, the armed forces, family conversations, and other interactions. Bulletproof fashion intervenes in the realm of security through commodification processes that, as mentioned, include a variety of emotions. Affective dimensions are integral to the corporate promotion of bulletproof products, drawing on notions such as what it means to be a good parent, the importance of patriotic attachment, or the need for a securitized citizenry. The emotions that "stick" to bulletproof products—to borrow from Sara Ahmed's notion of "sticky" emotions[89]—do so partly via commodification mechanisms, helping to explain why and how a technology initially associated with the armed forces finds a place in the civilian realm. Attending to emotions helps to shed light on the corporate normalization of armored apparel for private citizens, which in turn rests on the normalization of guns and gun violence in U.S. society.

The emotional components of bulletproof objects transcend their function as artifacts of security in a practical sense, that is, their capacity to avert physical harm. Indeed, it is hard to know whether many of these products would work in an actual active shooter situation. For obvious reasons, they are tested in controlled settings. Even if they are effective at stopping bullets under such conditions, product testing cannot reproduce real-world scenarios. For instance, would children be able to effectively deploy their bulletproof backpacks as shields to protect themselves from a mass shooter? Importantly, do these individual solutions promote security in a deeper sense, including for children? After all, the promotion of bulletproof gear does not prevent gun violence, and it seems to take for granted the proliferation of lethal weapons in everyday life. And still the emotional promise contained in those products can be compelling: to alleviate fear, decrease anxiety, and offset concern.

From the perspective of emotions, it can be argued that bulletproof fashion does more than potentially protect bodies, including from the angry or hateful actions of others. It offers a tool for consumers to manage disturbing emotions, such as fear and sadness, and it encourages other affective experiences such as the possibility to express love and feel pride. Whether wearing a bulletproof garment or backpack effectively provides a sense of relief, or instead heightens unpleasant emotions—for instance, through reminders of a dangerous world—is an open question. Writing about gun culture in the United States, Harel Shapira argues that certain defensive behaviors by private citizens—such as carrying a gun in everyday life—show the inscription of a fearful society "onto the armed body," as the gun carrier adjusts bodily movements and conduct to avert potential threats.[90] Body armor comes with its own set of indications, which can also shape emotions and embodied experience.

Regardless of the actual effectiveness (or lack thereof) of bulletproof products, the promise of "peace of mind" is insistent. This emotional state has become a precious commodity itself, and the intense yearning for such feelings may reveal something about the times we live in, how we interpret its challenges, and how we respond individually and collectively. To the extent that achieving peace of mind through individualized consumer products may replace interest in collective efforts to tackle root causes of insecurity, these products become part of neoliberal and militarized approaches that leave the insecurity associated with gun violence intact.

Notes

1 The survey, conducted in August 2019 soon after two mass shootings, revealed that "48% of U.S. adults [were] 'very' or 'somewhat' worried, compared with 39% in 2017 after one gunman killed 58 people in Las Vegas and 38% in 2015 after a San Bernardino shooter left 14 dead" (Megan Brenan, "Nearly Half in U.S. Fear Being the Victim of a Mass Shooting," *Gallup*, September 10, 2019, https://news.gallup.com/poll/266681/nearly-half-fear-victim-mass-shooting.aspx.).
2 Eva Illouz, *Emotions as Commodities: Capitalism, Consumption and Authenticity* (London and New York: Routledge, 2018), 7.
3 Zygmunt Bauman, "Consuming Life," *Journal of Consumer Culture* 1, no. 1 (2001): 9–29, 24.
4 Chethana Achar, Jane So, Nidhi Agrawal, and Adam Duhachek, "What We Feel and Why We Buy: The Influence of Emotions on Consumer Decision-Making," *Current Opinion in Psychology*, Special issue on "Consumer Behavior," edited by Jeff Joireman and Kristina M Durante, 10 (2016): 166–70, 166.
5 Kari Marie Norgaard and Ron Reed, "Emotional Impacts of Environmental Decline: What can Native Cosmologies Teach Sociology about Emotions and Environmental Justice?," *Theory and Society* 46, no. 6 (2017): 463–95, 470.
6 Natalie Dreier, "Back to School: Stores Offer Bulletproof Backpacks in Bricks-and-Mortar Locations," *Dayton Daily News*, July 31, 2019, www.daytondailynews.com/news/national/back-school-stores-offer-bulletproof-backpacks-bricks-and-mortar-locations/vMiGCPlXFpyymisvteIxNP/.
7 *Fox 35 Orlando*, "Bulletproof Backpacks Selling Locally for Back-to-School," July 26, 2019, www.fox35orlando.com/news/bulletproof-backpacks-selling-locally-for-back-to-school.
8 Scott Johnson, "Disney Seeks to Shut Down Avenger and Princess-Themed Bulletproof Backpacks," *The Hollywood Reporter*, August 6, 2019, www.hollywoodreporter.com/lifestyle/lifestyle-news/disney-seeks-shut-down-avenger-princess-themed-bulletproof-backpacks-1229580/.
9 Anne D'innocenzio, "Mass Shootings Give Rise to Bullet-Resistant Backpacks," *The Associated Press*, August 9, 2019, https://apnews.com/article/d877dab3c5b74caea23b8621eb9b84c4.
10 Shawn Vestal, "In the Congressional Void on Gun Safety, We Offer Kids a Political Education with Drills and Bulletproof Backpacks," *Spokesman Review*, August 25, 2019, www.spokesman.com/stories/2019/aug/25/shawn-vestal-in-the-congressional-void-on-gun-safe/.
11 David Yaffe-Bellany, "Bulletproof Backpack Is in Demand," *New York Times*, August 6, 2019, Section B, 5.
12 Yaffe-Bellany, "Bulletproof Backpack Is in Demand."

13 Sara Ahmed, *The Cultural Politics of Emotions* (London: Routledge, 2014), 11.
14 Sally Holloway, Stephanie Downes, and Sarah Randles, *Feeling Things: Objects and Emotions Through History* (Oxford: Oxford University Press, Oxford Scholarship Online, 2018), 2.
15 Holloway, Downes, Randles, *Feeling Things*, 2.
16 See the demonstration recorded on video, "Does a Bullet Proof Hoodie Actually Work???," *DemolitionRanch*, Video, April 11, 2020, www.youtube.com/watch?v=GJXRYdF0mac&list=RDCMUCBvc7pmUp9wiZIFOXEp1sCg&start_radio=1&rv=GJXRYdF0mac&t=695
17 See City of Houston Mayor's Office of Public Safety and Homeland Security, "RUN. HIDE. FIGHT.® Surviving an Active Shooter Event," accessed December 4, 2020. https://violenceresponse.com/. The Federal Bureau of Investigation's website also has a video illustrating the strategy: Federal Bureau of Investigations (FBI), "Run. Hide. Fight," accessed July 10, 2022, www.fbi.gov/video-repository/run-hide-fight-092120.mp4/view.
18 Barry Glassner, *The Culture of Fear: Why Americans Are Afraid of the Wrong Things* (New York: Basic Books, 1999).
19 "Our Story," *Wonder Hoodie*, accessed September 30, 2020, https://wonderhoodie.com/pages/our-story.
20 "Denali Backpack," *Bullet Blocker*, accessed October 15, 2020, www.bulletblocker.com/bulletblocker-nij-iiia-bulletproof-denali-backpack.html.
21 "Talos Ballistic NIJ IIIA Bulletproof Inserts Medium Tapered 10x12," *Talos Ballistics*, accessed December 4, 2020, https://talosballistics.com/product/talos-ballistics-bulletproof-inserts-medium-tapered-10-x-12/.
22 Chris Espinili, "Bulletproof Armor for School Children?" *Bulletproof Zone*, July 17, 2019, https://bulletproofzone.com/blogs/bullet-proof-blog/should-you-buy-a-bulletproof-backpack-or-bulletproof-backpack-armor.
23 "About Us," *ThykSkynn*, accessed February 24, 2021, https://thykskynn.com/about-us/.
24 See, for example, Frank Edwards, Hedwig Lee, and Michael Esposito, "Risk of Being Killed by Police Use of Force in the United States by Age, Race–Ethnicity, and Sex," *Proceedings of the National Academy of Sciences* 116, no. 34 (2019): 16793–8; Chaeyoung Cheon, Yuzhou Lin, David J. Harding, Wei Wang, and Dylan S. Small, "Neighborhood Racial Composition and Gun Homicides," *JAMA Network Open* 3, no. 11 (2020): e2027591; "Gun Violence Is a Racial Justice Issue," *Brady*, accessed November 25, 2021, www.bradyunited.org/issue/gun-violence-is-a-racial-justice-issue; "Impact of Gun Violence on Black Americans," *Everytown Research & Policy*, accessed November 25, 2021, https://everytownresearch.org/issue/gun-violence-black-americans/.
25 Nicolette Erestain, "What Does Body Armor Have to Do with the Coronavirus (COVID-19)?" *Bulletproof Zone*, March 24, https://bulletproofzone.com/blogs/bullet-proof-blog/what-does-body-armor-have-to-do-with-the-coronavirus.
26 "Every Life Matters. Choose MC Armor for the Ultimate Protection," *MC Armor*, February 24, 2020, https://mc-armor.com/blogs/blog/every-life-matters-choose-mc-armor-for-the-ultimate-protection.
27 "Protecting Lives with Ballistic Removable Inserts by MC Armor," *MC Armor*, March 9, 2020, https://mc-armor.com/blogs/blog/protecting-lives-with-ballistic-removable-inserts-by-mc-armor.
28 Gale Catalan, "The Ultimate Ballistic Body Armor Guide for Preppers and Survivalists," *Bulletproof Zone*, August 25, 2018, https://bulletproofzone.com/blogs/bullet-proof-blog/the-ultimate-ballistic-body-armor-guide-for-preppers-and-survivalists. Note that this article was later modified, and the picture described here was replaced by a different one. The name of the author of the blog post also changed, though the original date remained the same.
29 Allison Ford, "The Self-Sufficient Citizen: Ecological Habitus and Changing Environmental Practices" *Sociological Perspectives* 62, no. 5 (2019): 627–45, 631.
30 Allison Ford, "Emotional Landscapes of Risk: Emotion and Culture in American Self-Sufficiency Movements," *Qualitative Sociology* 44, no. 1 (2021): 125–50.

31 "ArmorMe," Video, *ArmorMe*, accessed October 1, 2020, www.armorme.com/.
32 "Everyday Civilian Protection," *Innocent Armor*, accessed December 5, 2020, https://innocentarmor.com/pages/about.
33 "Tips for Keeping your Child Safe in an Active Shooter Incident at School," *TuffyPacks*, accessed November 28, 2020, https://tuffypacks.com/images/pdfs/TuffyPacks-Parents-Guide.pdf.
34 "Multiple Scenarios: You Never Know," *ArmorMe*, accessed October 1, 2020, www.armorme.com/.
35 "Our Story," *ArmorMe*, accessed October 1, 2020, www.armorme.com/about.
36 "Active Attacker Response Training," *AVS*, accessed December 4, 2020, https://violenceresponse.com/active-attacker-response/.
37 "Bulletproof Panels and Inserts," *Talos Ballistics*, accessed December 4, 2020, https://talosballistics.com/bullet-resistant-panels-and-inserts/.
38 "How Much is Your Life Worth?" *Innocent Armor*, June 21, 2020, https://innocentarmor.com/blogs/news/how-much-is-your-life-worth.
39 For an elaboration of the concept of "ontological security" and its relation to routines, predictability, continuity, and trust, see Anthony Giddens, *Modernity and Self-Identity: Self and Society in the Late Modern Age* (Stanford: Stanford University Press, 1991).
40 Examples of how grief can motivate or be incorporated into collective action can be found in movements of "grieving mothers" in relation to various issues of political significance as well as those of people mobilizing to address gun violence. See, for example, Helena Flam, "The Politics of Grief and the 'Grieving' Mothers," pp. 978–83 in *The Blackwell Encyclopedia of Social and Political Movements*, eds. David A. Snow, Donatella Della Porta, Doug McAdam, and Bert Klandermanns (Malden: Wiley-Blackwell, 2013); Mary Bernstein, Jordan McMillan, and Elizabeth Charash, "Once in Parkland, a Year in Hartford, a Weekend in Chicago: Race and Resistance in the Gun Violence Prevention Movement," *Sociological Forum* 34, no. S1 (2019): 1153–73. At the same time, sadness can be associated with withdrawal from some types of activism and can have a more general depressive impact, in ways that also affects activism. See Jamie N. Albright and Noelle M. Hurd, "Associations between Emotional Responses to the Trump Presidency and Activism among Underrepresented College Students," *Journal of Community Psychology* 49, no. 7 (2021): 2298–315; James M. Jasper, *The Emotions of Protest* (Chicago: The University of Chicago Press, 2018).
41 "Paramedics and Ambulance Crews," *Safeguard Clothing*, accessed December 3, 2020, www.safeguardclothing.com/articles/stab-proof-vests-for-paramedics/.
42 "Guard Dog Proshield Scout—Level IIIA Bulletproof Backpack," "Customer Reviews," *Bulletproof Zone*, accessed December 2, 2020, https://bulletproofzone.com/collections/bags-backpacks/products/guard-dog-proshield-scout-bulletproof-backpack.
43 Isabel Rosales, "Testing out the Sold Out Bulletproof Backpacks Made in Florida," *ABC Action News*, updated February 21, 2018, www.abcactionnews.com/news/region-tampa/exclusive-testing-out-the-sold-out-bulletproof-backpacks-made-in-florida.
44 "Tactical One," *Leatherback Gear*, accessed November 8, 2020, www.leatherbackgear.com/products/tactical-one?variant=32484445225014.
45 "Guard Dog Proshield Prym Pinkout—Level IIIA Bulletproof Backpack," *Bulletproof Zone*, accessed December 2, 2020, https://bulletproofzone.com/collections/bags-backpacks/products/guard-dog-proshield-prym-pinkout-level-iiia-bulletproof-backpack.
46 "Proshield Flex—Bulletproof Backpack," "Buy One & We Give," *Guard Dog Security*, accessed December 5, 2020, https://guarddog-security.com/products/proshield-flex-charcoal.
47 "Proshield Flex—Bulletproof Backpack," "Buy One & We Give."
48 "Donation Program," *Wonder Hoodie*, accessed September 30, 2020, https://wonderhoodie.com/pages/donation-program.
49 Barbara Sutton and Kate Paarlberg-Kvam, "Fashion of Fear for Kids," *InVisible Culture: An Electronic Journal for Visual Culture* 25 (2017), https://ivc.lib.rochester.edu/ready-fashion-of-fear-for-kids/.

50. Bernstein, McMillan, and Charash, "Once in Parkland, a Year in Hartford, a Weekend in Chicago."
51. Isabel Fattal, "The Power of Grief-Fueled Activism," *The Atlantic*, March 2, 2018, www.theatlantic.com/education/archive/2018/03/the-power-of-grief-fueled-activism/554699/.
52. Ephrem Fernandez, Anna Callen, Sheri L. Johnson, Carina Gaspar, Cheyenne Kulhanek, and Carmen Jose-Bueno, "Prevalence, Elicitors, and Expression of Anger in 21st Century Mass Shootings," *Aggression and Violent Behavior* 55 (November 2020): 101483.
53. Audre Lorde, "The Uses of Anger," *Women's Studies Quarterly* 25, no. 1/2 (1997): 278–85; Jasper, *The Emotions of Protest*.
54. "Tuffypacks 12" X 18" Ballistic Shield Level IIIA Bulletproof Backpack Insert," *Bulletproof Zone*, accessed December 2, 2020, https://bulletproofzone.com/products/tuffypacks-12-x-18-ballistic-shield-level-iiia-bulletproof-backpack-insert.
55. "Bite Resistant Arm Guards & Clothing," *Bac-Tactical*, accessed December 3, 2020, https://bac-tactical.com/product-category/bite-resistant-arm-guards/.
56. "Tips for Keeping your Child Safe in an Active Shooter Incident at School."
57. "Active Attackers," (mobile banner), *AVS*, accessed June 12, 2021, https://violenceresponse.com/.
58. Rosanna Smart and Terry L. Schell, "Mass Shootings in the United States," *RAND Corporation*, Updated April 15, 2021, www.rand.org/research/gun-policy/analysis/essays/mass-shootings.html.
59. "Active Attackers," AVS.
60. "Active Attacker Response Training," *AVS*, accessed June 12, 2021, https://violenceresponse.com/active-attacker-response/.
61. Carrie M. Rockwell, "How are You Protecting Your Company's Field Personnel and Corporate Environments?," *Wonder Hoodie*, October 17, 2019, https://wonderhoodie.com/blogs/bulletproof-blog/how-are-you-protecting-your-company.
62. Rockwell, "How are You Protecting Your Company's Field Personnel and Corporate Environments?"
63. "About Bulletproof Zone," *Bulletproof Zone*, accessed December 2, 2020, https://bulletproofzone.com/pages/about-bulletproof-zone.
64. Mark Warr and Christopher G. Ellison, "Rethinking Social Reactions to Crime: Personal and Altruistic Fear in Family Households," *American Journal of Sociology* 106, no. 3 (2000): 551–78; Richard P. Eibach and Steven E. Mock, "The Vigilant Parent: Parental Role Salience Affects Parents' Risk Perceptions, Risk-Aversion, and Trust in Strangers," *Journal of Experimental Social Psychology* 47, no. 3 (2011): 694–7. https://doi.org/10.1016/j.jesp.2010.12.009.
65. "Testimonials," *Wonder Hoodie*, accessed September 28, 2020, https://wonderhoodie.com/.
66. "Scout Backpack," *Bullet Blocker*, accessed October 15, 2020, www.bulletblocker.com/bulletblocker-nij-iiia-bulletproof-scout-backpack.html.
67. "Built-For-You Panels," *Bullet Blocker*, accessed October 15, 2020, www.bulletblocker.com/bulletblocker-nij-iiia-bulletproof-builtforyou.html.
68. "Canvas Classic Pack," *Bullet Blocker*, accessed October 15, 2020, www.bulletblocker.com/bulletblocker-nij-iiia-bulletproof-canvas-classic-pack.html.
69. "Tuffypacks Swissgear Scansmart Backpack + Level IIIa Bulletproof Armor Plate Package," *Bulletproof Zone*, accessed December 2, 2020, https://bulletproofzone.com/products/swissgear-scansmart-backpack-level-iiia-bulletproof-armor-plate-package.
70. "The Artic," *Bulletproof Everyone*, accessed December 3, 2020, https://bulletproofeveryone.com/the-arctic-female-bulletproof-puffer-jacket/.
71. "About Us," *TuffyPacks*, accessed November 28, 2020, https://tuffypacks.com/about.
72. "Active Violence Solutions," *AVS*, accessed December 4, 2020, https://violenceresponse.com/.
73. Ariana Ricardo, "Practical Tips on Staying Safe this Holiday Season," *Bulletproof Zone*, December 17, 2019, https://bulletproofzone.com/blogs/bullet-proof-blog/practical-tips-on-staying-safe-this-holiday-season (the author of this post was later changed but the date remained the same).

74 "Reviews," *Innocent Armor*, accessed December 5, 2020, https://innocentarmor.com/pages/reviews.
75 "AR500 Armor Rimelig 11x15 Level IIIA Lightweight Backpack Soft Body Armor," *Bulletproof Zone*, accessed December 2, 2020, https://bulletproofzone.com/collections/bags-backpacks/products/ar500-armor-rimelig-11-x-15-backpack-iiia-soft-body-armor.
76 Harvey Molotch, *Against Security: How We Go Wrong at Airports, Subways, and Other Sites of Ambiguous Danger* (Princeton: Princeton University Press, 2012), 3.
77 Gavin Brent Sullivan, "Collective Pride, Happiness, and Celebratory Emotions: Aggregative, Network, and Cultural Models," in *Collective Emotions* (Oxford: Oxford University Press, 2014), https://doi.org/10.1093/acprof:oso/9780199659180.003.0018; Alessandro Salice and Alba Montes Sánchez, "Pride, Shame, and Group Identification," *Frontiers in Psychology* 7 (2016): 557; Jasper, *The Emotions of Protest*.
78 "School Programs," *TuffyPacks*, accessed November 28, 2020, https://tuffypacks.com/school-programs.
79 Ahmed, *The Cultural Politics of Emotions*; Jasper, *The Emotions of Protest*.
80 "Your Top Bulletproof Armor Specialist," *Bulletproof Zone*, accessed December 2, 2020, https://bulletproofzone.com/.
81 "Medical Lab Coat," *Bullet Blocker*, accessed October 15, 2020, www.bulletblocker.com/bulletblocker-nij-iiia-bulletproof-lab-coat.html.
82 "Leather Biker Vest," *Bullet Blocker*, accessed October 15, 2020, www.bulletblocker.com/bulletblocker-nij-iiia-bulletproof-biker-leather.html.
83 "Talos Ballistics NIJ IIIA Bulletproof Bravo Flight Jacket," *Talos Ballistics*, accessed December 4, 2020, https://talosballistics.com/product/talos-ballistics-nij-iiia-bulletproof-bravo-flight-coat/.
84 "Patriot Vest," *Bullet Blocker*, accessed October 15, 2020, www.bulletblocker.com/bulletblocker-nij-iiia-bulletproof-patriot-vest.html.
85 "Tested by Security Experts," *ArmorMe*, accessed October 1, 2020, www.armorme.com/.
86 "Real Proof: Shot by MC Club," *MC Armor/Miguel Caballero*, accessed November 8, 2020, https://mc-armor.com/pages/david-blaine-was-shot-by-miguel-caballero.
87 "I Shot Myself on Purpose—Bulletproof Everyone," *Bulletproof Everyone*, Video, September 18, 2018, www.youtube.com/watch?v=NEDJI9PhfAM.
88 "EPIK Trauma Kits AR500 Armor," *AVS*, accessed December 4, 2020, https://violenceresponse.com/product/ar500-epik/.
89 Ahmed, *The Cultural Politics of Emotions*, 25.
90 Harel Shapira, "How to Use the Bathroom with a Gun and Other Techniques of the Armed Body," pp. 194–206 in *The Lives of Guns*, eds. Jonathan Obert, Andrew Poe, and Austin Sarat (New York: Oxford University Press, 2019), 195.

4
AESTHETICS OF SECURITY
Emotions, Bodies, and Bulletproof Fashion

Fences, window bars, border walls, body armor—these and other security-oriented objects often denote fear or a defensive stance. Yet they might also be aesthetically pleasing. What embodied sensibilities, affective dispositions, and stylistic preferences do different security artifacts invite or evoke? Teresa Caldeira's notion of an "aesthetics of security" points to how security-oriented objects can become symbols of status, distinction, and taste by combining protective and aesthetic elements.[1] Drawing on Caldeira's work, D. Asher Ghertner, Hudson McFann, and Daniel M. Goldstein also highlight aesthetic dimensions, "asking what security looks, feels, sounds, smells, and even tastes like."[2] In that vein and keeping in mind the *fashion* aspect of "fashion of fear," this chapter delves into the aesthetic components of bulletproof apparel for civilians. How does the form of these products entwine with their function to promise more than security? Through aesthetic features, bulletproof apparel can encapsulate style, desire, and fantasy as well as the sensibilities and values associated with different social groups. However, (protective) function and (aesthetic) form coexist in uneasy tension, as even stylish and attractive designs may not be enough to fend off the unpleasant emotions that these products sometimes elicit.

Bulletproof apparel consists of an armored "fence" of sorts, designed to be worn on the body and to shield the self from potentially dangerous others. Sociologist of fashion Joanne Entwistle noted that clothing works as an "interface between the individual and the social world."[3] In that sense, bulletproof clothing "hardens" that boundary between self and other, producing a fortress body. Bulletproof apparel, however, is not merely protective but also aesthetically shaped through fashion, and it shares cultural meanings with other forms of dress and accessories constituting what Terence Turner called "social skin."[4] The aesthetic components that make the apparel inconspicuous are often important to the commercialization of the products and to their potential appeal. Furthermore, aesthetics relate to how the product is meant to feel, as various products are geared toward the preferences, styles, and

DOI:10.4324/9781003326854-4

cultural identities associated with distinct groups. They mark differences and inequalities among people, signaling power, wealth, beauty, or other social attributes. Whereas some customers considering security-oriented garments may seek an overt militarized aesthetic—whether bulletproof or not—others prefer to blend in with civilian society. In the latter case, fashionable "normal" looking clothing may somewhat ameliorate the aversive feelings associated with reminders of danger, even as armor reshapes the body and might foster attunement to potential threats.[5]

Fear, anxiety, and concern about unsafe worlds help prompt interest in bulletproof fashion, and companies offer to relieve unpleasant emotions through ballistic apparel intended to protect from injury or death. Additionally, through a variety of product designs and representations, companies appeal to the tastes of different kinds of consumers: A casual fleece vest for women, a wool topcoat for men, a feminine laced biker vest, a natty navy hoodie for kids, a white medical lab coat, and many other garments are offered with bullet-resistant features. The balance between function and form fluctuates in different depictions; and the portrayals of people/bodies wearing the products help evoke varied emotions, moods, and affective experiences, such as feeling sexy, strong, outgoing, adventurous, or distinguished, among others. These representations sometimes make security the focal point and at other times they highlight features that may make one forget what is distinctive about the products: ballistic protection. Through a sleight of hand, bulletproof fashion hides what lies beneath. Still, the very existence of these products points to how a security-oriented milieu influences dress and fashion. It also shows the entanglement of bulletproof fashion with individualized notions of security amid a lack of confidence in the state and other publicly oriented approaches: Self-reliance and consumer choices are apparently what is left to address social problems.

The visual and textual representations of bulletproof fashion on company websites reveal the significance of the aesthetic, emotional, and social dimensions of this type of apparel. Indeed, bulletproof fashion needs to be understood in relation to a broader social field where a range of identities, experiences, and inequalities interact with concerns about security. One important dimension is gender, which in various advertising materials serves to organize the products along binary lines—that is, clothing for men or women—even as some products are marketed regardless of gender. Given the prominence of this distinction, especially for adult products, I pay particular attention to gendered tropes while also showing intersections with other aspects of social location such as class and race-ethnicity. In the case of children, I also consider the aesthetics of the products in relation to certain notions of childhood. The discussion of fashion, aesthetics, and security helps situate bulletproof products in the broader context of social and political concerns, which in turn shape sartorial styles.

Fashion, Aesthetics, and Security

Clothing is a pervasive fact of social life. As Joanne Entwistle and other scholars point out, in most social situations, and across cultures, the body is dressed in some way, even if minimally or by way of painting, tattoos, or jewelry. Clothing can operate as a mechanism of self-expression, a way to display group belonging, a site of social control, and a means of resistance to social norms.[6] At its most basic level, clothing has a protective function, for instance, against the elements, rough terrain, or the unwanted gaze toward intimate body parts. Body armor extends the protective role of clothing in contexts of fear of gun-related threats. Part of the novelty of certain bulletproof apparel for civilians, however, is the concealment of its protective features, and its fashionable appearance. Therefore, aesthetics can be an important component of these products. In Catherine Baker's definition, the notion of aesthetics alludes to "the creative and representational practices with which artists and other creators engage the senses and emotions to convey human imagination and experience."[7] Aesthetics are intimately connected to fashion.

In *Thinking through Fashion*, Agnès Rocamora and Anneke Smelik refer to fashion as "dress, appearance and style" and "as both material culture and as symbolic system," among other dimensions.[8] Diana Crane and Laura Bovone note that fashion describes "systems that produce new styles of clothing and attempt to make them desirable to the public."[9] These aspects of fashion are relevant to the bulletproof apparel industry. Armored wear has traditionally been the province of military and security forces—which have a fashion of their own, too—but it has taken corporate promotional work to persuade civilian audiences about the need and desirability of bulletproof attire. The garments' aesthetics are a key aspect of their potential appeal. While participation in everyday civilian life comprises diverse aesthetic presentations and types of clothing, they usually do not include a conspicuous bulletproof element. Still, clothing that is obviously militarized or appears to be bulletproof (even if it may not be) can also constitute a fashionable style. Scholars, activists, and fashion writers have analyzed the expansion of military styles into civilian life and attire, from the use of "camo," cargo pants, and khaki fabrics, to decorative designs that resemble military regalia.[10] This is just one manifestation of "how war and the military shape the ways that bodies move and appear," as Baker pointed out.[11] Whether visible or invisible, the militarized components of fashion are symptomatic of the lingering influence of the security apparatus into the realm of culture. Moreover, as military and security forces have been traditionally male dominated, this militarization of fashion also bears the marks of certain types of masculinity, associated with strength and power.

Writing about the sociology of clothing and fashion, Crane and Bovone observe that "clothing brands transmit sets of values that imply an ideology and specific life styles."[12] They also note that the "nature of the symbolic values attached to fashionable clothing depends on the cultural and political history of the country and the characteristics and variety of the ethnic groups of which it is composed."[13] When considering the companies selling bulletproof apparel in the United States, the security ideologies that undergird these products immediately come to mind. Armored clothing points to social anxieties about the vulnerability of the body to violence, and the role of securitization as one hegemonic response. In some cases, ballistic apparel serves to project a "warrior" outlook, complementing the role of guns and fostering a sense of strength and immunity to danger. Still, a number of covert armor designs also reveal a desire to blend in, which is achieved through "normal," even fashionable, civilian aesthetics. If the body is to be distinguished, the implicit message seems to be, *let it be on account of fashion*. The varied aesthetic configurations of the products, then, appeal to different social identities based on class, gender, race-ethnicity, and age, among others.

What does the commercialization of these garments and accessories tell us about contemporary social life in U.S. society? As fashion studies demonstrate, clothing has been influenced not only by personal preferences, or the whims of the fashion industry, but by broader social phenomena. For instance, we can think of fashion in relation to war, economic crisis, religious norms, and the political standing of a nation. In *Fear and Fashion in the Cold War*, Jane Pavitt shows how prominent concerns of the era, including the specter of nuclear weapons, political conflicts, and new technological developments, profoundly shaped fashion. Among other characteristics of the period, Pavitt notes that

> inasmuch as 1960s fashion was concerned with revealing flesh, it also demonstrated a concern for armouring the body. Figure-hugging catsuits were often shown with chain mail, rigid plastic or metal breastplates and protective coverings for limbs. These body coverings are a kind of hybrid of clothing and jewellery design, and beg the question: what did the vulnerable body need protection from?[14]

This question remains relevant today, as fashionable clothing and accessories can still function as evidence of the vulnerability of the body and the fears that surround it. For example, colorful face masks to protect against COVID-19—even in their most creative and "fun" designs—may remind us of human vulnerability to potentially deadly viruses. On a different register, the promotion of bulletproof jackets, dresses, and backpacks—no matter how stylish—is one response to the anxieties produced by mass shootings and other forms of gun violence by civilians and/or state actors.

In her analysis of fashion in the context of societal responses to terrorism, Rhonda Garelick shows how security concerns can find their way to fashion, shaping styles and norms about dress:

> As terrorism breeds, even encourages, a tenuous grip on our bodily integrity, threatening us with dissolving borders of myriad kinds, fashion steps up, seemingly to allay or control these anxieties, while actually reproducing symbolically the very things we fear, normalising and encouraging an internalised (unconscious) culture of surveillance.[15]

Garelick notes how security concerns sometimes translate into violent or unpleasant practices, including those that target the body and its clothing. For instance, security measures may involve guards palpating or stripping the bodies of people crossing through checkpoints, especially members of racialized groups construed as potentially dangerous. Garelick also discusses how anxieties about breaches to national borders get repackaged into a preoccupation with bodily contours, managed through technologies that render the body's clothing "transparent"—the body scanning machines in airports being a paradigmatic example of this phenomenon. Juxtaposing the hyper-visible bodies of security scanning machines and contemporary gendered fashions, Garelick notes that certain forms of dress used by celebrity women also render the body extremely visible. Here, the mechanism is not airport technology but clothing that, with transparent materials and scant coverage, amounts to what has been touted as a "super-naked dress."[16]

Interestingly, while some bodies become hyper-visible through fashion, others mimic the security state's desire for impenetrable and fortified borders, including via fashionable clothing. By forting up the body, the companies selling bulletproof fashion, and the individuals who consume it, reiterate the ideologies that peg bodily security to militarized technologies. At the same time, not everyone wants to be conspicuously armored, so fashionable bulletproof products offer concealed protection. Covert armor still needs to be comfortable enough to be palatable to civilians, and companies aim to create ballistic apparel that is lightweight in comparison to that used in security and military operations.[17] Commenting on hard armor, a post in the Bulletproof Zone company blog reminds us that not everyone "need[s] to look like Robocop."[18]

In the United States, "hardened" security responses sometimes follow mass shootings, including calls to further arm the citizenry, or in the case of bulletproof fashion companies, through the promotion of body armor. By way of aesthetics, bulletproof fashion hides its protective function, but this trick does not resolve the tension between the fencing of bodies and the openness of an ideally "free" society. Companies then must navigate the contradictions between the unpleasant emotions associated with insecurity and those linked to aesthetic appreciation. A central dilemma they face is this: How does one make the fortress body beautiful, or at least "normal" looking? In practical terms, how is this tension translated into the products advertised to different sectors of the population? In some cases, this may indeed lead to a "Robocop" aesthetics, as the armed/armored body of the cyborg appeals to certain masculinity scripts, enhancing body size and projecting power. However, the products analyzed in this study show a wider range of expected consumers and aesthetic designs that incorporate armor in inconspicuous ways.

As is the case with other clothing and apparel, bulletproof fashion companies are not exempt from the inequalities already existing in society. The cost of many of the products is high, making them inaccessible, especially to those most socially marginalized. In that sense, bulletproof fashion becomes another form of social distinction and status. As in other product advertisements, individuals associated with bulletproof fashion in the company materials I analyzed did not appear economically destitute but seemed to be at least middle-class, and in some cases wealthy. The still images in various companies tended to depict white-appearing models, an exception being Thyk Skynn: All models on its website appeared to be people of color, largely with physical features associated with Blackness. Companies such as

Wonder Hoodie and Innocent Armor had diverse representation, including individuals who appeared to be white, Black, and Asian. Though some companies had a roughly similar representation of masculine and feminine individuals, many of the people featured in the group of companies as a whole tended to be masculine. In the case of Guard Dog Security, groups of all or mostly feminine individuals appeared on different banners, and images of hands holding specific products, such as pepper spray, had conventionally feminine red painted nails. As we shall see, various companies were offering products to both men and women at the time of the analysis, or included gender-neutral products such as backpacks—sometimes distinguished with gendered patterns or colors. One company, Aspetto, specialized in suits for men, which was reflected in the visual representations on the business's website for civilians. Most companies also included some representation of children and youths in their online materials.

Bulletproof fashion, as well as other security-oriented products, targets varied sectors of the population. As we shall see, this is signaled not only through the bodies of the people portrayed but also through the aesthetic form of the products and the textual narratives that accompany them.

Bulletproofing Childhoods

Children appear prominently in discussions of mass shootings—usually as potential victims. Institutional responses to such forms of gun violence include active shooter drills, security protocols, and police presence in educational spaces. In some cases, it may also include the consideration of bulletproof whiteboards, armored backpack inserts, and the like.[19] Parents who provide bulletproof products to their children, such as armored backpacks or vests, draw attention to the possibility of students being shot during schooltime. This is also the case for parents, teachers, and school administrators who may discuss with children what to do in the event of an active shooter situation. Hence, adults have to walk the fine line between scaring children and striving for their well-being. Product design mediates this boundary through aesthetic features that make bulletproof apparel and accessories for children inconspicuous, even "cool" or evocative of children's worlds. For children to be able to laugh, play, and learn, they cannot be constantly scared. The form of the product has a function in that regard.

As Kate Paarlberg-Kvam and I argued in our previous work on the topic, the design features of bulletproof apparel for kids, such as colorful fabrics and child-oriented motifs, may help protect more than the bodies of children but the sense of innocence culturally associated with childhood, and with socially and economically privileged children in particular.[20] The affective dimensions of the product aesthetics rest on the ability of *form* to downplay practical *function* (protection from bullets), underscoring normalcy and even fun. Flowers, contemporary designs, varied color schemes, kids-movie characters' images, and other stylistic features help children blend in. And to the extent that the products pass for regular backpacks and jackets, they might help guard against the negative feelings elicited by reminders of danger. Commenting on an armored backpack insert, Andrew F., a Bulletproof Zone customer, noted: "These fit absolutely perfectly into both my kids elementary school character backpacks."[21] Although his children initially "were a little apprehensive" about using the products, their "unassuming look," combined with relatively light weight, were among the factors that might have encouraged the children's acceptance.[22]

In a Bulletproof Zone blog post image, a mixed-gender group of elementary school-aged children are running in what appears to be school grounds. We can only see their backs as they run toward a set of stairs in front of them. The group includes children with blonde, brunette, and darker-colored hair with straight and curly textures, perhaps belonging to different ethnoracial groups. They are all wearing backpacks with an assortment of colors and patterns. While the scene may seem benign enough, the blog post's subheading suggests something more ominous: "Parents Are Now Buying Bulletproof Backpacks for Their Kids and for Good Reason."[23] That is, the incidence of active shooter events, which have gained public attention and "shocked the world." In the context of such events and the existence of products that promise protection, a TuffyPacks customer expressed gratitude:

> I am so happy to have found this. I bought three. One for both my kids and one for my husband . . . just my kids having them is incredibly reassuring. I am angry that we even have to think about the possibility of a school shooting, OR 'mad gunman'; at work, but at least now we can do something. THANK YOU.[24]

As schools and workplaces are described as sites of danger, companies promote a variety of security-oriented products in addition to bulletproof materials. For instance, Bullet Blocker advertises a School Safety & Survival Pack, which consists of an armored backpack, a first-aid kit, and a variety of items for the event of having to shelter in place, including duct tape, a space blanket, tactical light sticks, a whistle, and a 14 in 1 multi-purpose tool, among other elements displayed on a picture and described through a written list. Given that this is a precautionary measure, the child so equipped is presumably expected to go every day to school with all such elements, in addition to more typical school supplies. What message does this type of equipment convey about the "safety" of the school and what emotions might they elicit?

Some of the companies' images of small children or teens project a wholesome feel, such as the photo of an adult white woman helping a white boy put on the jacket, a Black woman holding the hand of a Black girl in a video, or the picture of a blonde woman wrapping her arms around two children of different ages. While we do not know what the relation is between the women and children depicted, the images convey motherly care and a sense of comfort. Yet some pictures also portray defensive or fearful stances, such as teens crouching behind their backpack or partially covering their face with the backpack. This tension between the disturbing emotions associated with imminent danger and the desire to uphold a sense of normalcy seems particularly difficult to navigate when it comes to children, as adults may be wary of unduly scaring them. As with other armored products, the appearance of children's bulletproof apparel plays a significant role in grappling with that tension.

To illustrate, the aesthetic enhancement of kids' security products is highlighted in Bulletproof Zone's online materials. A blog post stated: "Who would have ever thought that this adorable backpack is bulletproof? A bulletproof bag is a must-have item for your little ones while they are at school."[25] Several customer reviews echo this theme, such as one by Gwen J., who commented: "Great Backpack. I purchased this at the request of my daughter who has anxiety about safety at school. She loves the backpack. The aesthetic and function is even better than the old backpacks she used to carry."[26] Bulletproof Zone additionally sells a transparent backpack deemed good "for security checkpoints at school, the airport, or a stadium," which includes a panel made with Kevlar that comes in solid colors or patterns with labels such as "Sunflower," "Cherry," and "Camo." One customer review by Justin R. praised these products, saying that the children loved "the look and how light they are."[27]

Gender normativity is one dimension of the social construction of the "normal," which in some cases is achieved with colors or patterns associated with girls and boys. Bullet Blocker's youth backpack, the Scout, came in pink and blue colors, likely to cater to girls and boys respectively (though, of course, anyone can use any color in theory). They also included compartments for storing "school supplies and personal treasures" and a removable lunchbox in matching colors.[28] This armored backpack looked like any other school bag, and the references in the description also highlight the normalcy aspirations connected to children's worlds, including school as integral to their everyday lives, as well as small things that make childhood special ("personal treasures"). It might also convey a sense of discovery and exploration connected to being a "Scout." Similarly, a pink backpack by the same company, the Acadia, evoked the lives of children, probably girls given the color. The product's image shows how the bag could fit pens, a small pink notebook, an electronic device, a water bottle, and, hanging from the zipper, a small teddy bear in matching colors. The Acadia was touted as ideal for children six to ten years old, also with space for "protecting trinkets and treasures."[29] In other words, it offered to preserve children's lives, play, fantasy, and everyday routines.

Customers appreciate the "normal" look of various children's products. Bullet Blocker's Defender backpack is featured with a picture of what might be a teen boy about to board a school bus; the backpack is blue and looks like so many other bags that children use every day. Indeed, one customer testimonial reads, "Love that it looks like a normal kids backpack."[30] Similarly, parents and grandparents emphasized the common appearance of the Junior Pack, a bag recommended for preschoolers and first graders and "ideal for children under 49 inches." Two customer reviews describe the product as follows: "Cute, pink, light weight and similar enough to regular backpacks to not draw undo [sic] attention. I have instructed my granddaughter how to carry in case of such a horrible tragedy with someone shooting at innocent children. She used it every day since I gave it to her to go to school" and "Looks like a cool, normal backpack (great purple-pink color that my daughter loves), and gives me peace of mind to know she's at least a little bit safer now at school."[31]

In these depictions, a sense of security is achieved through ballistic protection as well as the normalcy projected by the product, including the gender normativity and age appropriateness that the objects' aesthetics convey. The emphasis on cuteness and colors linked to girlhood make this defensive backpack more appealing for users such as a "granddaughter" and a "daughter." The form of the backpack might help store away disturbing thoughts about a potential "horrible tragedy." At the same time, insistence on normalcy actually constructs a peculiar idea of what is normal: In addition to gender/age assumptions, it is the fortress body, the fortified childhood, and individually-driven security.

The products and the images that advertise them reproduce culturally embedded differences, including but not only gender distinction. As companies draw on "common sense" assumptions to market their products, they incorporate symbols and messages that reproduce social differences and hierarchies. In the case of children, it may include symbols that while often taken for granted can contribute to stereotypes about certain groups in society. For instance, TuffyPacks ballistic backpack inserts can be tailored with patches featuring school symbols and logos, exemplified mostly by animal mascots, but in one case, the advertisement includes an image of a Native American person wearing a headdress with feathers—the kind of imagery that various sports teams and schools across the nation have adopted but which have also been denounced for perpetuating racist stereotypes and creating hostile environments for Native students.[32]

Considering the bulletproof products for kids, it becomes apparent that the "security" they embody may not really be for all children. The products are mounted on already existing structures of inequality, such as those based on class and race-ethnicity. With respect to bulletproof products, one aspect that involves the social stratification of children is the prohibitive cost of some apparel and accessories. For instance, Bullet Blocker's Youth Nylon Jacket—depicted as a "bullet resistant child's jacket [that] provides fashion and safety"—was advertised with a price tag of $ 670; a bulletproof hoodie for kids, by Wonder Hoodie, had a promotional price of $ 450; and a school-themed TuffyPacks ballistic insert was posted with a reduced price of $ 129 (down from $ 169). These prices are surely unaffordable to many families, while still accessible to affluent and wealthy groups, among which white people are more likely to be represented.

Additionally, there are documented disparities in the treatment of children of different social classes and ethnoracial groups when it comes to school misbehavior, including those interpreted as security threats. Schools attended by relatively large numbers of students of color are particularly likely to rely on heavy-handed punishment and overt "exclusionary" security approaches, such as metal detectors.[33]

Aesthetics of Security 95

In "Fashion of Fear for Kids," Kate Paarlberg-Kvam and I noted the implicit class and racial distinctions embedded in children's bulletproof products, including the aesthetics of concealment:

> Some children seem to deserve to be protected, both from the constant threat and from knowing about it; others are to be protected against with highly visual symbols of militarization. As such, the proliferation of ballistic apparel for children both reflects and reproduces neoliberal structures of inequality; it both asserts a threat and pretends to ameliorate it for those who can pay.[34]

We noted that while in contemporary U.S. society children of color are more likely to be considered sources of misbehavior and even crime, the security apparatus is in many cases not designed to protect them but to protect *against* them. In that sense, the protection of children's worlds encapsulated in bulletproof products with child-oriented designs may not equally apply to all children but those already deemed more "innocent" and worthy of protection.

As we shall see in the following chapter, some stakeholders interpret the existence of bulletproof garments as a societal and political failure: an inability or unwillingness to adequately deal with the problem of gun violence. These products also reverberate in the work of artists who rely on aesthetics as a form of social commentary and critique. The *Back to School Shopping* exhibit by multi-media artist WhIsBe ironically overflew with "fun" colors and the bright aesthetics associated with children.[35] But upon closer inspection, one can see that among the colorful balls in a "claw machine"—like those in children's arcades—were red, orange, pink, purple, and light blue faux guns of several types. Supposedly on sale, the exhibit included bulletproof-like vests with colorful designs and cartoon characters, such as Ninja Turtles and Pikachu. These vests were meant to look like overt—rather than concealed—body armor, and in that sense, the artist added a twist by making visible that which is generally hidden in actual bulletproof fashion for kids. By incorporating the children's motifs, the jarring combination of a world of danger and one of children's play is exposed.

In a video of the exhibit, children and adults appear to be having fun while trying on the vests and playing with the toy guns in this immersive experience. Yet as the video continues, we can see a broader frame of violence, tragedy, and suffering, through news clips about the Sandy Hook Elementary School shooting and commentary on the problem of gun violence. A description of this art project mentions that the artist

> uses subversive formulas that collide innocent images with provocative messages, while simultaneously making subtle alterations on known consumer products; irrevocably disrupting their intended meaning. With this project, WhIsBe targets the message: Don't let this be the future generation's "Back to School Shopping."[36]

Fortressing Adult Bodies

As in the case of bulletproof apparel for children, the representation of the products for adults also appeals to different emotions and sensibilities via aesthetics. Whereas an overt bulletproof vest might signal "danger," stylish and creative designs that conceal the ballistics function can help tame reminders of ominous threat, creating the illusion of normalcy. Additionally, evocation of travel, adventure, leisure, and valued occupations provides a different emotional texture to ballistic products that in their traditional version signal the risks faced by security personnel. For instance, Talos Ballistics explained that its "NIJ IIIA Bulletproof Double Duty Day Pack was made with fun in mind. It has tons of style and doesn't loose [sic] any of the function from a normal backpack."[37] Another armored backpack by the same company, the Trekker, was said to be "great whether you are backpacking up the side of a beautiful mountain or just strolling along on the city streets."[38] The evocation of nature's beauty and a carefree stroll can help temper feelings of fear and dread that might be associated with bulletproof products. Aaron L., a Wonder Hoodie customer, remarked:

> Almost every friend of mine wants to try it on. It is fun, makes me feel safe and confident. . . . I don't need a suitcase when I travel to foreign countries, but I will bring my bulletproof hoodies.[39]

Although in this statement foreign countries implicitly appear as sites of potential danger, travel may also be for leisure purposes, and the association of the garment with feelings of enjoyment, safety, confidence, and distinction adds to the product's allure.

Various bulletproof products designed for adults contain a fashionable dimension that is absent in more traditional body armor. They help enlist emotions that make the products more acceptable for civilian use. Unless consumers seek a militarized look specifically (military-inspired designs such as "camo" are by now part of mainstream clothing[40]), usually the goal for civilian bulletproof fashion is hiding the ballistic features. The desire for normalcy, and for blending in, is evident in a comment by a customer identified as Mrs. V., who praised an Innocent Armor vest for women: "I love my puffy vest. It's comfortable. It doesn't 'stand out in a crowd'. It's not heavy. It easily molded around my shape. I can happily wear it every day, every where [sic]. Exceeded my expectations."

In contrast, the visibility of "tactical" body armor can have a function for law enforcement or military personnel, or for those individuals who want to emulate militarized aesthetics even if not part of security-oriented institutions. For instance, in a blog post addressing "today's sheriffs," Safeguard Clothing discussed the presumed external effects, including emotional, of overt ballistic garments:

> An overt vest is worn over the uniform, and is typically of a bulky design— this may provoke a variety of reactions from civilians. Some neighborhoods,

for example, may greet the sight of a law enforcement representative dressed in an obvious ballistics vest as an insult, or, conversely, find it highly unnerving. On the other hand, it may alert potential criminals to the fact that a sheriff or sheriff's officer is in the vicinity, and prepared for trouble.[41]

In this description, overt body armor appears as potentially threatening or angering. Regardless of whether the point of bulletproof gear is merely defensive, it may be interpreted as aggressive too, and some users seem to worry that overt armor might make them a target. Customer Cristina C., a retired police officer, came to value civilian bulletproof apparel: No longer donning a uniform, she expressed a sense of vulnerability, "especially with all these horrific shootings happening these days." She added: "Wearing this comfortable, stylish, non revealing protective vest, I really feel safe."[42] Still, there are companies that do sell overt vests for civilians, and in the case of Thyk Skynn—as we shall see—with fashion-oriented designs and decorations.

A comment posted on the Innocent Armor website, by Ross K., hints at concerns regarding overt armor while extolling the advantages of covert ballistics:

> I've been looking for body armor for my wife to wear that doesn't look like body armor. . . . I've always felt that someone wearing armor in public is like open carrying, you're advertising that you are protected and they'll assume you're probably carrying a gun. A friend referred me to Innocent Armor and I'm so glad they did. She absolutely loves it and I have a little more peace of mind that she's protected when I'm not around.[43]

Besides explaining the perceived benefits of inconspicuous bulletproof clothing, the comment incidentally draws on gender scripts in which women appear as needing protection, while men are assigned the role of protectors. Body armor becomes a stand-in for a masculine figure. This is similar to sociologist Jennifer Carlson's observation regarding male gun owners who encourage women to also arm themselves but to replace the masculine protector in his absence.[44]

Some of the affective connotations in bulletproof apparel representations are laced with gendered assumptions and expectations, including references that reproduce and reinforce the gendering of bodies and emotions. Some of these references are explicit, and some provide visual or textual elements that can activate audiences' feelings and imagination. The public may fill in the missing pieces in text and images, drawing on the social contexts from which these cultural productions emerge. The following sections explore some of the connections between bodies, emotions, and representations of security condensed in adult bulletproof fashion promotional materials, looking specifically at how they address several types of men and women. The analysis reveals the affective dimensions of these representations, highlighting the role of gender in intersection with other social statuses, such as race and class, in the promotion of bulletproof fashion.

Feminine Bulletproof Fashion

On the companies' websites as a whole, women appear in various roles and situations, including those involving stereotypically feminine attributes. In some of the depictions, there is an emphasis on bodily appearance and positive qualities that evoke pleasure or joy while simultaneously reminding of fear by alluding to the need for protection. For instance, Talos Ballistic described its Bulletproof Circe Leather Vest for women as "sophisticated," "form-fitting," and "feminine," adding that the "pliability and softness you will experience on the outside of this vest discreetly hides four NIJ IIIA bulletproof panels hidden on the inside. It is built to protect you from unforeseen dangers yet look attractive."[45] Similarly, in describing a bulletproof vest for women, Thyk Skynn explained that "the cut is specifically designed to shape the body of the woman to provide protection without sacrificing your look."[46] Appearance is important in these statements, consistent with femininity expectations directing women to care about their looks. Similarly, the following description of a women's bulletproof garment underscores bodily appearance and connected feelings:

> The BulletBlocker NIJ IIIA Bulletproof Woman's fitted Jacket has been designed and tailored to flatter any female figure. This is the best concealable body armor for a variety of social settings. Whether going to the bus stop in the morning, out with the girls on a Friday night or going for a spin on the back of a motorcycle, this form-fitting coat had been designed to make you look and feel great.[47]

The promise to the woman who wears this armored jacket includes good looks and enhanced positive feelings, such as those derived from fulfilling feminine standards of beauty and behavior. The product is "flattering"; the user rides in the back of—rather than drives—the motorcycle; and she goes out at night with "the girls" despite these friends presumably being adult women. The playful language, activities, and feelings referenced make one almost forget that the point of this product is to provide physical/personal security.

Various companies promote positive emotions through the aesthetics and style of their bulletproof products. For example, Thyk Skynn described the fashionable look of one of its armored garments as "fun": "The W1–001 is designed with our fashion-forward female customer in mind. This vest brings white vinyl, pink glitter, and sleek cuts together to give our ladies a fun addition to their closet."[48] Given the ethnoracial representation on this Black-owned company website—seemingly all people of color, though with different skin shades and hair colors and textures— it can be assumed that "our ladies" are likely to be women of color. In this way, the company offered these women both security and fun feelings through bulletproof fashion. Positive emotions are also evident in the comments of Michelle Renee, an Innocent Armor customer, regarding a bullet-resistant jacket: "My fashionable favorites are the Leather Jacket and the Down Vest. Perfect wardrobe additions for casual & contemporary chic dressy attire with 'Safety' center mass protection!!! Highly recommended, and a great self love investment."[49] The effusive tone and the reference to love underscore once again the positive emotions that may be associated with this type of product, in this case derived from the combination of aesthetics and security, and implicitly, the pleasures of consumption.

Some of the portrayals of women on different websites are markedly gendered, and sometimes sexualized, evoking emotions associated with sex appeal. From the svelte ginger-haired white woman donning a stylish MC Armor/Miguel Caballero red jacket to the slim and curvaceous dark-skinned woman wearing a tight and revealing bulletproof dress by Thyk Skynn—some of the images emphasize sexually alluring femininity that fits specific gendered scripts in intersection with race and class. These interconnected social statuses work in tandem to represent various types of bodies secured by bulletproof fashion, while also conveying specific affective tonalities.

For instance, MC Armor/Miguel Caballero's bulletproof products include a series of high-end, elegant attires, all modeled by the ginger-haired white woman mentioned earlier. She appears in different scenes projecting elegance, affluence, and sophistication according to dominant race, class, and gender ideologies. She embodies an idealized type of delicate and privileged white femininity. Her body is slender; her long hair cascades over her shoulders; and her gait and posture fit socially valued modes of femininity in its upper-class, white, heteronormative versions. In one series of images, the woman is coming out of a pristine-looking vintage car, with someone holding her hand—seemingly a male partner—to help her out of the vehicle. In another garment's photo series of the same brand, the model is sitting next to a modern fireplace wearing a white blouse, black skirt, and stiletto shoes. In this and other images, her facial expression looks self-assured, even aloof. The affective tone conveyed is anything but a preoccupation with potential gun injury, even as she wears bulletproof clothing. Indeed, the aesthetic form of the apparel completely hides its protective function, and the scenes and settings represented have emotional connotations that revolve around wealth and fashion.

A different type of sexually alluring femininity appears on Thyk Skynn's website, which as mentioned, portrays people of color, particularly with physical features associated with Blackness. Perhaps the most sexualized image of the set analyzed is that of a slim dark-skinned woman with long straight black hair, wearing high heels and a skin-tight bulletproof dress. The clothing reveals the sides of her breasts as well as her body contours through the naked space between the straps connecting the front and back of the dress. She has long eyelashes and long nails painted with dark polish, and she adopts sexy postures in different pictures. The company specified that the dress is suitable for women of different body sizes, yet the model wearing this garment fits conventional notions of slim feminine beauty. The protective function of the product almost disappears, as the body takes center stage. While women unapologetically displaying their sexual bodies can be an empowering move when done on their own terms, feminists have noted how sexualized media depictions often objectify women. Such representations can serve to uphold stereotypes, including those at the intersection of gender and racial ideologies. For example, stereotypes that associate Black womanhood with excessive or exotic sexuality have been deployed to justify sexual violence and infringements on bodily autonomy against Black women.[50] These considerations are particularly pertinent in the context of a product meant to protect the body.

Notably, in this woman's representation, sexualization appears juxtaposed with signals of grief and mourning inscribed on the model's body. One of the woman's arms has a tattoo that reads "Forever in my heart. R.I.P. Betty," surrounded by drawings of two roses and a dove with open wings.[51] Viewers are not privy to the causes of death of the person commemorated, but in the context of the model posing with a bulletproof dress, a kind of intertextuality emerges between tattoo and attire. Indeed, one may wonder whether gun violence has something to do with the referenced death, further reinforcing the message about the need for bulletproof apparel. In this series of images, specific intersections of gender, race, and sexuality emerge in representations of femininity, as the woman of color is sexualized and literally marked by loss. At the same time, the tattoo also points to a story that the woman herself may want to tell through her body inscription: one that includes meaningful affective connections and a different realm of beauty reflected by the rose and dove symbols inscribed on the body.[52]

In addition to sexuality, another area that reveals specific representations of bulletproof fashion pertains to care and nurturing qualities associated with womanhood, particularly motherhood. In that sense, it is not surprising that different companies appeal to mothers directly or include images that evoke motherly care. For instance, Wonder Hoodie refers to its body armor as "loved by moms and law enforcement alike," and has been particularly concerned with including women and children among its consumer base.[53] Some of the images on other companies' websites, while not as explicit, represent situations that could be interpreted as involving motherhood, or at least gendered care. To illustrate, an ArmorMe video depicts a slender Black woman holding the hand of a Black girl who is wearing a backpack. The adult woman, who could be the girl's mother, is wearing a stylish coat and trousers and looks professional. The pair is walking outside, next to a building, and greenery appears in the background. A caption reads "ArmorMe. For protection wherever you go."[54] The woman smiles in the girl's direction, and the scene conveys love and care—emotions expected of mothers and those with carework duties. This image contrasts with the pictures previously discussed, in that the adult woman is not sexualized but projecting social class comfort and connection to a child. Positive affects apparently flow from such a bond and from the ability to give the child protective gear.

Another depiction linking women to children, though more implicitly (as no child is in view), appears in a video describing the Civilian One backpack by the company Leatherback Gear, which shows how the product can function as a "diaper bag." The model showing the bag is a slim white woman with blonde hair, and she wears a pair of skinny jeans and a NASA T-shirt. In the posted video, she gathers several items that are spread on the floor and puts them inside the backpack: baby wipes, diapers, a small rubber toy, pink sneakers, colorful books, and other things such as a laptop computer, water bottle, and car keys. This woman looks conventionally feminine, with long straight hair, nails with red polish, and a ring with a gem on one of her fingers. According to one customer, the featured backpack is a "Great bag for soccer moms."[55] The model in the video looks happy and confident—an affective state that is reinforced by the active beat of the background music. She seems ready to face whatever the day might bring, whether fending bullets, working on her computer, or taking care of her child's needs. In this type of image, security-oriented apparel becomes part of the products that modern women "need" to perform their duties, which might combine unpaid care work and employment. Positive feelings displace emotions such as fear or alertness, emotional states visibly present in other materials. As mentioned in the previous chapter, sometimes the affective dimensions of the product connect with how they function as tokens of love. A comment by Mario G., an Innocent Armor customer, illustrates the point, as he saw the potential for a bulletproof backpack to become a diaper bag and a gift for women in his life: "I bought one for me, one for my wife to use as a diaper bag, and one for my Mom for mothers day."[56]

Somewhat acknowledging that women are often engaged in multiple activities, some garments are designed for the "active woman" or the "busy woman," though not necessarily in reference to women's work activities. For instance, Talos Ballistics described its Woman's Raven Vest as

> prefect [sic] for today's busy woman. Great to wear when on the go, at the field watching the game, or while taking a stroll in the woods. The 12-oz. 100% cotton sandstone duck shell and Sherpa-fleece lining embraces you in soft warmth when the temperature turns cool.[57]

In addition to lifestyle features reminiscent of suburban middle or upper-class settings (e.g., easy access to green spaces and sports/recreation facilities), the description also has an affective tone that is leisurely and comforting, including through the notion that the garment "embraces" the woman who wears it—perhaps the way a loving partner would. Another description by Talos did mention work, in tandem with heteronormative relations: The "Woman's Falcon Leather Jacket is the perfect three season jacket for driving into the city for work or riding on the back of your boyfriend[']s motorcycle."[58] Referring to a Leatherback Gear backpack, a review by a customer named Michelle E. mentions its job-related utility: "I take it into work everyday and it looks professional and put together. The security of knowing it's bulletproof is amazing! Love it!"[59]

In other instances, there are references to specific employment or careers, such as the Bullet Blocker Medical Lab Coat. This garment is touted as "ideal for men and women in the medical, pharmaceutical, or consultation fields who desire a layer of lightweight anti-ballistic protection."[60] The young woman portrayed using this product contrasts with some of the other images in which bodily appearance and sexuality are emphasized. In this case, bodily appearance is downplayed by a non-descript white lab coat. The woman's black, thick-framed glasses and a hairstyle consisting of a ponytail add to her serious look. In the text's depiction, the security-oriented features of the garments are highlighted, remarking that they allow users to "covertly and safely get the job done."[61]

As in the case of the woman with the lab coat, some company websites include models who seem "regular" women, that is, women of diverse body shapes and sizes who do not fit strict mandates of thin, glamorous, and/or sexy femininity. These women do not look like fashion models and sometimes wear gender-neutral bulletproof attire, such as fleece vests, and do not pose like models. Some of these women appeared visibly content, including with smiles on their faces. This is the case, for example, for the image of a brown-haired woman wearing a Bullet Blocker Women's Fortress Fleece and a blonde woman wearing the Talos Ballistic Delta Flight Jacket.

One of the images that stood out among those of women on the companies' websites was that of a dark-skinned, full-bodied woman wearing a red jogging suit with a Thyk Skynn vest. What was notable in this woman's image was a device attached to her ankle, which appeared to be an electronic ankle monitor like the ones applied to people who are under surveillance by the criminal justice system (i.e., as an alternative to detention or incarceration). Inscribed in her vest were the words "love" and "peace." A complex juxtaposition of words, objects, and affects appeared in relation to this woman's body. On the one hand, the incorporation of an ankle device as part of the attire can help perpetuate criminality stereotypes applied to communities of color and trivialize the suffering associated with such devices.[62] In fact, a stylized item reminiscent of an ankle "shackle" included in a Gucci fashion presentation was criticized for "[g]lamorizing [. . .] house arrest," among other expressions of dismay.[63] On the other hand, and considering that Thyk Skynn is a Black-owned business, the inclusion of such a device might be interpreted as a perhaps resistant appropriation of a stigmatized symbol, however controversial the strategy. Interpreted in tandem with the promotion of a bulletproof vest, the ankle device may signal the embodied vulnerability of people of color to different forms of violence, including through reminders of their disproportionate representation in the carceral system.[64] While monitoring devices carry stigma and evoke criminality, the inscription "love" and "peace" on the vest contradicts the negative traits attributed to those accused of criminal behavior.

Other images representing women of color convey meanings that include strength, creativity, and style. Thyk Skynn's website featured women of color of diverse body shapes and sizes, posing with creative attires that include various textures, fabrics, furs, and materials combined into unique styles. The attractive designs resulting from the overall combination of clothing items, beyond the vests, make one forget the ballistics aspect, even as the models outwardly wear the vests (which in fact can be used with or without armor). The affective connotations of some of these images might be pride, conveyed through posture and the uniqueness of the apparel displayed. On other companies' websites, bodily strength is apparent in the representation of a couple of women. For instance, Innocent Armor's bullet-resistant down vest for women was modeled by a woman of dark skin and black hair, with visibly toned and delineated arm muscles. In the picture, she is standing with one hand in her pocket, looking confident. Leatherback Gear also presented a woman of color whose body projects strength, and who in one of the pictures is sitting in ways often associated with masculinity. She is taking space with legs open, the backpack on the floor in-between her legs. By contrast, MC Armor/Miguel Caballero featured a lighter-skinned woman, wearing a ballistic-resistant tank top, who also looks strong and has an assertive pose but shows markers of conventional femininity, such as nails painted with red polish.

These various representations of women in bulletproof fashion convey meanings involving sexuality, care relations, employment, leisure, and femininity. They represent distinct notions of womanhood shaped by intersections of race, gender, and class discourses. Considered together, they convey that bulletproof fashion for women can be sexy, stylish, and practical; it can be useful for care work and certain professions; it can help enhance beauty and express identity; and it could protect against gendered and racialized vulnerabilities. They might also help embody a sense of power. Through aesthetic devices and representational choices, the promotional materials of bulletproof fashion for women emphasize affective dimensions beyond fear.

Masculine Bulletproof Fashion

Bulletproof garments and accessories for men both overlap and differ from those offered to women. While some types of body armor are for men in general, others are designed to appeal to specific types of masculinities, including men with particular hobbies, leisure interests, and occupations. They also include distinct aesthetic sensibilities, fashion preferences, and group belongings. As in the case of women's bulletproof apparel, representations of men's products involve emotions conveyed or solicited through a sense of style, scene setting, and activities associated with diverse types of garments.

Per the reviews posted on different companies' websites, various male customers appreciated more than the functionality of ballistic garments and accessories. This emerges in comments on how different men feel about the aesthetic appearance of the products. For instance, Andrew, a Bulletproof Everyone customer, expressed satisfaction with a vest called The Freedom: "Had my vest for a few weeks now. I love the look. Weight is manageable for extended wear and most would never even know you had anything on. It[']s comfortable and stylish."[65] The combination of style, comfort, and inconspicuousness influenced positive reactions in this case. The name of the garment already has positive connotations, as "Freedom" remits to a cherished cultural value (albeit one not equally available to all social groups historically or currently). Rocky, an Innocent Armor customer, praised a bullet-resistant men's vest saying, "It does not look like body armor at all, so you don't stand out. It really is a great looking, stylish vest and the protection offers peace of mind for the security/self-defense professional."[66] Here inconspicuousness, aesthetics, and functionality combine to produce positive feelings, too. And Andrew, a 16-year-old who won a contest co-sponsored by Innocent Armor, commented in an interview, "I always thought bullet-resistant clothing was a product of science fiction! I think it's very cool that there is clothing that can protect you and remain stylish at the same time."[67] This statement conveys both the heady feelings linked to innovation and positive assessments related to both protection and style.

Some of these affective connections emerge from representations that highlight "hegemonic masculinity" ideals of technical competence, bodily strength, confidence, and assertiveness.[68] Some of these attributes are conveyed through crossovers with the military realm—that is, a male-dominated field that cultivates emotional toughness and physical fitness and that enhances the power of its members through access to weapons and body armor. Additionally, references to guns, allusions to armed activities such as hunting, representations of men in protective roles, and male models' assertive bodily postures also convey cultural notions of masculinity. A number of male models, across companies, have a "rugged" look, including a stubble or beard, denim jackets, adventure-oriented clothing, or militarized types of gear. The outdoor settings in which some of the pictures were taken enhance that sense of ruggedness. Other fashion styles represent urban forms of masculinity, including stylish professionals, men in formal attire or casual-elegant clothes, and men in garments reminiscent of Black hip-hop artists' and entertainment industry celebrities' fashion. In some representations, the bodies of the men photographed become particularly important to the look—whether it is the beard, the tattooed body, rippling muscles, imposing body size, or confident pose. Bulletproof wear can then further enhance attributes culturally associated with hetero-masculinity, such as toughness. It may also foster fantasies of invulnerability and impenetrability, in some cases complementing other "man gear" such as guns.

Certain bulletproof items are directed to groups of men with specific interests or hobbies. For instance, some garments are marketed for motorcycle enthusiasts, hinting at how emotions, bodies, and masculinized worlds become entwined. A large muscular man wearing a Bulletproof Leather Biker Vest appeared in a couple of pictures on Bullet Blocker's website. His skin is olive or tanned; he wears a cowboy hat and exhibits a tattooed arm. In one picture, he is standing with imposing presence; in another one, he is riding a large motorcycle. The company explained that the vest's "single back panel is perfect for displaying your club's colors or any other type of decorative emblems. A perfect addition to your protective gear for any season."[69] The references to the bikers' colors and insignias highlight the importance of group belonging, in this case, within the realm of masculine biker cultures. The male model projects strength through his body form and posture, and the motorcycle enhances that image as a powerful object that also affords a sense of freedom. In another depiction of this type of clothing, Talos Ballistics named the garment "Men's Rebel Open Collar Leather Biker Vest,"[70] also accentuating notions of masculinity associated with autonomy and independence, captured by the word "rebel" (perhaps even evoking romanticized notions of rebellious men).

As we can see, the concept of freedom emerges explicitly or implicitly in representations of certain products, and it entails positive affects that are coupled with masculinity in the promotional materials. It is the freedom to explore, discover, or follow the open road while protected with bulletproof garments. In its description of one of its backpacks, Bullet Blocker encourages potential customers—in this case cued through images of a white male model in an outdoors setting—to "[h]ave confidence diving into any adventure with the Bulletproof 30/50 backpack."[71] With this product, "the opportunities of exploration are endless."[72] In this case, the backpack not only offers protection through the ballistics feature but also a wide universe of free exploration and adventure where the dominant emotion is not fear but confidence. The figure of the male explorer is part of the appeal.

Relatedly, a type of rugged masculinity surrounds certain products, for example, those directed to men who work or spend time outdoors. Referring to its Bulletproof Denim Defender Jacket, Talos Ballistics explained that the "classic jacket is one that every outdoorsman has at home and on the road," now with "added protection" provided through bullet-resistant components.[73] The model wearing the jacket appears to be a white man, with short hair and a stubble, eyes focused forward, and arms slightly curved on his sides as if in gunslinger pose, with one of his hands grabbing his pants' pocket. He has a serious face and an overall rugged look. He seems ready to act if needed. Given that clothing can be an expression of identity, the name "Defender" merges garment and user into an embodiment of strength associated with "protector" masculinities. The emotion projected is one of confidence, or even defiance. Fear is not part of the picture.

Among a range of masculinities, militarized masculinity embodies a particularly powerful stance. The marketing of gear reminiscent of that used by the military not only highlights quality aspects but also appeals to certain sensibilities. Descriptors such as the word "tactical" or product lines named "Spartan" are evocative of military worlds. While women have increasingly entered the armed forces, they are still a minority,[74] and even when militarized products are presented in gender-neutral terms, they likely connote masculinized aesthetics, fantasies, and affects. An example of these types of connections is Bullet Blocker's Condor Compact Assault Pack 126, modeled by a bearded white-appearing man in a forest setting. "Assault packs" for the military are meant to be sturdy and fit for a mission. The idea of "assault" connotes physical power to attack, which also entails affective dispositions, such as aggressiveness and fearlessness. In this case, the bag also offers a layer of security through its ballistics protection. For men to be associated with "assault," even if not literally intended, is also a way of glorifying an aggressive masculinity, for both military and civilian men. A "tactical" look can also be achieved through the association of men with guns and fabric patterns such as camouflage, even if the bulletproof product itself is not overtly militarized. An Innocent Armor bulletproof garment, for instance, was modeled by a Black man with dark glasses, muscular arms, fatigue pants, and a bulletproof fitted T-shirt. He also appears to have a firearm holstered at his waist, which in addition to body armor, contributes to forting up the body.

The connection of men to guns is especially obvious in relation to tactical or hunting gear; however, it also veers into other realms of bulletproof clothing—that of casual garments such as jackets. A number of these jackets are just meant to be stylish, but others additionally have design features for gun owners. In the case of bulletproof products, the garments are meant to shield against armed attack, but can help those who carry guns to feel further empowered, and embody the individual autonomy linked to guns. Bullet Blocker's men's Ranch Coat—a bullet-resistant garment described as "rugged"—was "designed for those who carry concealed" guns and includes "a discreet internal pocket that allow[s] you to draw easily from with your strong hand."[75] In this description, attributes linked to certain masculinities such as strength and ruggedness are explicitly mentioned. Traits such as assertiveness or decisiveness—needed to draw a gun—are more implicitly embedded. In this case, a sense of security is enhanced through concrete design features (gun carry compartments) and materials (ballistics) as well as through implicit allusion to affective dimensions or physical attributes evoking hetero-masculinity.

In addition to the more physical masculinity conveyed by the adventure or tactical-looking apparel, other products cater to competencies associated with the realm of the mind, for instance, in certain types of professional or intellectual work. Bullet Blocker's Messenger Bag is said to be "great for tech-savvy individuals who need a safe place to store their electronic gadgets when commuting to school, a job, or a business trip."[76] This description appeals to attributes that are culturally more likely to be applied to men, such as technical expertise, and the person carrying the bag appears to be a man (only part of the body is in view). Another item entailing occupational expertise is the medical lab coat, which while dubbed "unisex" is depicted in the main picture by a male model, seemingly a doctor who wears the coat open, revealing his professional attire underneath (he is wearing a button-up shirt with a tie and long formal pants). In the product description, there are also pictures of a young man and woman wearing the lab coat, but they both seem more informally dressed (i.e., less authoritative than the previous man mentioned).

Other masculinities such as those in various kinds of urban spaces have also been addressed by different companies' products, including Aspetto, MC Armor/Miguel Caballero, Thyk Skynn, Innocent Armor, Bulletproof Everyone, and others. As in the case for women, MC Armor/Miguel Caballero's Black collection is meant to offer ballistic protection and has an "exclusive style," in this case portrayed by light-skinned men in cityscapes.[77] Space is critical to the construction of distinct identities, but certain attributes may still cross over varied geographies. Though these masculinities differ from the "adventure" or militarized masculinities previously described, some of the city men also exhibit aspects of ruggedness, donning a stubble, and showing intent and confidence through their facial expression. One picture in the Black collection portrays a conventionally handsome man wearing a bulletproof "executive vest" of pique fabric (the Sinatra); he is walking in New York City in the Plaza Hotel area. Another man, wearing a bulletproof Harrington-type jacket (the Brando), is in the driver's seat or next to the vintage car that also appears in the feminine picture series of the same company (in fact, the woman previously described is in the background of one of these images, sitting in the front passenger seat of the car). The affect that these men display is serious, including the "Brando" model's tough gaze, characteristic of men in countless movies. Here too fear is displaced by a tough masculinity, now armed with extra security through a "discreet" and "exclusive" bulletproof garment. These men convey readiness in the face of a dangerous world. They have the looks, the resources, and the body armor. It is also worth noting the references to famous white men, such as Frank Sinatra and Marlon Brando, which add to the message of social success, class exclusivity, and masculine desirability.

Aspetto, a company whose civilian branch specialized in formal attire for men, presented a large variety of suits that could be tailored to be bullet resistant. A white man with a clean-cut beard appeared to be the model for all the suits at the time of the analysis. The company described "a focus on high-fashion" aimed to avert "the bulky look synonymous with traditional bulletproof clothing."[78] Indeed, it was hard to tell whether the pictures of the suits were of the ballistics version or not. Through the dialog box with specifications, one could select to add armor to the garments. The company aspired "to produce America's toughest, and most stylish, bullet-resistant suit on the market."[79] In this description, "tough" operates as a signifier of what one would wish for a body shield intended to avert injury but also cues into a particular aspect of hegemonic masculinity, to be "tough" (even though looks are emphasized too, a concern more often associated with femininity). As if to not forget normative versions of manhood, even the male mannequin in one of the videos documenting the testing of the suits showed a tough facial expression as well as rippling muscles on his chest and abdomen (a similar mannequin also appeared in a test of Thyk Skynn products).

Thyk Skynn offers a variety of vest designs for men and seems to cater especially to Black men, perhaps attentive to the racialized vulnerability to gun-related harm that Black men disproportionately face in U.S. society. Yet ballistics protection is not the only notable feature. Bulletproof vests combine with a range of clothing styles, layering arrangements, and fabrics. At the time of the analysis, all the male models featured appeared to be Black and exhibited a variety of fashions. There is the model with the beige-colored vest whose attire includes symbols of wealth and status, such as a gold watch and large Gucci labels on white shoes. Another model dresses in all-black clothing, including hat and neck gaiter partially covering the face, leather boots, and a more tactical-looking black vest. Another model appears in all-white attire, except for dark sunglasses, including a white vest, a sweatshirt, sweatpants, and a durag on the head. While some of the vests are worn on top of informal clothing such as hoodies, one of the models wears it on top of formal attire, such as a professional business suit. Another model exhibits all-black attire that includes a vest with leathery elements and fabrics of different textures, with an attached hood covering the head. And showing a more revealing attire, a model wears an open vest directly on his naked torso, exposing his muscular chest, arms, and abdomen—all covered in tattoos. He is also wearing a Von Dutch cap, silver necklace, torn jeans, and work boots. As mentioned earlier, certain styles are reminiscent of entertainment industry celebrities', including those who adopted conspicuous body armor as part of their attire. Rapper 50 Cents reportedly started wearing bulletproof vests in the 2000s, after having been shot multiple times. Others adopted similar garments, not just for security reasons but as an expression of fashion—particularly a "tough" appearance—including through garments that seem bulletproof without being so.[80] The latter adds a layer of ambiguity about the nature of the garment as viewers may not know whether a particular vest has ballistic components or not. In fact, Thyk Skynn vests can be worn with or without ballistic panels.

Thyk Skynn has developed multiple styles drawing from the experiences, fashion, and sensibilities of members of Black communities in the United States, including elements that have been mainstreamed. The portrayal of men's clothing conveys not only masculine strength but also pride in identity, creativity, and symbols of economic success. This is in contradistinction to the stigmatization and vulnerability of Black men to various types of violence (e.g., police violence, mass incarceration, and civilian gun violence). While the ballistic protection component is what is distinctive in many of the brands, Thyk Skynn also has put a premium on style and fashion in unique ways and included a discourse of holistic protection. "We believe in Protecting your Energy, mentally, spiritually and physically," said the company in an online statement.[81] Some of the vests that the Black men models were wearing read "no truth, no life,"[82] raising the question of whose truths have prevailed over time and whose lives have been lost. In the context of current events, and historically, one could think about the multiple forms of marginalization that have put Black people in harm's way, and the societal silence and coverups that have too often prevailed (and denounced by racial justice activists).

All in all, bulletproof products for men appeal to different groups in ways that not only distinguish men from feminine traits and affects but also embody various types of masculinities that convey power, for instance, through an emphasis on expertise, technical competence, physical strength, or association with guns or armed activities. Aside from the use of camo—which has been popularized across genders and age groups—the transfer of a "tactical" aesthetic seems to be more straightforward for men, likely due to the masculine connotations traditionally linked to security and military forces. While in the case of white men, bulletproof clothing may serve to further bolster the power they have in the racial hierarchy, for men of color who have been disproportionate targets of violence, body armor may function to ameliorate the sense of vulnerability linked to injustice while drawing on aesthetics that resonate with different groups.

DIY Bulletproof Clothing?

Aside from corporate-developed body armor, the idea of bulletproof clothing has also captured the imagination of artists engaged in social justice efforts, such as micha cárdenas, Patrisse Cullors, Edxie Betts, and Chris Head. In recognition of the socially rooted vulnerabilities experienced by economically marginalized people of color, queer, gender nonconforming, and trans individuals, the artists worked together to create "DIY [Do It Yourself] bulletproof clothing at low to no cost" as the basis of the art project *Unstoppable*.[83] This artistic intervention aimed to generate awareness and dialogue about ways to resist "the murder of black people, in particular black trans women."[84] State violence was at the center of the project's critique, in consonance with the Black Lives Matter movement that inspired the initiative:

> Governments today kill both through direct acts of state violence, such as police killing black people, and through neglect, choosing not to prosecute the murders of trans women, or looking the other way when civilians and paramilitaries arm themselves and commit murder. In this state of necropolitics, where the government facilitates death for communities it deems unwanted, we must act to physically protect ourselves now, as we do not even know where the next bullet might come from.[85]

The artists experimented with different materials, such as used tires and Kevlar airbags retrieved from car junkyards, to test their resistance to bullets and develop instructions on how to make protective garments. The project's blog includes pictures of Edxie Betts wearing the apparel developed, videos of shooting tests performed in the desert, an image of a hand holding a bullet after having been fired, photos of an art exhibition featuring the tested artifacts, a prototype dress made with tires, and a group of people engaged in a public conversation based on the project. In various parts of the website, the artists warn that they cannot guarantee that following the instructions provided would protect users from gun injury. After all, different tests yielded inconclusive results, and as the disclaimers emphasized, "This is an art project."[86]

Whereas the bulletproof fashion produced by companies consists of "normal" looking clothing that is unaffordable to many, the *Unstoppable* armor incorporated discarded or relatively cheap materials, which are presented in raw form in the images: pieces of tire arranged in overlapping layers to be inserted into a backpack, steel-belted tires dressing the torso of a mannequin, recovered Kevlar strapped around Edxie Betts as a tube dress and held together with a red belt. Not incidentally, Edxie Betts identifies as a "black, filipin@, black footed, trans femme, gender non conforming, queer anti-authoritarian art healer."[87] The project centers on marginalized communities, the lives of those who are often absent in corporate depictions. The rudimentary garments portrayed in this art project are a far cry from the sleek, fashionable, and inconspicuous bulletproof apparel on corporate websites. They indirectly highlight the disparities between the protection available to different sectors of the population, and the "precarity" that socially subordinated groups are forced to contend with.[88]

In some ways, the project's images perform both the vulnerability and resourcefulness of marginalized groups, in a context of injustice and what Betts called "dystopia." A will to resist is embedded in the project, apparent in Betts's firm facial expression in a banner image of the art exhibit[89] as well as in Betts's remarks: "Lets flip the script and tear at the pages of this living dystopia imposed on our psyches and bodies. Direct action saves our lives."[90] A sense of urgency is palpable in the project, as artists grappled with how to create defenses against the violence associated with racism, trans misogyny, and class inequalities (even as cárdenas discovered that much information about bulletproof materials was posted on white supremacists' online sites, among others).[91] Opposed to such ideologies and distinct from corporate approaches, participants in this art project maneuvered in a complex space. They, too, handled guns and bullets, engaged in shooting tests, and saw some promise in the idea of bulletproof garments, yet their efforts emerged from the experiences of marginalized communities in a context of social disempowerment.

While this art project dealt with practical issues, such as how to develop inexpensive protective garments to guard against gun violence and other forms of aggression directed toward marginalized populations, cárdenas recounts interlocutors' reactions that pointed to the need to address the roots of the problems:

> a lot of the feedback I've gotten about *Unstoppable* questions whether I'm only addressing the symptoms of violence, and not the causes – a Band-Aid approach. I'm not saying I agree with this perspective on the *Unstoppable* project, but it did get me thinking about ways in which people who are regularly targeted by violence can actually *feel* safer on a day-to-day basis.[92]

The project stirred public dialogues about both violence and community efforts to create health and safety. This type of public engagement was one important outcome of the project, and so was the opportunity to "make perceptible to audiences the kind of urgency that many trans women and black people feel on a daily basis."[93] In some sense, *Unstoppable* not only tested affordable materials that might resist bullets, but through aesthetic practices that stimulated community engagement, the project fostered collective explorations of whether the fortress body is a solution, and what other approaches might be needed.

The commercial and "artivist" versions of bulletproof fashion draw attention to different subjects and social problems; they also stand apart by the profit motive that drives the corporate production of bulletproof garments and by the critical edge of the artivist project. Still, both approaches resort to some shared repertoires—notably the reliance on body armor—based on an overlapping lack of confidence in the state as the guarantor, or at least sole guarantor, of security (albeit for different reasons). As we can see, the idea of fortressing the body has gained currency as part of subjectivities of security that cross the political, ideological, and social spectrum.

Conclusion

The visual and textual representations of bulletproof apparel in corporate online materials, as well as in some artistic interventions, reveal how aesthetics, emotions, and inequalities contribute to the configuration of different types of fortress bodies. Bulletproof garments circulate in the civilian sphere, revealing the "capillary" dispersion of a security apparatus that transcends the state.[94] The diverse fashion designs that the corporate websites offer point to that dispersion, as different social groups are addressed not only through a security discourse but through images and narratives that aim at various desires, identities, and lifestyles. Fashion is intimately linked to the affects that different security products reflect and (re)produce, in ways that exceed fear and project more pleasant emotions as well. In contrast to the fashionable bulletproof garments that companies commercialize, which hide the securitization of society through "normal" looking aesthetic designs, the garments in art projects such as *Unstoppable* or *Back to School Shopping* expose such securitization and open it up to scrutiny. They do so in tandem with a critical indictment of the society that makes it possible for bulletproof clothing to be a viable consideration.

Pervasive social hierarchies shape bulletproof apparel, as evidenced by not only aesthetic representations but also the materiality and costs of the products. Within the market-based realm of security, in this case consisting of bulletproof products, children in well-off families might get to save their lives in the face of gun violence, while others are implicitly excluded. Adults who can afford the products are promised security and the possibility to blend into their workplaces, sites of recreation, and spaces of leisure, thanks to fashionable design. Consumers might also embody sex appeal, beauty, strength, and other traits unevenly distributed along gender, race, class, and sexuality lines. The *Unstoppable* art project precisely underscores the specific vulnerabilities of those who often fall through the cracks of corporate fantasies of security. It does so not only by outlining specific forms of violence but also because the garments' raw aesthetics and the use of discarded materials expose such marginalization.

The online depictions analyzed show that different types of consumers and producers have become interested in bulletproof apparel as a response to gun violence. A range of social actors across the ideological spectrum, and across the corporate and artistic worlds, engage with the idea of fortressing the body. Thus, it is important to ask: How do different stakeholders, beyond those appearing on the websites, react to bulletproof fashion and how do their perspectives mesh with distinct social and political experiences? Such is the focus of the following chapter.

Notes

1 Teresa Pires do Rio Caldeira, *City of Walls: Crime, Segregation, and Citizenship in São Paulo* (Berkeley: University of California Press, 2000), 292.
2 D. Asher Ghertner, Hudson McFann, and Daniel Goldstein, "Security Aesthetics of and beyond the Biopolitical," pp. 1–32 in *Futureproof: Security Aesthetics and the Management of Life*, eds. D. Asher Ghertner, Hudson McFann, and Daniel Goldstein (Durham: Duke University Press, 2020), 4.
3 Joanne Entwistle, *The Fashioned Body: Fashion, Dress & Modern Social Theory*, 2nd ed. (Cambridge: Polity, 2015), 7.
4 Terence S. Turner, "The Social Skin," *HAU: Journal of Ethnographic Theory* 2 (2012): 486–504, 486.

5 See, for example, Harel Shapira's study on the act of holding, shooting, and carrying a gun, applying Marcel Mauss's concept of "techniques of the body": He finds that "a particular kind of society is inscribed onto the armed body, one that is gendered, racialized, and fearful" (Harel Shapira, "How to Use the Bathroom with a Gun and Other Techniques of the Armed Body," pp. 194–206 in *The Lives of Guns*, eds. Jonathan Obert, Andrew Poe, Austin Sarat [New York: Oxford University Press, 2019], 195). Drawing on "cyborg anthropology," Tessa Diphoorn, found that bulletproof vests worn by security personnel were experienced as part of the users' bodies and had emotional dimensions, too: "the vest made them feel safe and more confident in their work" (Tessa Diphoorn, "It's All About the Body": The Bodily Capital of Armed Response Officers in South Africa, *Medical Anthropology* 34, no. 4 [2015]: 336–52, 344).
6 See Entwistle's, *The Fashioned Body*, on the connection between body and dress from a sociological perspective. For the influence of politics and major events such as wars, social upheaval, and cultural change, see, for example, Eugenia Paulicelli, "Fashion, the Politics of Style and National Identity in Pre-Fascist and Fascist Italy," *Gender & History* 14, no. 3 (2002): 537–59; Jane Pavitt, *Fear and Fashion in the Cold War* (South Kensington, London and New York: V & A Pub, 2008); Betty Luther Hillman, *Dressing for the Culture Wars: Style and the Politics of Self-Presentation in the 1960s and 1970s* (Lincoln: University of Nebraska Press, 2015); Djurdja Bartlett, ed., *Fashion and Politics* (New Haven: Yale University Press, 2019); Lucy Adlington, *Women's Lives and Clothes in WW2: Ready for Action* (Barnsley: Pen and Sword History, 2020).
7 Catherine Baker, "Introduction. Making War on Bodies: Militarisation, Aesthetics and Embodiment in International Politics," pp. 1–30 in *Making War on Bodies*, ed. Catherine Baker (Edinburgh: Edinburgh University Press, 2020), 9.
8 Agnès Rocamora and Anneke Smelik, "Thinking Through Fashion: An Introduction," pp. 1–27 in *Thinking Through Fashion: A Guide to Key Theorists*, eds. Agnès Rocamora and Anneke Smelik (London: I.B. Tauris. 2016), 2.
9 Diana Crane and Laura Bovone, "Approaches to Material Culture: The Sociology of Fashion and Clothing," *Poetics* 34, no. 6 (2006): 319–33, 320.
10 See, for example, Women of Color Resource Center, *Fashion Resistance to Militarism*, Video DVD, directed and edited by Kimberly Alvarenga, Executive Producer Christine Ahn (Oakland, 2006); Timothy Godbold, *Military Style Invades Fashion*, with an Introduction by Colin McDowell (London: Phaidon Press, 2016); Laura Shepherd, "Militarisation," pp. 209–14 in *Visual Global Politics*, ed. Roland Bleiker (New York: Routledge, 2018).
11 Baker, "Introduction. Making War on Bodies," 1.
12 Crane and Bovone, "Approaches to Material Culture," 322.
13 Crane and Bovone, "Approaches to Material Culture," 324.
14 Pavitt, *Fear and Fashion in the Cold War*, 70.
15 Rhonda Garelick, "Bombshell: Fashion in the Age of Terrorism," pp. 105–23 in *Fashion and Politics*, ed. Djurdja Bartlett (New Haven: Yale University Press, 2019), 123.
16 Garelick, "Bombshell: Fashion in the Age of Terrorism," 119.
17 The weight of the apparel varies depending on the product and company, but for instance, Guard Dog Security boasted a civilian armored backpack that is only ounces heavier than a similarly sized non bullet-resistant backpack; ArmorMe mentioned that armored panels may add 1.5 to 3 pounds to the weight of a normal backpack; and various types of clothing may be 4 to 5 pounds heavier than their regular counterparts, according to Bullet Blocker.
18 Nicolette Erestain, "Why Is Hard Body Armor So Heavy?" *Bulletproof Zone*, July 1, 2019, accessed December 2, 2020, https://bulletproofzone.com/blogs/bullet-proof-blog/why-is-hard-body-armor-so-heavy.
19 Liz Halloran, "Bulletproof Whiteboards and the Marketing of School Safety," *NPR*, May 4, 2013, www.npr.org/2013/05/04/180916246/bulletproof-whiteboards-and-the-marketing-of-school-safety; Travis M. Andrews, "Florida School Lets Parents Buy Bulletproof Panels for Students to Put in Backpacks," *Washington Post*,

November 7, 2017, www.washingtonpost.com/news/morning-mix/wp/2017/11/07/florida-school-lets-parents-buy-bulletproof-panels-for-students-to-put-in-backpacks/.
20 See Barbara Sutton and Kate Paarlberg-Kvam, "Fashion of Fear for Kids," *In Visible Culture: An Electronic Journal for Visual Culture* 25 (2017), www.google.com/url?q=http%3A%2F%2Fivc.lib.rochester.edu%2Fready-fashion-of-fear-for-kids%2F&sa=D.
21 "Tuffypacks 11" x 14" Ballistic Shield Level IIIA Bulletproof Backpack Insert," *Bulletproof Zone*, accessed December 2, 2020, https://bulletproofzone.com/collections/tuffypacks/products/bulletproof-zone-11-x-14-ballistic-shield-bulletproof-backpack-insert
22 "Tuffypacks 11" x 14" Ballistic Shield Level IIIA Bulletproof Backpack Insert," *Bulletproof Zone*.
23 Chris Espinili, "Bulletproof Armor for School Children?" *Bulletproof Zone*, July 17, 2019, https://bulletproofzone.com/blogs/bullet-proof-blog/should-you-buy-a-bulletproof-backpack-or-bulletproof-backpack-armor.
24 "Product Reviews," *TuffyPacks*, accessed November 28, 2020, https://tuffypacks.com/.
25 Ariana Ricardo, "Is Ballistic Protection Affordable?" *Bulletproof Zone*, February 20, 2020, https://bulletproofzone.com/blogs/bullet-proof-blog/is-ballistic-protection-affordable.
26 "Guard Dog Proshield II, Multimedia Level IIIA Bulletproof Backpack," *Bulletproof Zone*, accessed December 2, 2020, https://bulletproofzone.com/collections/guard-dog-security/products/guard-dog-proshield-ii-multimedia-level-iiia-bulletproof-backpack.
27 "Bulletblocker NIJ Level IIIA Clear Backpack," *Bulletproof Zone*, accessed December 2, 2020, https://bulletproofzone.com/products/bulletblocker-nij-level-iiia-clear-backpack?_pos=1&_sid=0345087f7&_ss=r.
28 "Scout Backpack," *Bullet Blocker*, accessed October 15, 2020, www.bulletblocker.com/bulletblocker-nij-iiia-bulletproof-scout-backpack.html.
29 "Acadia Pack," *Bullet Blocker*, accessed October 15, 2020, www.bulletblocker.com/bulletblocker-nij-iiia-bulletproof-acadia-backpack.html.
30 "Defender Backpack," *Bullet Blocker*, accessed October 15, 2020, www.bulletblocker.com/bulletblocker-nij-iiia-bulletproof-defender-backpack.html.
31 "Junior Pack," *Bullet Blocker*, accessed October 15, 2020, www.bulletblocker.com/my-child39s-pack-39.html.
32 See, for example, Richard P. Mills, "Memo to the Presidents of Boards of Education and Superintendents of Public Schools," The State Education Department, The State University of New York, April 5, 2001. https://aistm.org/2001nysed.htm.
33 See Pedro Noguera, "Schools, Prisons, and Social Implications of Punishment: Rethinking Disciplinary Practices," *Theory into Practice* 42, no. 4 (2003): 341–50; Aaron Kupchik and Geoff Ward, "Race, Poverty, and Exclusionary School Security: An Empirical Analysis of U.S. Elementary, Middle, and High Schools," *Youth Violence and Juvenile Justice* 12, no. 4 (2014): 332–54; Aaron Kupchik, "Rethinking School Suspensions," *Contexts* 21, no. 1 (February 2022): 14–19.
34 Sutton and Paarlberg-Kvam, "Fashion of Fear for Kids."
35 See, *TeleSUR English*, "An Artist Creates Bulletproof Vests for Children," Video, June 18, 2019, www.youtube.com/watch?v=0GoYPFR1yd0; Roselle Chen, "Tiny Bulletproof Vests Centerpiece of New York Art Exhibit on School Shootings," *Reuters*, June 17, 2019, www.reuters.com/article/us-usa-guns-art/tiny-bulletproof-vests-centerpiece-of-new-york-art-exhibit-on-school-shootings-idINKCN1TI2M5; Lily Darling, "WhIsBe's 'Back to School Shopping' Rebelliously Shows the Importance of Gun Control," June 26, 2019, *Kulture Hub*, https://kulturehub.com/whisbe-back-to-school-shopping/.
36 WhIsBe, "Back to School Shopping," Video, June 10, 2019, www.youtube.com/watch?v=gIqQQNwoDPE.
37 "Talos Ballistics NIJ IIIA Bulletproof Double Duty Day Pack," *Talos Ballistics*, accessed December 4, 2020, https://talosballistics.com/product/talos-ballistics-nij-iiia-bulletproof-double-duty-day-pack/.
38 "Talos Ballistics NIJ IIA Bulletproof Trekker Backpack," *Talos Ballistics*, accessed December 4, 2020, https://talosballistics.com/product/bulletproof-trekker-backpack/.

39 "Testimonials," *Wonder Hoodie*, accessed September 30, 2020, https://wonderhoodie.com/
40 For illustrations of the different ways in which military styles made their way into civilian fashion, see, for example, Godbold, *Military Style Invades Fashion*.
41 "Secure Protection for Today's Sheriffs: A Guide to Body Armor," *Safeguard Clothing*, accessed December 3, 2020, www.safeguardclothing.com/blog/secure-protection-for-todays-sheriffs-a-guide-to-body-armor/.
42 "Bulletproof Women's Down Vest," *Innocent Armor*, accessed December 5, 2020, https://innocentarmor.com/collections/womens-clothing/products/bullet-resistant-womens-down-vest.
43 "Bullet Resistant Women's Leather Jacket," *Innocent Armor*, accessed December 5, 2020, https://innocentarmor.com/collections/womens-clothing/products/bullet-resistant-womens-leather-jacket.
44 Jennifer Carlson, "Mourning Mayberry: Guns, Masculinity, and Socioeconomic Decline," *Gender & Society* 29, no. 3 (2015): 386–409.
45 "Talos Ballistics NIJ IIIA Bulletproof Circe Leather Vest for Woman," *Talos Ballistics*, accessed December 4, 2020, https://talosballistics.com/product/bulletproof-circe-leather-vest/.
46 "W021 | Bulletproof Vest," *Thyk Skynn*, accessed February 24, 2021, https://thykskynn.com/product/bulletproof-vest-global-shipping-level-3a-kevlar-panels-light-weight-luxury/.
47 "Women's Fitted Leather Jacket," *Bullet Blocker*, accessed October 15, 2020, www.bulletblocker.com/bulletblocker-nij-iiia-bulletproof-women39s-fitted-leather-jack39.html.
48 "W1–001," *Thyk Skynn*, accessed February 24, 2021, https://thykskynn.com/product/w1-001/.
49 "Bullet Resistant Women's Leather Jacket," *Innocent Armor*, accessed October 4, 2022, https://innocentarmor.com/collections/womens-clothing/products/bullet-resistant-womens-leather-jacket
50 See for example, the analyses of Patricia Hill Collins, *Black Feminist Thought: Knowledge, Consciousness, and the Politics of Empowerment* (London: Routledge, 2000); Patricia Hill Collins, *Black Sexual Politics: African Americans, Gender, and the New Racism* (New York: Routledge, 2005); Janell Hobson, *Body as Evidence: Mediating Race, Globalizing Gender* (Albany: SUNY Press, 2012); Seanna Leath, Morgan C. Jerald, Tiani Perkins, and Martinque K. Jones, "A Qualitative Exploration of Jezebel Stereotype Endorsement and Sexual Behaviors Among Black College Women," *Journal of Black Psychology* 47, no. 4–5 (2021): 244–83.
51 "01–001: Bulletproof Dress," *Thyk Skynn*, accessed February 24, 2021, https://thykskynn.com/product/luxury-bulletproof-dress-fashion-level-3a-kevlar-for-women-ballistic-vest/.
52 As viewers, we do not know the context of the photo shoot or the tattoo or its meanings for the model, but it presumably became a more permanent feature of the model's body than the clothing worn for a photo shoot. Thus, one can speculate that it reflects something that she wants to express. In that sense, it is interesting to keep in mind that while tattoos by women in different cultures and time periods became sexualized (see, Margo DeMello's *Body Studies*), women have also resorted to tattoos to tell other stories, resist oppression, and form affective bonds with other women (Heidi Gengenbach, "Tattooed Secrets: Women's History in Magude District, Southern Mozambique," pp. 253–73 in *Bodies in Contact: Rethinking Colonial Encounters in World History*, eds. Tony Ballantyne and Antoinette Burton [Durham: Duke University Press, 2005]); Margo DeMello, *Body Studies: An Introduction* (New York: Routledge, 2014).
53 "Premium Bulletproof Clothing," *Wonder Hoodie*, accessed September 30, 2020, https://wonderhoodie.com/collections/wonder-hoodie-bulletproof-clothing.
54 "Instant Protection with Bullet-Proof Backpacks," *ArmorMe*, accessed October 1, 2020. www.facebook.com/watch/?ref=external&v=2381422922126933.
55 "Civilian One," *Leatherback Gear*, accessed November 8, 2020, www.leatherbackgear.com/products/civilian-one?variant=32484444241974.
56 "Reviews," *Innocent Armor*, accessed December 5, 2020, https://innocentarmor.com/pages/reviews.

57 "Talos Ballistics NIJ IIA Bulletproof Woman's Raven Vest," *Talos Ballistics*, accessed December 4, 2020, https://talosballistics.com/product/talos-ballistics-nij-iiia-bulletproof-womans-raven-vest/.
58 "Talos Ballistics NIJ IIA Bulletproof Woman's Falcon Leather Jacket," *Talos Ballistics*, accessed December 4, 2020, https://talosballistics.com/product/bulletproof-womans-falcon-leather-jacket/.
59 "Sport One," *Leatherback Gear*, accessed November 8, 2020, www.leatherbackgear.com/products/sport-one?variant=32484445749302
60 "Medical Lab Coat," *Bullet Blocker*, accessed October 15, 2020, www.bulletblocker.com/bulletblocker-nij-iiia-bulletproof-lab-coat.html.
61 "Medical Lab Coat," *Bullet Blocker*.
62 For an analysis of ankle monitors and stigma, see Lauren Kilgour, "The Ethics of Aesthetics: Stigma, Information, and the Politics of Electronic Ankle Monitor Design," *The Information Society* 36, no. 3 (2020): 131–46.
63 Maria Sherman, "Gucci, Guys, What Are You Doing?" *Jezebel*, October 9, 2019, https://jezebel.com/gucci-guys-what-are-you-doing-1838905627. See also, Danielle James, "Gucci Is Trying to Make House Arrest Fashionable and People Aren't Having It," *Hello Beautiful*, October 11, 2019, https://hellobeautiful.com/3061315/gucci-house-arrest-ankle-bracelet/.
64 See, for example, Ashley Nellis, "The Color of Justice: Racial and Ethnic Disparity in State Prisons," *The Sentencing Project*, 2021, www.sentencingproject.org/app/uploads/2022/08/The-Color-of-Justice-Racial-and-Ethnic-Disparity-in-State-Prisons.pdf.
65 "The Freedom," *Bulletproof Everyone*, accessed December 3, 2020, https://bulletproofeveryone.com/the-freedom-IIIA-bulletproof-vest/.
66 "Bullet Resistant Men's Down Vest," *Innocent Armor*, accessed December 5, 2020, https://innocentarmor.com/collections/mens-clothing/products/bullet-resistant-down-vest.
67 "Blue Coat Music Contest Winner Andrew Luna," *Innocent Armor*, accessed March 10, 2020, https://innocentarmor.com/blogs/news/blue-coat-music-contest-winner-andrew-luna.
68 Raewyn Connell, *Gender and Power: Society, the Person and Sexual Politics* (Palo Alto: University of California Press, 1987); Raewyn Connell and James W. Messerschmidt, "Hegemonic Masculinity: Rethinking the Concept," *Gender & Society* 19, no. 6 (2005): 829–59.
69 "Leather Biker Vest," *Bullet Blocker*, accessed October 15, 2020, www.bulletblocker.com/bulletblocker-nij-iiia-bulletproof-biker-leather.html.
70 "Talos Ballistics NIJ IIA Bulletproof Men's Rebel OC Leather Biker Vest," *Talos Ballistics*, accessed December 4, 2020, https://talosballistics.com/product/talos-ballistics-nij-iiia-bulletproof-mens-leather-biker-vest1/.
71 "Bulletproof 30/50 Backpack," *Bullet Blocker*, accessed October 15, 2020, www.bulletblocker.com/bulletblocker-nij-iiia-bulletproof-30-50-backpack.html.
72 "Bulletproof 30/50 Backpack," *Bullet Blocker*.
73 "Talos Ballistics NIJ IIA Bulletproof Denim Defender Jacket," *Talos Ballistics*, accessed December 4, 2020, https://talosballistics.com/product/talos-ballistic-nij-iiia-bulletproof-denim-defender-jacket/.
74 Council on Foreign Relations (CFR), "Demographics of the U.S. Military," July 13, 2020, www.cfr.org/backgrounder/demographics-us-military.
75 "Ranch Coat," *Bullet Blocker*, accessed October 15, 2020, www.bulletblocker.com/bulletblocker-nij-iiia-bulletproof-ranch-coat.html.
76 "Leather Messenger Bag," *Bullet Blocker*, accessed October 15, 2020, www.bulletblocker.com/bulletblocker-nij-iiia-bulletproof-leather-messenger-bag.html.
77 "Made to Order: The Black Collection," *MC Armor*, accessed November 8, 2020, https://mc-armor.com/pages/the-black-collection.
78 "How Is Aspetto Bulletproof Clothing Made?" *Aspetto*, accessed November 28, 2020, https://apparel.aspetto.com/#/about-us.
79 "How Is Aspetto Bulletproof Clothing Made?" *Aspetto*.

80 Elizabeth Flock, "The Rise of Bulletproof Fashion—It's No Longer About Safety," *US News*, May 10, 2013, www.usnews.com/news/articles/2013/05/10/bulletproof-garb-about-safety--and-making-a-statement; Ruth La Ferla, "A Look That's Bulletproof," *New York Times*, January 20, 2010, www.nytimes.com/2010/01/21/fashion/21BULLET.html.
81 Thyk Skynn, "thykskynn," *Instagram*, accessed February 6, 2022, www.instagram.com/thykskynn/?hl=en.
82 "1–011," *Thyk Skynn*, accessed February 24, 2021, https://thykskynn.com/product/bulletproof-vest-for-civilians-level-3a-body-armor-light-weight-kevlar-panels/.
83 "Unstoppable," November 29, 2015, https://michacardenas.sites.ucsc.edu/unstoppable/.
84 "Unstoppable."
85 "Unstoppable."
86 "Unstoppable."
87 "Unstoppable," Institute for New Connotative Action (INCA), 2015, http://incainstitute.org/unstoppable/.
88 Judith Butler, *Frames of War: When Is Life Grievable?* (London: Verso, 2009).
89 See, "Unstoppable," Institute for New Connotative Action (INCA).
90 "Materials Testing #1 and New Designs with Edxie Betts," November 29, 2015, https://michacardenas.sites.ucsc.edu/unstoppable/.
91 Priyanka Kaura, "Imagine Otherwise: micha cárdenas on Wearable Technologies for Racial Justice," June 1, 2016, https://ideasonfire.net/11-micha-cardenas/.
92 "micha cárdenas—Bulletproof Art, Technology, and Social Justice," Fall 2016, www.uwb.edu/ias/newsletter/2016-fall/micha-cardenas-bulletproof-art.
93 micha cárdenas, "What If We Got Free," April 19, 2016, https://contemptorary.org/what-if-we-got-free/.
94 Michel Foucault, "Entrevista sobre la prisión: El libro y su método," in *Microfísica del Poder*, 3rd ed., eds. and trans. Julia Varela and Fernando Alvarez-Uría (Madrid: La Piqueta, 1992), 97.

5
FEELING AND THINKING ABOUT BULLETPROOF FASHION

Stakeholders' Perspectives

How do different groups of people feel and think about bulletproof fashion? After all, while bulletproof garments may be considered niche products, this does not impede companies from speaking to broad sectors of society or aiming to mainstream bulletproof apparel. By referring to incidents of gun violence, especially mass shootings in schools, companies communicate to parents that it is wise to armor children. Partnerships with charities or school programs raise companies' profiles, presenting them as socially responsible enterprises connected to broader communities. Company websites also address scenarios that include work, leisure, adventure, and different lifestyles, and potential product users include teachers, doctors, travelers, gun enthusiasts, and children, among others. Customers, in turn, sometimes leave product reviews online, including comments about their security concerns. In the previous two chapters, we saw how companies pitch their products to different publics through their online materials. This chapter shifts attention to how members of the public react to such products. Focus groups with different stakeholders allow for an exploration of the ways in which people interactively construct meaning about bulletproof fashion in relation to wider security discourses.

In these discussions, the emotional contours of focus group participants' attitudes helped signal what is at stake with body armor as a security strategy. Individual attitudes commonly include cognitive and affective dimensions, and in stakeholders' narratives, what they *thought* and how they *felt* about bulletproof apparel often appeared in tandem or in mutually embedded ways. Attitudes can be understood as more than individual preferences or evaluations but as also reflecting shared, albeit contested, social norms and cultural expectations.[1] Their emotional components draw attention to what matters to individuals and communities—in this case, regarding security. Indeed, emotional expressions or efforts to contain emotion hint at significant aspects of social settings, ideological standpoints, and cultural expectations, whether in workplaces, organizations, social groups, or political movements.[2] To highlight how emotions and cognitions are entwined in the context of social movements, sociologist James Jasper elaborated on the observation that "[m]ost feeling is a form of thinking, or rather feeling-thinking."[3] Here, I borrow this language of "feeling-thinking" to foreground the significance of emotions in security-related appraisals.

Participants in this study shared varied perspectives on the products, the industry, and the circumstances that prompt interest in armoring the body. Mothers, teachers, health care workers, gun violence prevention advocates, gun rights supporters, law enforcement officers, activists in organizations addressing police violence, and those addressing sexual and gender violence—all had something to say about bulletproof fashion (see Chapter 1 for the demographic characteristics of focus group participants). Many of these narratives injected feeling into evaluations about the wisdom, effectiveness, and usefulness of bulletproof apparel for civilians. These emotional dimensions were not just a matter of added emphasis but consisted of feeling-thinking manifestations, unfolding sometimes vehemently and in interaction with members of the group. Emotions were interlaced with other factors that likely shaped participants' perspectives, such as ideological and political orientation, occupational status, parental experiences, and social location, for instance, in terms of race-ethnicity, class, gender, and sexuality hierarchies. All focus groups were shown pictures of ballistic products—bulletproof jackets, vests, backpacks, and lab coats for civilians—including those designed for men, women, and children, and advertised for people who are teachers or health care personnel. The images served as a prompt to the discussion and provided concrete points of reference, eliciting varied reactions.

When asked to consider such garb, participants expressed an array of emotional responses such as dismay, anger, sadness, empathy, and excitement, among others, though not everyone expressed emotion. In articulating their views, participants sometimes bridged different social scales: the micro level of individuals (e.g., feeling personally unsafe), the meso level of organizations (e.g., schools as sites of potential mass shootings), and the macro level of social systems (e.g., the workings of capitalism and militarism). As other scholarly contributions show, emotions also cross scales, in the sense of not only constituting individual experiences but also forming part of different groups or organizational cultures and influencing national and international policies.[4] In this study, some focus group participants noted how emotions such as fear help account for the marketing of ballistic products in tandem with broader social dynamics. In presenting their views, participants' emotions were also at play. They referred to emotions both in personal terms and in the sense of "public feelings."[5]

In addition to emotions, what social experiences became salient as different people reflected on bulletproof fashion? While a portion of the group discussions focused on civilian armored apparel, participants referenced emotional themes such as economic injustice, racism, children's worlds, gender inequality, gun politics, policing, and the impact of the pandemic. For instance, different participants' feeling-thinking responses included appraisals that pointed to corporate opportunism—a theme that elicited emotions and cut across different, though not all, focus groups. To elaborate, various participants perceived bulletproof fashion as an opportunistic approach that failed to address the deeper causes of insecurity. Sam, from the teachers focus group, commented: "It feels, to me, a little bit like war profiteering. Like there's these tragedies in different schools, and these feelings of insecurity and fear, and they're sort of preying on that to sell products." Suzanne, from the mothers focus group, described this security strategy as something that she "can't get [her] arms around" and that "it's not going to accomplish anything." She saw it "as a business that's kind of seizing on a moment that is just kind of ugly and mean." Maya, from the group addressing police violence, summarized her assessment as follows: "Fear mongering and commodification of safety. Like they're saying, 'you should be afraid. There's so much violence.' They're not saying that there's going to be actions to end violence." And Bailey, from one of the organizations addressing sexual and gender violence, concluded:

> I don't think any of those products would make me feel safe or buying them would make me feel that anyone else is safe. I see it as a distraction. It's a monetization, like capitalism often does, to say 'buy something.' [. . .] So I just think it's definitely marketing to make money. It's about making money based on the fact that this is a fear that people have, and it's not really a security measure in the big picture of what's happening in our communities. It's not going to keep [the] people safe that need to be kept safe.

Whereas companies sometimes pose their mission almost in altruistic terms— framing their business as one dedicated to saving lives—various focus group participants did not see it that way. Instead, they decried what they perceived as companies taking advantage of the fear and sense of vulnerability that many people experience. As we shall see, however, these views contrast with those of other focus group participants who were more receptive to the idea of bulletproof apparel, and certainly, with those of satisfied customers who posted their comments on vendors' websites, even expressing gratitude to the companies.

The remainder of this chapter presents the perspectives about bulletproof fashion within each focus group. It is organized around different stakeholders to give a sense of feeling-thinking processes in the context of the group interactions in which they emerged, while also drawing connections, comparisons, and contrasts across groups. Although we cannot draw generalizations based on the focus groups, these discussions serve to explore a range of meaningful perspectives and experiences, and to gain insight into the emotional dimensions of bulletproof fashion in relation to wider social and political issues.

Parents: How to Best Protect Children

The focus group of mothers of school-aged children discussed school shootings as a topic of deep concern. These women's children go to school in a relatively affluent and predominantly white community—one not unlike many of the places where high-profile mass shootings have occurred. School mass shootings also prompted responses from the bulletproof apparel industry: It is one of the reasons associated with the sale of bulletproof products for kids, including backpacks, vests, bag inserts, and other school accessories. In the focus group, Linda mentioned the topic of school shootings:

> The concept of a school shooter, as an example, is something that terrifies, terrifies in our house, and has caused—not all of them, but one [child], in particular—has caused real issues for us to deal with. [. . .] We talk about it often, and it is not comfortable. And one of the things that makes it hard to talk about is the fact that there is no saying 'Don't worry. It won't happen.' Or, 'I can protect you from that.' Or . . . You can't say any of those things, because none of that is true. So I do think that those issues of things that we have read about in the news, that have happened other places and have yet to happen here, do feel close to some, in my house anyway, some kids.

Despite the emotional situation she narrated, Linda and other mothers in the group rejected the products bulletproof apparel companies sell to protect children. Instead, they talked about the need to tackle the roots of the problem. Their assessments were entwined with emotions—whether their own feelings, or those of children and youths. They argued that the bulletproof apparel strategy failed to address the underlying issues causing gun violence, including school shootings. In the words of Linda, it was akin to putting "lipstick on a pig."

The emotions and challenges of the pandemic also sharpened participants' rejection of bulletproof products, magnifying the sense that this approach was misguided. For example, Kate mentioned the pandemic as she considered the impacts on both medical personnel and children:

> [It] makes me immensely sad to see that those are options, spec[ially] . . . for medical staff? Oh, my God. They should not have to wear that. They are already encumbered enough with . . . whether it's Coronavirus time, they have to wear all that extra protective gear, or just in general, all the tools, medical instruments they have on them. It's just, it's ridiculous. It makes me really sad. And, of course, kids having to wear vests like that, I just can't even imagine. Their backpacks are already very heavy as is, especially this year, they have to carry everything with them, because they don't have lockers, because they . . . Coronavirus.

In the last part of the passage, Kate was referring to new school restrictions due to the pandemic: Children could no longer use lockers at school but had to carry their belongings back and forth from home in their bags. The pandemic certainly added another layer of emotion. Kate's assessment of bulletproof products was punctuated by a feeling of sadness, disbelief, and a hint of anger and frustration in her condemnation ["it's ridiculous"]. While according to some companies and media coverage, the pandemic prompted increased interest in this type of product, in Kate's case, it seemed to accentuate her rejection of this security approach.

Like Kate, Monica worried about kids having to go to school fitted with ballistic products, and similarly reacted with sadness. She additionally referred to the need to examine the root causes of gun violence:

> I think it's sad, it's not looking at . . . it's very reactive and not proactive [. . .] it's not adjusting the issues in our culture, in our country, and so it's almost accepting that this is going to happen. Whereas, again, other countries are not faced with these issues. So I would rather focus on all of the things that we talked about earlier that cause insecurity and unstableness, and the anger, and look at that to try to think about what might cause somebody to have these issues. I feel very similar that it was very sad to see those images [of bulletproof products], and I wouldn't want it. [. . .] Imagine a child who's already nervous about this and then wearing these things. I think it is very tough and very sad.

Here again, sadness and empathy for children's experiences appear strongly in these mothers' rejection of bulletproof products. Monica pointed to the need to address causes of insecurity, and in her narrative, anger functions as a red flag signaling issues that, depending on how they are handled, might lead to violent and destructive behavior. Suzanne additionally observed that armored garments do not "even begin to address the root of the problem. And it would just scare any child to death [, . . .] it's just so scary." In these women's accounts, emotions figure prominently. Anger (of potential perpetrators) and fear (of potential victims) point to the events that bulletproof products are meant to protect against, namely, gun violence. However, the existence of the product itself, as a symptom of social and political failures, also elicited emotional responses such as sadness, bewilderment, and anger.

Whereas the customer testimonials on companies' websites include those of parents and grandparents who viewed ballistic apparel as a viable protection measure, participants in the mothers group were troubled by the products and wanted deeper solutions. Similar reactions also emerged in other focus groups that included parents but that were not organized around parental status.[6] For instance, Sam, a father in the teachers focus group, pondered:

> I want my kids to be safe, but am I going to get them Kevlar backpacks or anything? I don't know. I wouldn't do it. [. . .] It just seems like that's not a good way to prevent something from happening.

Walter, from the law enforcement focus group, similarly dismissed the idea for his children, elaborating on the emotional dimensions of the pandemic to make his point:

> I think my kids are already living in enough fear, having to wear a mask every day. I don't know that I want to put them in a bulletproof vest too, scare them

even more. My daughter is already having anxiety about getting freaking COVID, getting a cold. So I don't know if I want to add to that, although it sounds like an interesting product.

Bulletproof vests are staples of police officers' gear, yet bulletproof products for children seemed a different matter, and as such, they were news for Walter. While apparently curious about the product, he was inclined to draw a line when it came to his children. The pandemic prompted Walter to reflect on the experience of fear, and in the case of bulletproof apparel, his own children's fear functioned as a disincentive. Similarly, when asked about bulletproof products, Scott, a father in the teachers group, also addressed the question in emotional terms, bringing up his child:

> My five-year-old is in kindergarten this year; the idea of putting a bulletproof vest on him to [go to] school is just absolutely terrifying [; . . .] there's no physical harm necessarily in wearing something like that, but I'd worry a lot about kind of the mental stress.

Rather than the "peace of mind" promised by companies, in Walter's and Scott's assessments—as in the mothers group—the products *themselves* were likely to magnify unpleasant emotions, specifically for children. This is a theme that also arose in other focus groups. Participants rejected bulletproof apparel anticipating the emotional and literal burden that such gear would mean for kids—including their own—as well as for other people such as medical personnel. Yet as we shall see, condemnatory emotional reactions also related to what the product symbolizes: a social and political inability or unwillingness to prevent mass shootings and other forms of gun violence. In such contexts, then, parents fear for their children and are compelled to have emotionally difficult conversations about their safety. As Sara Ahmed argues, "[f]eelings may stick to some objects, and slide over others,"[7] and the disturbing emotions associated with gun violence, and its broader implications, seemed to "stick" to the objects that would purportedly offer protection. In that sense, bulletproof clothing and accessories can become sites of intense emotional "stickiness." Which emotions are more likely to attach to these products—whether dread, relief, disgust, fear, excitement, or others—is likely influenced by people's broader social experiences, ideological commitments, and social locations.

Teachers: Who Should Bear the Burden of Security at School?

Given the media attention to mass shootings in schools, the implementation of active shooter drills, and proposals to arm teachers, participants in the teachers focus group were interested parties in school security discussions. Indeed, many of the security policies and initiatives implemented at schools directly affect their lives, yet these teachers said they did not always feel heard. They commented on active shooter drills, metal detectors, the presence of firearms in schools, and their own individual strategies to achieve a measure of security. Furthermore, one of the teachers, Grace, was personally invested in the topic because a young member of her family was killed during a school shooting. The experiences, policies, and societal debates around school security formed the backdrop of the teachers' assessments of bulletproof fashion, but despite their personal connection to the topic, none of them found the idea of bulletproof gear in school settings compelling.

These teachers were certainly concerned about the possibility of a school shooting, and they also grappled with both institutional responses to gun violence and the trade-offs resulting from their own personal security strategies. Reflecting on one kind of intervention debated in the public sphere—arming teachers—Scott commented:

> I pretty vehemently oppose arming teachers and things. I'm a big believer in the statistic that when people buy guns for the houses, you're more likely to have someone inside your house use the gun on themselves than on an intruder, and I feel the same way with schools. If we start introducing weapons or things, that we're going to increase all sorts of unnecessary violence.

Scott's comment is consistent with studies that found that the presence of guns in the home increases the risk of death (by homicide or suicide).[8] Similarly, Sam rejected the idea of having powerful firearms at school, recalling: "[I]t made me nervous when I learned that our campus service officer had an AR15 in a safe in his office. [. . .] having that in a school seems like you're asking for trouble." In contrast, Grace—who rejected the idea of arming teachers as terrifying—did support having

> a professional in the building who has a gun, because the reality is, when I imagine a moment where there is a shooter outside my door, I don't want to be wondering how long it's going to take [. . .] a police responder, a first responder to get there. We know it's going to be about seven minutes, and it's too late by then.

Teachers in this group weighed different types of information and their own feelings and experiences as they determined to what extent they would support the presence of guns at school by authorized personnel and as a protective measure.

Group members also commented on their own security strategies. For instance, after the Parkland shooting, Amelia decided to keep her "classroom door locked at all times," which meant that "anybody who wants to come see [her] or talk to [her], they get a locked door at all times." This situation is far from ideal for a teacher like Amelia, who is also deeply invested in making her students feel welcomed. Likewise, Grace reported that she keeps her doors locked at school. As mentioned, the possibility of a school shooting was not an abstract or distant possibility for Grace, given the toll that such an event took on her own family. Still, she grappled with the tension between wanting to feel safe and implementing fortressing strategies:

> For my own just mental health, I have to keep reminding myself like we live in a free and open society, and because of that, I think there's always some risk of exposure to danger. Right? I don't want to live in a society that's locked up and completely 100% secure, because then you're not really living. So I have to keep framing things that way, that open public spaces are a positive and a good thing and reminding myself that that's like living. That's life.

Grace's observation recognizes human vulnerability, while still wanting to avert the risk of preventable violence. At the same time, her observations point to what might be lost in the move to "futureproof" individuals and societies.[9] These observations also relate to fortressing the body through bulletproof fashion.

When discussing bulletproof products specifically, none of the teachers lent support to this approach. They considered it a superficial measure at best. In the words of Sam: "[T]hey're individual solutions to the bigger problems that we need to take care of as a society." In the same vein, Carolyn remarked that

> it's kind of sad that they're even made, and it's definitely a Band Aid to a bigger problem and not a solution. But I do understand why some parents might buy it for their children, and how sending their children to school wearing that, or wearing it yourself, does provide a certain level of security to ease your mind and worries. But I definitely don't think it's a solution to our issues.

In Carolyn's narrative, her own emotions and the emotions of others shape her perspectives on bulletproof products. She expressed sadness about the products' existence but also empathy for worried parents and children who might welcome them. She assessed the promised emotional function of the products (peace of mind) vis-à-vis the practical function (protection), ultimately finding this approach wanting.

Similarly, Grace prefaced her assessment with emotional markers, and she too rejected the idea of bulletproofing kids: "I think it's sad, like that a kid would have to think 'I have to put on my bulletproof jacket' to go to school." She further reflected on something that Carolyn, the youngest teacher in the group, had mentioned earlier: That growing up she "never thought of school being a place that didn't possibly have a school shooting." Thus, Grace lamented how the notion of a school shooter has become part of childhood imaginaries and experiences in contemporary United States:

> [I]t's so disturbing. That should never happen. It should never be. I feel like that's where we're failing our children; they should feel secure. These are adult problems, and the adults should be able to find solutions to the problems, not dress the kids in bulletproof vests.

Grace's comments were deeply felt, given her family's experience with a school shooting: "I don't see school the same, so it's hard for me to feel safe in school, and it's hard for me to send my kids to school and feel that they're going to be okay." Still, she was unconvinced about the wisdom of adopting bulletproof products and did not want to place the burden of security onto children. Instead, Grace expected political leaders to address the problem and was dismayed by the refusal of many politicians to even talk about guns.

Among the bulletproof garments and accessories that are in the market, those made for children tend to attract special attention—perhaps precisely due to the emotional dimensions of armoring children. At the same time, some ballistic products are marketed for teachers, whether meant to be used on their bodies (e.g., bulletproof vests) or to be deployed in the classroom (e.g., bulletproof whiteboards). In considering the possibility of bulletproofing teachers, Scott commented:

> [B]oth my wife and I are teachers. If someone was like, "Hey, will you wear this bulletproof vest to school?" [. . .] if it ever came to where that was like a real necessity for teaching, I'd probably consider a different profession, just because that's. . . . I just feel like it's a whole extra boatload of stress and strain and possibly trauma on some kids who already have a very stressful, hard, difficult life.

Scott addressed the difficulties teachers face but included the trauma that kids may experience too. The conditions of teaching and learning are entwined, and bulletproof gear seems to represent a deep degradation of both. While a school shooting is surely terrifying, these teachers did not find solace in body armor. The emotional function of these products did not resonate with them. And neither did they find much practical utility in the products. Instead, they expected other types of solutions at the social, policy, and political levels.

Advocates Addressing Sexual and Gender Violence: Beyond Security-Oriented Objects

Members of organizations addressing sexual and gender violence were keenly aware that guns can play a role in the scenarios they deal with. Guns can be a tool of victimization, might be used for self-defense, and are sometimes linked to accidents and unintended uses.[10] One of the advocates in this line of work, Tina, mentioned that the potential presence of guns "factors in when you're initially speaking to someone [experiencing domestic violence] and helping them kind of assess the danger of the situation they're in." In such cases, guns are seen as potentially increasing the lethality of an abusive relationship. Andrea agreed that "gun violence is a huge issue" but also warned that "anything can be used as a weapon, at the end of the day, in our field." Wendy in turn countered the "perception that having a gun always makes you safer, when, in fact, we know that among victims of gender-based violence that have a gun, it's often turned around and used on them."

Indeed, research on the topic "suggests that victims of intimate partner and family-related disputes are more likely to be killed if a firearm is present in the home" and that women are especially likely to be victimized in this way.[11] Given that these considerations pertain largely to domestic and intimate-partner violence situations, it is not surprising that as group participants commented on bulletproof garments, the discussion veered to other sorts of gun violence: After all, what is the use of these products for people who face the greatest threat of violence, including gun violence, at home? Are they supposed to use the products in their households day and night? These advocates agreed that bulletproof products do not seem helpful but are revelatory of deeper problems that require systemic solutions and a focus on prevention.

Tina situated ballistic apparel in social context and pointed to the emotions that the images of bulletproof products elicited for her:

> I see those images, and I just think about the kind of level of anxiety that as a society we have to walk around with currently. Obviously, the divisiveness as a country, but concerts, movie theaters, parades, anywhere that you're going in crowds of people now, and in 2020—I know I can't just be speaking for myself—but it's like this constant level of. . . . And even being in this field working in these high stress [environments], you know, I've worked in jails, prisons, where loud sounds, you have like an automatic internal reaction to tense up. And even working with the population that we do now, you hear people with elevated voices in the background, and you start to uh, uh, uh make sure is it happy? Is it sad? Are people fighting? You know, it's a constant state of trying to run to help or run to save yourself.

In Tina's narrative, emotions such as anxiety are ubiquitous, and bulletproof products fit that emotional universe. She added, "[I]t's a wonder we're not all on anti-anxiety medication the way the society is right now." Her work assisting survivors of gender-based violence sensitized Tina to the added burden of a milieu of generalized anxiety: "I just think about the people that we serve and having to walk around with that weight on your shoulders on top of what you're going through." This reflection came up as Tina recalled the active shooter trainings implemented in her building, an exercise that has become increasingly common in the United States, and was also mentioned in the teachers, law enforcement, and gun prevention advocates focus groups.

Andrea also connected the discussion of bulletproof products with that of active shooter trainings, reflecting on the difficulties of talking about these issues with children:

> I've had to try to explain the whole active shooter drills to very little kids. What does that even mean that they're even experiencing that in kindergarten, first grade, when they don't even know what that is, but they have to go hide in a closet like a fire drill?

Andrea's viewpoint is implicit in the questions she posed, also conveying an emotional tone in her indictment. Rather than accepting the new normal of active shooter trainings, her questions encourage us to interrogate the kind of society in which these drills and associated security objects are seen as a necessity. Also with a critical perspective, a number of researchers, educators, mental health professionals, and parents have raised concerns about the potentially negative emotional impacts of certain active shooter drills, particularly on children.[12]

These advocates also linked their reflections about bulletproof apparel to the particularities of U.S. society when it comes to guns—something that also emerged in other focus groups. For instance, Sienna, who identified as Indian, observed:

> So I think even comparing just living in America versus different countries, and how they handle gun violence, and what their rates of gun violence are, it's like it's incredible to me that we still have such a, you know, "it's my right [to have a gun]," it's this and that, when it causes so many issues. And the people being affected are often the most vulnerable groups. You know, a child with a gun at 12 is still a child. They just now have this weapon of violence.

Rather than seeing guns as a source of safety, Sienna emphasized the problem of gun violence and raised questions about assertions of gun rights in a context in which even children might gain access. Transnational comparisons of the legal status of gun ownership also emerged in other focus groups, sometimes to critique its premises and consequences, or conversely, to support its wisdom.

In the case of Rose, who grew up in a home with guns in "hunting territory," the contemporary gun-related mindset in the United States differs from what she experienced growing up. Her observation mirrors gun studies scholars' analyses of gun culture shifts: from a focus on hunting and recreation to one increasingly concerned with self-defense.[13] Rose felt that the staunch claims of self-defense associated with current gun ownership justifications are misguided:

> [There are] grown people saying 'I need these guns to protect myself'—and what that translates into—so now second-graders need bulletproof vests to protect themselves? We really need to take a step back and say, 'what exactly is happening here?' Right? Like, how is this the way we wanted our country and our society to be functioning?

As in Andrea's case, Rose's questions are incisive and heartfelt. Her reflection moves from the realm of individual decision-making to what is a stake at the societal level. Bulletproof products for children, in particular, operate as a wake-up call in her analysis:

> When we start putting kids in backpacks that are bulletproof, you really have to take a look at what we're doing. We just do. I mean, it just, as a parent, it

takes me to a . . . and a grandparent, I just . . . takes me to a very different place, and it does not make me feel safe. I don't feel a sense of security with that at all.

In Rose's assessment, bulletproof products do not instill the promised peace of mind but prompt a confrontation with the state of society. Her emotions help open a social critique. Here too, rather than normalizing guns and the body-fortressing solutions proposed by the market, Rose demands a reckoning with the problems that produce insecurity in the first place.

In that vein, the group discussed the role of other protective products aimed at people who experienced sexual/gender violence or are afraid of being victimized in that way, for example, anti-rape garments, apps, and devices. These products relate to a fashion of fear universe,[14] and companies that sell bulletproof garments sometimes sell other security gadgets as well, including for women specifically. Guard Dog Security, for instance, offers a stun gun disguised in the shell of a cosmetic lipstick. According to Wendy, these types of products are "a distraction from the real issue, which is perpetrators" and "toxic masculinity." She explained:

There's actually a nail polish that you can . . . you dip your finger in the drink, and it tells you if there's a drug in it or not by changing color. So I just feel it's saying like it's easier to just make this nail polish and put the responsibility on the victim rather than actually addressing the real issue. Now having said that, I personally hate those devices. But I do, I have had clients in the past who have used them or wanted to use them, and I certainly don't, you know, if something is going to make somebody feel safer, I'm not going to be like, 'No, don't use that.'

Wendy's narrative points to perpetrators as the "real issue," although not just qua individuals but in relation to the broader phenomenon of "toxic masculinity" (a dimension also seen as important in some analyses of gun violence, including mass shootings).[15] While empathizing with those who find a sense of security in devices, Wendy shared her personal aversion and described them as a superficial approach. Likewise, Bailey brought up another example of what they saw as a "lip service" intervention in relation to violence, this time in prisons:

[O]ne of the many things that State Department of Corrections in New York has done is change their shower curtains, so that there is a place that you can look in to see if someone is being raped or not. And, man, what a low bar. Right? That's like . . . that's the thumbs up. Right?

Bailey's ironic tone underscored their critique of the reliance on security-oriented objects to address problems that require more substantial solutions.[16]

Overall, members of this group did not see much promise in security strategies dependent on devices, whether bulletproof or containing other protective features. Instead, they drew attention to prevention, education, and the need for broader and deeper approaches to address the root causes of multiple forms of violence.

Gun Violence Prevention Advocates: Pointing to Everyday Violence and Oppression

In this study, gun violence prevention advocates comprise the group most directly involved in tackling gun-related harm. They all identified as Black (one of them as Black/Native) and highlighted the experiences of underserved communities. Whereas mass shootings in schools have captured the public's attention, members of this group explained that such events are not the primary form of gun violence in the areas they serve (namely, economically and socially marginalized communities of color), and thus not the main focus of their work. In fact, as researchers have pointed out, though mass public shootings—in schools or other places—are extremely disturbing and damaging, they are a relatively small proportion of overall gun violence. Furthermore, Rosanna Smart and Terry L. Schell report that these types of incidents "are responsible for less than 0.5 percent of all homicides."[17]

Referring to schools more specifically, Mark—an advocate for gun violence solutions at the local and national levels—observed that it is very rare to have "mass shootings in school in the Black and Brown communities." A CNN analysis of ten years of K-12 school shootings in the United States, starting in 2009, is consistent with Mark's observation regarding *mass* shootings; however, it also notes the disproportionate impacts of more general forms of gun violence in schools attended by students of color: "While school shootings disproportionately affect urban schools and people of color, *mass* shootings are more likely to occur at white, suburban schools" (emphasis mine).[18] Byron, also actively involved in gun violence reduction, additionally alluded to forms of gun violence that affect youths outside educational settings: "[A] lot of schools are having active shooter drills, right? But that's only for large places and institutions." He wondered about the solutions available for youths once they leave school and venture into the streets to go home. Members of this group drew attention to everyday forms of gun violence in urban communities and assessed bulletproof fashion in that context. They highlighted social disparities in experiences of gun violence and in relation to the solutions offered.

These advocates' perception was that, generally, bulletproof gear does not seem to have been made with people of color in mind—in terms of both their representation and the kinds of scenarios that these artifacts are meant for. Starting with Mark, participants suggested that bulletproof garments appear to be mainly for affluent white communities, for example, for those who fear mass shootings in schools. Relatedly, the cost of the products was highlighted, noting that many people in marginalized communities would not be able to afford such garments. The issue of costs was also raised in other focus groups, including law enforcement officers, advocates addressing sexual/gender violence, and members of organizations tackling police violence. In this group, the implicit question was: Who are the beneficiaries of this security approach, particularly when it is out of reach for people disproportionately bearing the brunt of gun violence?

As we shall see, within this group, emotions about bulletproof gear were entwined with reflections on racism, the social neglect of underserved communities, the political tensions associated with certain types of body armor, and objections to the notion of equipping children with ballistic products. Beverly, a community development worker, started her comments on bulletproof fashion with emotional references:

> When I look at that advertisement, it just, it makes me feel more unsafe. It makes me feel sad. It makes me feel not included because, like [Mark] said, there were no Black or Brown faces [. . .], nothing to reflect safety needed in the urban communities. Although there are some Black-owned businesses that do create fashionable bulletproof vests, I still don't think that, you know, that is something . . . it's just heartbreaking that we even have to consider that within the school.

Sadness and other feelings accompanied Beverly's rejection of bulletproof fashion. She agreed with other participants that such products seem unhelpful to the kind of gun violence affecting their communities. Mark also underscored the financial costs: "[I]f you have to pay your rent, I'm not sure you're going to want to spend $500 on a bulletproof vest for your children that they're going to grow out of in like a year or two." On the one hand, Beverly and Mark critiqued the politics of representation and access, but on the other, they were not demanding "inclusive" or more affordable bulletproof fashion but much deeper responses to the problem of gun violence.

In her commentary on bulletproof apparel, Donna indirectly alluded to the emotions of privileged communities and how that relates to certain responses to gun violence. She saw the commercialization of ballistic products as a way to "calm" affluent members of society, in lieu of broader transformations. Referring to bulletproof gear, she said:

> I don't think it was ever meant to be brought down to the city communities. It was meant for the mass shooting in these influential areas to give these parents something to be calm about because a lot of new organization was coming out saying, 'we need to change the laws. We need to change the gun laws.' And the NRA [National Rifle Association] wasn't having it.

Byron similarly raised questions about equity. In his case, he pivoted between noting the impossibility of fitting everyone with bulletproof gear and rejecting the solution altogether: "[J]ust like the gun is a false sense of safety, the vest is a false sense of safety as well." Recounting his emotional reaction to the images of bulletproof gear, Byron commented: "I had to shake my head and look down upon. For me, it would be, what messages we giving to the community? If we, number one, if we can't give them to everybody, you know." Similar to participants in other focus groups, Byron also worried about the potential emotional effect of the products:

> But that's trauma, just putting that on a kid and the kid wondering why this coat is so much heavier than my last-year coat. [. . .] And you got to explain that to the kids, like, "Oh, but this is going to make you safe."

Byron and other members of this group were unimpressed by bulletproof fashion, and they analyzed the products' implications in ways that intersected race, class, and politics.

As shown in the following comments, focus group participants alluded to body armor in relation to racism, police violence, and social protest. Among the political and emotional situations they addressed was the use of (overt) body armor by ideologically opposed groups: On the one hand, members of right-wing organizations; on the other, protesters against police violence and racial injustice. In interpreting these comments, it can be useful to remember the role of emotions in racist or xenophobic expressions—for example, disgust or hatred—as well as in the responses of communities targeted, including anger or pride.[19]

Donna referred to right-wing group members who use bulletproof vests in the context of vigilante activities:

> [T]hey're coming out here with cammies [camouflage garments] and boots acting like they're toy soldiers out here because they feel that they coming to the neighborhood to decrease the crime. They want to act like they're policing us now, so that's why they're coming in here wearing vests.

In Donna's view, these activities prompted individuals at the opposite end of the political spectrum to also resort to protective gear:

> Now I have seen my brothers, my Black brothers and sisters, proud brothers and sisters, in turn creating a militant opposition, where they are now coming into the communities with vests because, in my opinion, you see all the white brothers and sisters coming out here, MAGA[20] crowd with flags, with cammies and bulletproof vests. So now, okay, so you're coming out here with your racism. Now I have to protect my community from you. So now I'm going to be wearing the vests and stuff like that.

Donna's mocking description of right-wing groups as "toy soldiers" can be interpreted as a form of affective resistance to a scene that can be scary and intimidating to many: a vigilante group asserting its power while displaying militarized gear and emblems with white nationalist/supremacist connotations. In that sense, Donna's narrative provides a context for what she describes as a "militant" self-defense tactic from members of Black communities, who also rely on bulletproof vests and who assert their pride.

Byron, in turn, elaborated on protesters' use of body armor in the aftermath of the police murder of George Floyd, a Black man: "We actually had a group come into our community, a fairly new group that came from, you know, all the George Floyd protests. [. . .] And, they were leading protests, but they were leading protests with bulletproof vests." While he expressed an affinity with people protesting police violence against Black people—implicit in his comments that he "support[s] BLM [Black Lives Matter] 100%"—he had some reservations regarding the use of body armor by some protesters in the group he mentioned. Consistent with his concern about the equity implications of bulletproof products, he commented: "[I]f you're in our community, and you're leading a protest, and you guys have bulletproof vests [. . .] what message are we giving to the community? We're safe, but you're not safe? I mean, I don't understand it." Ultimately, Byron did not have much faith in the kind of protection that bulletproof gear offers, so he was not advocating for it more generally. In his view, "It's not the apparatus that make the community safe." In Donna's description, we can infer how tactical gear by far-right groups serves to heighten a sense of insecurity in communities of color, prompting self-defense responses that may include bulletproof vests; in Byron's case, there is a glimpse of the tensions that these protective strategies can generate within communities directly affected by gun violence, police violence, and racial injustice.

In this focus group, bulletproof products—both overt and covert—were seen as symbols of inequality, as part of intimidation tactics by right-wing organizations, as a self-defense tool in communities of color, and as an ultimately ineffective approach to security. Emotions such as fear, disappointment, anger, sadness, and confusion appear explicitly or implicitly in the narratives. They point not only to the shortcomings of bulletproof fashion but to ingrained social problems, hierarchies, and inequalities.

Activists in Organizations Addressing Police Violence: Expansive Critiques of Power

Bulletproof fashion sparked a lively discussion among activists in organizations addressing police violence. Members of this group had activist experiences that were broader than their critique of policing, including matters of racial, social, economic, and environmental justice. Consistent with such orientations, their assessments of bulletproof garments were situated within expansive critiques of systems of power and inequality. As part of their political activism, participants were aware of the risk of violence, including with firearms, in recent protest situations; and they spoke about body armor as a potential protective measure in that context. Indeed, in addition to police presence, a number of demonstrations around 2020 included armed protesters or counter-protesters, and some events resulted in injuries or fatalities.[21] More generally, however, this group rejected bulletproof apparel as an adequate response to the problem of gun violence in U.S. society. Participants' narratives included both their own emotional responses as well as observations about the role that emotions play with respect to the bulletproof fashion market. They expressed indignation at societal failures to address the root causes of gun violence and noted how fear is mobilized to justify the commercialization of bulletproof products. They saw a capitalist logic mediating this particular approach to security.

Still, within this group, Maya and David alluded to the use of body armor by social justice/anti-racist protesters in recent times. David said he considered this possibility himself, given the heated situations he faced during the protests that erupted in the summer of 2020. He felt concerned about his personal safety, so he decided to check out different types of body armor. He hesitated, asking himself, "Do I want to get a bulletproof vest?" but soon realized that body armor was outside his price range. He noted,

> it's available to a certain class of individuals to kind of further insulate and protect themselves. And certainly, the folks who are in the communities that were being tear gassed and facing riot cops in [town], they have no access to that. It's off the table.

Maya in turn, while critical of the "fear mongering" she associated with the commercialization of bulletproof fashion, described situations in which the fear of being injured by a gunshot had a certain immediacy—like the protests David described.

Maya's comments pointed to the potentially differential interpretations and security ramifications of ballistic apparel depending on the user, and how in some cases, it might be read as a sign of violent intent rather than as merely self-defense:

> [W]hen our activists show up in bulletproof vests, the police say that's why they're there, because we must be wanting to do something violent. Why else were our people wearing bulletproof vests, as opposed to, we're scared for our safety because you don't keep us safe. We have the police saying they want to hurt us. We have white supremacists that say they want to hurt us. We got all kinds of folks that say they want to hurt us. But you're telling us we're violent because we're prepared for bodily harm.

Both David and Maya grappled with the ambivalences connected to bulletproof garments: On the one hand, they rejected bulletproof fashion as an everyday security measure; on the other, they considered body armor as potentially protective in protest situations during volatile political times. Fear appears implicitly and explicitly in their accounts—as a response to concrete conditions of violence and as an emotion exploited by companies mainly interested in making a profit. Maya decried the "commodification of safety" and David similarly concluded, "[T]he commodification of security is grotesque."

In a similar vein, Greg and Santiago offered critical assessments of bulletproof garments, highlighting how they fit capitalist approaches to social problems.

Referring to the phenomenon of mass shootings in schools, Santiago commented with bitter irony:

> Let's not do anything about any of the underlying issues that caused this type of violence, the kind of alienation, desperation that people feel that ends up pushing them towards crazy acts like that. No, let's just give these kids bulletproof vests because in capitalism, they are more interested in treatments, not cures, because a treatment you can keep selling. A cure you can't.

Maya emphatically agreed: "I'm writing down 'treatments, not cures,'" and Greg also expressed agreement pointing to systemic factors. According to him, bulletproof garments represent

> a total failure of our government, of our system, to protect people that a private company has to vend products to people—to teachers, for lab workers, whatever it might be. It's just a . . . it's such an admission of failure.

He further observed that "in America, the form that an admission of failure takes, [is] separating the people from their money" and the "vacuum of safety has been filled by this blob of capitalism." Greg's perspectives were infused with emotions that revealed his deep dissatisfaction with the workings of society. He remarked: "[I]t's gross. It's infuriating. It makes me very angry to see those products. It does not make me excited or interested. It just reminds me of how deeply all of us have been failed by the system."

In this group, unpleasant emotions were strongly embedded in assessments of bulletproof fashion. Even in the more ambivalent perspectives about vests, we do not see "peace of mind" or a wholehearted endorsement of the products articulated. Instead, what predominates is fear, anger, disappointment, and a sense of injustice. Still, as in the description by Donna—in the gun violence prevention advocates group—we can see that body armor may be used or considered by social justice activists and not just people with right-wing sympathies or an affinity with "tactical" gear. Yet the interpretation of the uses of and feelings about the products may vary depending on political and experiential standpoints.

Health Care Workers: Denouncing Violence and Guns in Medical Settings

During the pandemic, risks to the health and safety of health care workers received increased public attention, yet longer-term risks such as violent situations in the workplace were already on the radar of companies that offer security-oriented products for this sector specifically. The focus group of health care workers discussed such risks but were unconvinced by the wisdom of bulletproof products. Participants found this solution generally "disturbing," and in one case even "disgusting" (the latter resembled reactions in the previous group, for example, Greg, who found it "gross," and David, "grotesque.") Still, one of these health care workers recalled a case in which nurses had requested body armor due to scary situations involving guns at work. Concerns about guns and the risk of shootings in health care settings are not limited to these nurses but have been salient enough to prompt various medical institutions to consider the implementation of active shooter trainings.[22] Members of this focus group had worked as nurses or in related functions in different types of spaces—large medical centers, educational facilities, maternity units, long-term care—and they assessed bulletproof apparel in the context of their occupational experiences. They reflected on the violence that health care workers sometimes encounter in medical settings, and more broadly addressed the presence of guns in U.S. society.

In reference to bulletproof apparel, Sophia, a nurse working as a case manager in a medical facility, commented: "[I]t's not a solution to anything, and it's kind of disturbing that people are thinking, 'well, this might be the future.' [. . .] I don't think it would make me feel much safer." Marie, a school nurse who also had previous experiences in medical facilities, was likewise disturbed by the products, and observed,

> we're really missing the boat if we all feel like we have to go to work with a bulletproof vest, or if I have to send my kids to school with a bulletproof backpack. But I totally understand the thought.

As in other focus groups, Marie showed empathy for those who might consider purchasing such products, despite thinking "that we could do better in trying to prevent these things from happening."

Claire reacted strongly to bulletproof fashion and connected the conversation to the proliferation of guns in U.S. society: "I think it's disgusting." She continued, "I don't understand why everybody feels the need to carry a gun. I just don't understand why we feel that need." She recalled an episode at a hospital, in which a patient's husband entered the facility with a gun, killed his wife, and then killed himself. Claire pondered,

> why do you need to carry a gun in a hospital? For what reason? They should be checked at the door. And why do you need to carry a gun into school? I mean, I don't understand our society these days.

While in the episode narrated, the intent of carrying a gun might have been precisely to use it—that is, for the man to shoot his wife—Claire's questions more broadly interrogate the place of guns in the United States. And her emotional response—confusion and repulsion—points to the seeming incommensurability of worlds and ideologies among diverse groups of people in the country, including those who see a need to restrict the circulation of guns and those who describe the right to bear arms as an inalienable right, with some degrees of variation.

Megan similarly gave examples of problematic cases of guns in health facilities and, as others in the group, expected better solutions than bulletproofing medical personnel. Nevertheless, she tried to put herself in the shoes of nurses who sought relief in body armor:

> [I]n the ten years that I worked in a medical center in Vermont, there were at least three occasions that a family member brought a gun into the mother/baby unit, the post-partum unit. And it was discovered by the nurses on every occasion, and those nurses were terrified. And they asked for bulletproof vests, and I believe they got them, because it kept happening. So, I agree that it is education that needs to happen, but I think we also have to. . . . We can't ignore the fact that there are active shooter situations in medical centers and community hospitals and shopping malls, and, all the time. And how do we protect people in that moment until we get to a point in our society where we feel like we don't have to be afraid anymore?

In the face of fear and societal failure to stem the circulation of guns in places where they do not belong, body armor seemed the best option for the nurses in Megan's account. Her rhetorical question about the here and now still conveyed a sense of hope that we may "get to a point" not ruled by fear: that as a society, we might create a world where health care practitioners do not feel the need to strap on ballistic garments.

Emotions also entered the discussion of bulletproof fashion in relation to the state of mind of gun violence perpetrators. Like Santiago—the social justice activist who mentioned the "desperation" and "alienation" of some shooters—Marie found part of the clue in societal and interpersonal failures to adequately tackle perturbed emotional states:

> I think the one thing that you do see in almost every situation like that is the [individual] being distraught over something, and somebody not recognizing it, and the lack of communication. [. . .] I think we can do better to prevent people from coming into a hospital and feeling like they have to end it all.

Certainly, psychological difficulties have been subject of concern for gun violence researchers, among a wider array of demographic, economic, cultural, political, and experiential factors. At the same time, researchers have also countered popular tendencies to simply attribute gun violence to mental illness and have warned against stigmatizing assumptions equating mental health disorders with dangerousness.[23] Instead, they call for nuanced and multifaceted approaches that would help disentangle "forms, and levels, of psychological symptoms and disorders and aspects of gun violence—both gun attitudes and actual firearm-related behaviors."[24] Scholars, practitioners, and advocates concerned about gun violence support the improvement of mental health services—which would also contribute to more general well-being—as well as welcome increased funding for research on gun violence, including from a public health vantage point.[25]

The perspectives of various participants in this study highlight key areas of concern related to guns: mental health, interpersonal relations, social supports, gun culture, and gun policy.[26] Among the health care workers, Claire pointed to the need for cultural changes and further regulation of guns, and Marie suggested the need to build better relationships and preemptively address the emotional states of people in distress. They saw more promise in such interventions than in bulletproof fashion as a protective measure. Similarly, Drew, a nurse working with children, highlighted the need for "better education, better resources" and added that "relationship building is a better bulletproof vest than a bulletproof vest."

As a protective measure, bulletproof garments direct attention away from perpetrators and the causes of gun violence, and toward potential victims. Like Wendy—the advocate who reflected on anti-sexual violence devices—Drew also objected to placing the onus of protection on those potentially targeted, in this case, by having to wear a particular type of clothing:

> I think it's disturbing to feel like we have to. . . . It's like it reminds me of a whole other category, like why do we have to dress a certain way? Essentially, it's dressing a certain way to try to give us the façade of safety. It's the same way that women are told, 'if you don't wear this, then,' you know . . . 'if you wear this, then you're going to . . . you're asking for trouble.' 'If you don't . . .' whatever. It's like we shouldn't have to wear something that is addressing a symptom instead of addressing the problem in the first place.

Combining Drew's objection and Megan's question about how to address the threat of guns, a tension emerges between approaches, such as restrictions on the circulation of guns (as Claire suggested) vis-à-vis the normalization of bulletproof clothing for everyday use (as companies promote). At the same time, across the focus groups discussed so far, participants also voiced the need to address the root causes of gun violence, including deeper systemic transformations.

What kinds of social arrangements, policy changes, and cultural shifts may help prevent and reduce gun violence? This question has been the subject of significant political and academic debate—and an emotionally contentious issue itself.[27] In the United States, guns are the center of deep ideological crevices, though there are also nuances in perspectives that cross these divides.[28] To some extent, differing viewpoints and emotions regarding bulletproof fashion reveal some of these dynamics and can be situated within the larger debate about the place of guns in U.S. society.

Gun Rights Supporters: Armor as Just Another Self-Defense Strategy

Gun rights supporters in the United States include myriad people who own guns, defend the right to bear arms, learn to use firearms, attend gun shows, practice in shooting ranges, join gun clubs, and become activists in gun rights organizations. Many legal gun owners base their decision to own a firearm on the desire to protect themselves or their loved ones; in fact, "personal safety/protection" was the top reason given by gun owners in a 2019 Gallup poll.[29] Given this security-oriented stance, it is pertinent to ask how bulletproof fashion fits within this framework.

Among the gun rights supporters focus group, their assessment of bulletproof products centered on the decisions of individuals and their right to self-defense. This was consistent with participants' perspectives on gun ownership, particularly on guns as instruments of self-protection.[30] In the context of this discussion, references to broader social systems appeared mainly in the form of critiques of government intervention, including initiatives perceived as interfering with the right to defend oneself. Practical aspects were also considered, such as the extent of protection offered by bulletproof products. Unlike participants in other focus groups who expressed anger, disgust, sadness, or other disturbing emotions in relation to these products, members of this group generally did not voice aversive or unpleasant feelings about bulletproof fashion (though one participant estimated that it may exacerbate a potentially "paranoid" mindset). Participants spoke as individuals with familiarity and expertise with guns, assessing the functionality of bulletproof garments in light of such knowledge, and pragmatically considering different scenarios. They weighed the possibility of injury and ways in which the garments might or might not work as expected but also found potential value in the products.

The affective tone in some comments about bulletproof fashion was rather positive. For instance, Eleanor, an experienced firearms educator, considered the garments to be a "cool" option and found the opportunity to test a ballistic product "kind of exciting." In contrast, she had a different emotional reaction regarding a policy proposal to further restrict body armor in New York, finding it "a little disturbing," due to its potential to encroach on self-defense rights.[31] Eric, who identified as a libertarian, coincided: "[I]f people feel the desire to protect themselves this way, it's a perfectly legitimate thing for them to do." Still, he considered the possibility of making oneself more "paranoid" than necessary, and to make his point, he drew a parallel with other experiences during the pandemic:

> You know, maybe we could call it like the "face shield effect," right? Because people are out there wearing face shields, which really don't protect you or anyone else from the Coronavirus, but they're doing it anyway. And I wonder if they're just poisoning their own mental state and making themselves more unhappy and worried than they really need to be. I mean, that's also a factor.

Similar to other focus groups, emotions entered the discussion of bulletproof fashion in relation both to the products themselves and to policy and political matters (though with different emphasis and content). As illustrated by Eric's comment, and as also emerging in other groups, we can see, for example, the influence of the pandemic in shaping perspectives on security. Participants in different focus groups drew on this experience to make sense of concrete features and emotional dimensions of bulletproof fashion.

When asked about bulletproof products as a security strategy, Roger—who identified as someone who likes guns, shooting, and politics—responded: "[T]hat's up to the person. I think that some of these things, may have some value." Still, after reflecting on the case of a seller who intentionally shot himself in body armor as a marketing pitch, Roger clarified that "it's not going to be like in the John Wick movie, where you can get shot multiple times and you don't even feel it." He mentioned that the following day the seller had a "bruise the size of a grapefruit and thought he was having a heart attack." Roger concluded: "I think it's more of a specialty product depending upon where . . . what you do for a living. I don't think it's something you could really sell in a mass market." Katherine, who grew up around guns and is a firearms instructor, also added a word of skepticism. She wondered about the utility of the products, noting that "anybody with any type of knowledge is going to know that—especially the more popular those get—aiming for the chest is not what they're going to do."

Eleanor seemed to be the most enthusiastic about the products, saying, "[M]y answer to these particular garments is why not? I mean, the lab coat. That's kind of cool." She pointed to their potential usefulness to pharmacists, for example, who face risks in the context of selling legitimate drugs that have value in the illegal market and who "deal with a lot of cash." Moving to a different scenario, this time involving children, Eleanor continued by telling an anecdote in which she had firsthand exposure to a bulletproof product:

> [W]hen I was teaching women a target instructional shooting clinic, a mom showed up with a backpack, a child's backpack that had . . . that she was considering purchasing for her child. And she asked—and it had the ballistic panel in it—and she asked us after the class if we could actually put some rounds into that vest, which we did.

As we shall see, Eleanor responded positively to the challenge, with feelings that seem to be associated with the pleasures of novelty, curiosity, and expertise (although later she also considered some downsides):

> [I]t was kind of exciting for us, because we had never had the experience of doing that. So it was very interesting to . . . and we shot it at several different distances, so that we could see the impact, [. . .] with the mom's permission, of course. Because she was going to buy another one for real purposes, you know, if this one met her expectations. And it did.

Eleanor conceded that as the test was not performed on a live person, it was hard to gauge how it would feel in the flesh, and the kinds of injuries the gunshots might leave, even if the armor protects vital organs. Still, she considered bulletproof garments potentially useful, including for children: "[H]opefully, those kids are going to be able to maneuver them. But it really comes down to preparedness and what they're willing to do." Unlike participants in other focus groups who found the idea of ballistic garments for school-aged children "terrifying," "sad," and potentially "trauma" inducing, Eleanor focused on what she perceived as a valid means of protection in case "something God awful happens." In this focus group, body armor was, with some caveats, one option within a broader self-defense repertoire that also included gun ownership and firearms proficiency.

While bulletproof products are meant to protect from attacks by gunfire, when asked about gun violence as a security concern, the discussion was more circumscribed: It centered on gangs, drugs, and criminal activity. In fact, rather than a merely descriptive term, "gun violence" had negative emotional connotations for Eleanor. She explained:

> [T]he phrase gun violence has always irritated me quite a bit. Because when we hear the word 'gun violence,' the word 'gun' is in 72-font, and the word 'violence' is in like 4. So it's really violence in general [. . .] regardless of the tool that's being used.

In this group, the proliferation of guns did not seem to be an issue, and when the use of guns was deemed problematic, it was associated with people already engaged in deviant or criminal activity. Roger advocated for "just better behavior. Don't get involved with gangs. Don't get involved with violent underworld activity, and that solves much of it." Differing from gun violence prevention advocates—who situated gun violence in the context of poverty, racism, and "systemic oppression"—Roger's framing of the problem was more individualistic, and so was the solution. From his perspective, law-abiding citizens need to have "situational awareness" and avoid or take precautions in "high-crime areas." They are also entitled to own a gun for self-defense, and in Eleanor's terms, "why not" bulletproof fashion.

Law Enforcement Officers: Considering the Intent and Context of Body Armor Use

Bulletproof garments have been primarily associated with military, police, and security forces. A common assumption is that members of these forces need this protection due to the risks associated with their jobs. The everyday use of body armor by civilians is more controversial. Within the law enforcement officers focus group, the reaction to civilian bulletproof garments was somewhat ambivalent. Their perspectives combined acceptance of the products, caveats about the context in which the garments should or should not be used, and indirect references to the social conditions that spark interest in body armor.

Within this group, Rosalie—a police officer in a large city—spoke in detail about ballistic products, reflecting on her own use of body armor for her job as well as the role that bulletproof garments may play in the lives of other people. She had a generally accepting attitude about these products but noted that one should have a specific reason to use them,

> based upon where you work and the type of environment that you're surrounded with, teachers, the medical profession, especially anybody working in emergency rooms and those kinds of situations. You never know what's coming through the door. [. . .] And we have to move along with what time is showing us. And I personally, even though my children are grown, I'm not adverse to the idea of children having some type of bulletproof thing done to their clothing, their outer clothing, their backpacks, especially when we're also teaching them about sheltering in place and going through all of those types of drills that now has to become, unfortunately, part of their training in school, in school with other kids. And in the emergency rooms, definitely.

Rosalie lamented the exposure of children to active shooter drills but accepted them from a pragmatic perspective. Her willingness to entertain bulletproof garments as a valid approach goes hand in hand with the normalization of active shooter drills. Phillip, from a rural area, also commented on such trainings at school before the pandemic. He noted that the active shooter issue was "hot and cold" but remarked: "I believe the active shooter is usually in communities like the one I live in, where it's a little bit quieter, and you don't expect it." As these law enforcement officers noted, active shooter drills have been incorporated in the lives of children in diverse types of communities and educational establishments, so armoring children is sometimes perceived as a logical next step. In Rosalie's account, for example, bulletproof fashion might be considered an addition to that repertoire of security measures.

Other police officers in the group, including those who have school-aged children, grappled with the meaning of these garments for kids. As mentioned before, Walter felt it would add to the fear and anxiety that his kids were already experiencing amid the pandemic, and Arthur rejected them partly on practical grounds, like children rapidly outgrowing costly garments. However, moving into the realm of emotions, Arthur also offered the following considerations:

> I have some mixed feelings with stuff like that, although I feel that if you feel that it's necessary, it's great that somebody makes those products. But then there's the other side of me that says, no one should live in that much fear. And, you know, and so, yeah, we can protect ourselves against gun shots, but, actually, it's probably more likely that we would get killed in a car accident. So what do we wear to protect ourselves from that?

Companies would respond that as we wear seatbelts to guard against car accidents, we should also seriously consider bulletproof garments.[32] And yet, Arthur's comments point to a deeper issue, with emotions at its center, when he says that "no one should live in that much fear." Indirectly, the question that might follow is why people are living in fear and what can be done to address the events that cause that fear in the first place. Brandon, who did not "feel one way or another on this topic" (bulletproof garments), observed that "it speaks more to the kind of climate that we live into where we got to have a discussion about whether we should send kids to school with bulletproof garments and backpacks." He still estimated that "it's better to be prepared for something that may happen than need it and not have it."

As members of law enforcement, participants also discussed the use of bulletproof garments by people not connected to security-related jobs. Here, the underlying question was whether such usage potentially represented danger. Let us remember that the issue arose in other focus groups, for instance, when Maya, a social justice and anti-racist organizer, talked about how such activists are likely to be perceived as possessing violent intent when wearing a ballistic vest. Donna, from the group of gun violence prevention advocates, alluded to the aggressive stance of right-wing vigilantes fitted with body armor and other militarized attire. And in the group of gun rights supporters, Eric implicitly responded to the presumption of dangerousness when he concluded that body armor "does not make a person dangerous." He based this view on the presumed likelihood of experiencing some sort of injury even if wearing body armor while being shot at.

Members of the law enforcement group weighed different situations regarding the potential dangerousness of people in body armor. For Rosalie, one indicator was the purpose of its use. She thought that bulletproof clothing should be linked to specific occupations and spaces that raise legitimate concerns about the risk of gun violence: "[I]t should not be something that you can just go in and buy. What is your purpose? What's in the purview of your job?" Rosalie also commented that she does not bring her bulletproof vest or gun home, suggesting that she strictly associated these objects with the risks her occupation entails. Since she only wears her vest while on the job, she expected that if "you're wearing your vest, you must be on too."

Brandon pondered other situations in which people might wear a bulletproof vest, not linked to particular jobs, and considered what kinds of body armor usage might indicate potential danger:

> For me, I think it would be what circumstances they were wearing the clothing. I mean, if we're talking about schools where kids are wearing bulletproof vests underneath their garments or kids with bulletproof backpacks, I don't think that would give me a second thought. But now if I'm working a protest where I have a bunch of people wearing tac[tical] vests and carrying long guns, I think it would definitely raise my suspicion, and it would definitely make me think twice about things and where I am and my officer safety and for the safety of the people who were there.

Here, factors such as age, social space, and the presence or not of guns shape perceptions of danger: School children are considered likely to be harmless, and overtly militarized protesters are perceived as potentially dangerous. Arthur additionally commented on his preparation to deal with someone in body armor:

> If somebody is wearing a vest and it's like covert, I don't know that we would even think twice about it [. . .] but I know that as a police officer, as a firearms instructor, when we go to the range and we train, we specifically do drills to how are we going to deal with someone who potentially could be wearing body armor. [. . .] I feel like if I confront that—because I have to because of my job—I'm probably just going to revert to my training and just deal with it in that manner.

Arthur did not describe the procedure—what exactly he was prepared to do—but conveyed confidence in his ability to deal with the situation based on his training. Overall, this group did not seem too concerned about other people wearing body armor, though when asked to reflect on this matter from the perspective of law enforcement, they did consider scenarios in which the use of bulletproof garments might be illegitimate or indicate potential danger. In fact, the conversation about bulletproof products apparently took some participants into uncharted terrain. For example, the existence of bulletproof backpacks for children was news for Walter; and Arthur mentioned, "I don't know if I would ever even think about like, what if I saw somebody wearing a bulletproof vest just walking around?"

Interestingly, a few weeks before this focus group, a bill had been introduced in the New York State legislature to ban the possession or purchase of "body vests" (certain types of bullet-resistant vests) by people other than law enforcement officers or those in occupations that require such gear according to the Department of State.[33] While the bill did not progress into law at that point, its presentation suggests that some people, including legislators, were troubled by the ready availability of body armor and how it might be used for purposes other than legitimate self-defense. Yet, at least for this group of law enforcement officers, the issue did not stir strong reactions though Rosalie offered some caveats about the conditions of use.

After the mass shooting in Buffalo, New York, in May 2022, the public debate on body armor was reignited. Among other voices, Buffalo Police Commissioner, Joseph Gramaglia, explained in a public hearing that the shooter had "legally purchased a military-style weapon and body armor," which gave him an advantage even over security personnel at the site.[34] In a media interview, Gramaglia mentioned that the officer "engaged the shooter; he got off numerous shots, and one of those shots hit the tactical armor that the shooter was wearing. That would've ended it and it didn't" partly due to the immunity offered by the body armor.[35] Asked whether he supported policies to restrict body armor for civilians, this Police Commissioner agreed.[36] Ultimately, the gun laws enacted in New York during the summer of 2022 included restrictions on body armor for the general population, while still allowing it for certain professionals, such as police and federal law enforcement officers.[37]

Conclusion

In stakeholders' narratives about bulletproof apparel, one can trace the influence of social, ideological, and political factors as well as the role that emotions play in security concerns. Conversations about bulletproof fashion offer a window into security-related assumptions, experiences, and emotions. The issue is not just what people *think* about different security risks or strategies but what makes them *feel* safe or afraid, what gives them peace of mind or aggravates their worries about their own safety and their loved ones'. How do they feel about fortressing the body, fitting children in ballistic backpacks, going to work in armor, or encountering demonstrators in bulletproof vests? How does it feel to live in a society in which many people experience "that much fear"? Attending to the emotional components of attitudes about bulletproof products helps us to further understand different security cultures and contexts in which these products find a place.

The various viewpoints and feelings about bulletproof fashion were often about more than the products per se. They point to deeper ideological divides and distinct "common sense" assumptions. Feelings of confusion, sadness, anger, disappointment, or excitement offer a glimpse into these differential stances and social worlds. A nurse is disgusted by bulletproof fashion and bewildered by people who feel the need to carry their guns everywhere. A firearms instructor expresses positive emotions regarding ballistic products and is disturbed by policy proposals to restrict them. A gun violence prevention advocate is sad about the existence of bulletproof garments and instead wants to tackle the systemic oppression she sees at the root of gun violence. A gun rights supporter assesses bulletproof fashion in pragmatic terms and refers to gun violence primarily as a matter of poor personal choices and behavior. And an activist in an organization addressing police violence finds the ballistic products for civilians infuriating and a sign of a failed system.

Some participants tried to put themselves in the shoes of those who have different experiences and perspectives about security-oriented products. For instance, a teacher expressed empathy for parents who may want those products for their children, even if she herself does not feel it is a solution; a member of an organization addressing sexual/gender violence did not try to discourage her clients from using security technologies she strongly rejects; and a nurse who would like to see deeper responses to security issues still understood, emotionally and intellectually, why other nurses sought body armor. As stakeholders' conversations indicate, body armor may find a home among people across ideological and political divides.

Beyond considerations about the effectiveness or concrete uses of bulletproof garments, different types of commentary show how these objects are bestowed with emotional power. As we have seen, varied emotional responses appear not only in the stakeholder focus groups but also in customers' reviews discussed in earlier chapters. For some people, a bulletproof garment represents peace of mind, functioning as a comfort object, a security blanket of sorts. For some critics, it embodies the fear and trauma of mass shootings, and might itself be traumatizing. Sadness may also be attached to the product, symbolizing the pain of an unequal and unsafe world. For others, it is a lightning rod for indignation and disappointment about societal and state failures to address gun violence more deeply. And in some political contexts, a bulletproof vest may be associated with emotions such as pride, defiance, anger, and/or fear.

Catastrophic events that affect large swaths of the population, albeit in distinct ways, can provide a common reference point, operating as an *interpretative force* in the sense of strongly shaping frames of meaning. A war, an environmental disaster, a widespread economic crisis, or a pandemic can function in this manner. In the context of this study, the global COVID-19 pandemic worked as an interpretative force that shaped and inflected perspectives on security, including on bulletproof fashion. As shown earlier, different stakeholders—for example, a police officer, a mother of a school-age child, a gun rights supporter—drew on the pandemic experience to substantiate or illustrate their perspectives about bulletproof garments. In making sense of these products and weighing the pros and cons, the fears, difficulties, and practices associated with the pandemic were brought into relief. These connections are not surprising if we view the pandemic as a multifaceted emotional phenomenon and one at the center of multiple crises of insecurity, broadly conceived. Such experience might prompt us to consider: What does security mean to us? What matters in that regard? In considering these questions, it is important to keep in mind that security-oriented objects, as is the case with other artifacts, might be more than just things or tools that we use and control. Objects populate our worlds and can take on almost agentic qualities, affecting our perception, reflecting our yearnings, mediating our relationships, and influencing our emotions in powerful ways.

Notes

1 David Voas, "Towards a Sociology of Attitudes," *Sociological Research Online* 19, no. 1 (2014): 132–44.
2 Arlie Russell Hochschild, "Emotion Work, Feeling Rules, and Social Structure," *American Journal of Sociology* 85, no. 3 (1979): 551–75; Arlie Russell Hochschild, *The Managed Heart: Commercialization of Human Feeling*, 20th anniversary ed. (Berkeley: University of California Press, 2003); Kari Marie Norgaard, "People Want to Protect Themselves a Little Bit: Emotions, Denial, and Social Movement Nonparticipation," *Sociological Inquiry* 76 (2006): 372–96; James M. Jasper, *The Emotions of Protest* (Chicago: University of Chicago Press, 2018).
3 Jasper, *The Emotions of Protest*, 7.
4 See, for example, Neta C. Crawford, "The Passion of World Politics: Propositions on Emotion and Emotional Relationships," *International Security* 24, no. 4 (2000): 116–56; Helena Flam, "Emotions' Map: A Research Agenda," pp. 19–40 in *Emotions and Social Movements*, eds. Helena Flam and Debra King (London and New York: Routledge).
5 Ann Cvetkovich, "Public Feelings," *South Atlantic Quarterly* 106, no. 3 (2007): 459–68.
6 Conversely, participants in the mothers focus groups also had other identities and experiences besides being parents but responded to the call to join the focus group as parents of school-aged children.
7 Sara Ahmed, *The Cultural Politics of Emotion* (Edinburgh: Edinburgh University Press, 2014), 8.
8 See, for example, Linda L. Dahlberg, Robin M. Ikeda, and Marcie-Jo Kresnow, "Guns in the Home and Risk of a Violent Death in the Home: Findings from a National

Study," *American Journal of Epidemiology* 160, no. 10 (2004): 929–36; Andrew Anglemyer, Tara Horvath, and George Rutherford, "The Accessibility of Firearms and Risk for Suicide and Homicide Victimization among Household Members: A Systematic Review and Meta-Analysis," *Annals of Internal Medicine* 160, no. 2 (2014): 101–10.

9 D. Asher Ghertner, Hudson McFann, and Daniel Goldstein, "Security Aesthetics of and beyond the Biopolitical," pp. 1–32 in *Futureproof: Security Aesthetics and the Management of Life*, eds. D. Asher Ghertner, Hudson McFann, and Daniel Goldstein (Durham: Duke University Press, 2020).

10 See the work of Carlson on women and guns, particularly in relation to self-defense: Jennifer D. Carlson, "From Gun Politics to Self-Defense Politics: A Feminist Critique of the Great Gun Debate," *Violence against Women* 20, no. 3 (2014): 369–77.

11 Aaron J. Kivisto, Lauren A. Magee, Peter L. Phalen, and Bradley R. Ray, "Firearm Ownership and Domestic Versus Nondomestic Homicide in the U.S.," *American Journal of Preventive Medicine* 57, no. 3 (2019): 311–20, 319.

12 Tim Walker, "Unannounced Active Shooter Drills Scaring Students without Making Them Safer," *National Education Association*, February 25, 2020, www.nea.org/advocating-for-change/new-from-nea/unannounced-active-shooter-drills-scaring-students-without.

13 David Yamane, "The Sociology of U.S. Gun Culture," *Sociological Compass* 11, no. 7 (2017), https://doi.org/10.1111/soc4.12497.

14 Olivia Fleming, "Wall Your Body: Bulletproof Clothing and Anti-Rape Wear," project presented at the National Conference of Undergraduate Research, University of Central Oklahoma, April 4–7, 2018.

15 Alison J. Marganski, "Making a Murderer: The Importance of Gender and Violence against Women in Mass Murder Events," *Sociology Compass* 13, no. 9 (2019): e12730.

16 The curtains used in prison facilities may be understood in the context of implementation of broader governmental efforts to address the problem of sexual violence in prison, including through the Prison Rape Elimination Act (PREA) enacted by Congress in 2003 (for more information on PREA, see the National PREA Resource Center website: www.prearesourcecenter.org/). Curtain businesses such as Gary Manufacturing mention PREA specifically (Gary Manufacturing, "PREA: Shower Curtains for Compliance and Prevention," accessed November 28, 2021, www.garymanufacturing.com/prea-shower-curtains-for-compliance-and-prevention/), and among the Corcraft products featured in the New York State government website is the "PREA shower curtain" (Corcraft, "Apparel & Textiles," accessed November 28, 2021, https://corcraft.ny.gov/apparel-textiles). See also New York State guidelines specifying the use of Corcraft PREA curtains: Corrections and Community Supervision, "Guidelines for Assignment of Male and Female Corrections Officers," February 21, 2019, https://doccs.ny.gov/system/files/documents/2021/09/2230.pdf.

17 Rosanna Smart and Terry L. Schell, "Mass Shootings in the United States," *RAND Corporation*, Updated April 15, 2021, www.rand.org/research/gun-policy/analysis/essays/mass-shootings.html.

18 "Ten Years of School Shootings," *Cable News Network (CNN)*, 2019, www.cnn.com/interactive/2019/07/us/ten-years-of-school-shootings-trnd/. Also, in an analysis of incidents of gunfire in schools from 2013 to 2019, Everytown for Gun Safety, AFT, and NEA report that "among the 335 shooting incidents at K-12 schools where the racial demographic information of the student body was known, 64 percent occurred in majority-minority schools" (13), that is, they happened "in schools in which one or more racial and/or ethnic minorities comprise a majority of the student population (relative to the US population)" (31). The report also observes that Black students are disproportionately affected. See, Everytown for Gun Safety, American Federation of Teachers (AFT), and the National Education Association (NEA), "Keeping our Schools Safe: A Plan for Preventing Mass Shootings and Ending All Gun Violence in American Schools," 2020, https://everytownresearch.org/wp-content/uploads/sites/4/2020/05/WEB-School-Safety-021120A.pdf.

19 See, for example, Audre Lorde, "The Uses of Anger," *Women's Studies Quarterly* 25, no. 1/2 (1997 [1981]): 278–85; Ahmed, *The Cultural Politics of Emotion*; Eduardo Bonilla-Silva, "Feeling Race: Theorizing the Racial Economy of Emotions," *American Sociological Review* 84, no. 1 (2019): 1–25.
20 MAGA, the acronym for Make America Great Again, is a slogan popularized by Donald Trump in the context of his electoral presidential campaigns. While not making any mention of race, MAGA has been interpreted by critics as a coded assertion of white nationalism or white supremacy, and studies have shown the crucial role that race has played in enlisting Trump supporter's allegiance. See, for example, Amanda Graham, Francis T. Cullen, Leah C. Butler, Alexander L. Burton, and Velmer S. Burton, "Who Wears the MAGA Hat? Racial Beliefs and Faith in Trump," *Socius: Sociological Research for a Dynamic World*, 2021, https://doi.org/10.1177/2378023121992600.
21 Robyn Thomas, "Armed Protesters Inspire Fear, Chill Free Speech," January 28, 2021, https://giffords.org/lawcenter/report/armed-protesters-inspire-fear-chill-free-speech/.
22 These trainings aim to account for the additional complexities that health care settings present, including in relation to patient care and infrastructure. See Heather Stringer, "Hospital Shooting Rates Bump Up Need for Active Shooter Drills," accessed November 28, 2021, https://resources.nurse.com/hospital-shooting-rates-active-shooter-drills; Charles Denham II, Gregory Botz, Charles Denham III, and William Adcox, "Effectively Responding to Active Shooters in Healthcare Facilities," *Campus Safety* 27, no. 1 (2019): 18–21, www.utph.org/dA/51dd5b938b/Campus%20Safety_Active%20Shooter%20in%20Healthcare%20Facilities%20(revised).pdf?language_id=1.
23 Jeffrey W. Swanson, E. Elizabeth McGinty, Seena Fazel, and Vickie M. Mays, "Mental Illness and Reduction of Gun Violence and Suicide: Bringing Epidemiologic Research to Policy," *Annals of Epidemiology* 25, no. 5 (2015): 366–76.
24 Rachel Wamser-Nanney, "Understanding Gun Violence: Factors Associated with Beliefs Regarding Guns, Gun Policies, and Gun Violence," *Psychology of Violence* 11 (2021): 349–53, 352.
25 2020 Mom et al., "Statement on Gun Violence Crisis from 60 National Organizations," June 6, 2022, www.aacap.org/aacap/zLatest_News/Statement_Gun_Violence_Crisis_from_60_National_Organizations.aspx; Nidhi Subbaraman, "United States to Fund Gun-Violence Research after 20-year Freeze," *Nature* 577, no. 12 (2019), https://doi.org/10.1038/d41586-019-03882-w; Kirsten Weir, "A Thaw in the Freeze on Federal Funding for Gun Violence and Injury Prevention Research," *American Psychological Association* 52, no. 3 (2021), www.apa.org/monitor/2021/04/news-funding-gun-research.
26 For a review of the areas addressed by "Gun Studies" in the United States, see Jennifer Carlson, "Gun Studies and the Politics of Evidence," *Annual Review of Law and Social Science* 16, no. 1 (2020): 183–202.
27 For a review of the different types of research and intervention to curve gun violence, see Carlson, "Gun Studies and the Politics of Evidence."
28 For example, in this study, it was not just gun rights supporters who supported the right to bear arms. Donna (a gun violence prevention advocate) and Maya (an activist denouncing police violence) also mentioned their support for Second Amendment rights. Roxanne Dunbar-Ortiz's history of the Second Amendment reveals nuances as well; the author herself became a gun owner and a proficient shooter but also advanced a critique of the historical underpinnings of the Second Amendment and the contemporary politics that surround it. See Dunbar-Ortiz, *Loaded: A Disarming History of the Second Amendment* (San Francisco: City Lights Books, 2018).
29 Gallup, "Guns," accessed October 3, 2021. https://news.gallup.com/poll/1645/guns.aspx.
30 This stance is typical of some of the shifts in gun culture, from an emphasis on hunting and recreation to the view of guns as essential to self-defense. See Carlson, "Gun Studies and the Politics of Evidence" and David Yamane, "The Sociology of U.S. Gun Culture," *Sociological Compass* 11, no. 7 (2017), https://doi.org/10.1111/soc4.12497.

31 From the description, Eleanor was likely referring to New York State Assembly Bill No. A352, "An Act to Amend the Penal law, in Relation to the Unlawful Purchase or Possession of a Body Vest," 2021–2022 Regular Sessions.
32 See, for example, "About Us," *Bac-Tactical*, accessed November 28, 2021, https://bac-tactical.com/about-us/.
33 See New York State Assembly Bill No. A352, "An Act to Amend the Penal Law, in Relation to the Unlawful Purchase or Possession of a Body Vest," 2021–2022 Regular Sessions. Information about the bill can be found on the NYS Senate website (www.nysenate.gov/legislation/bills/2021/a352) and the NYS Assembly website (https://assembly.state.ny.us/leg/?default_fld=&leg_video=&bn=A00352&term=2021&Summary=Y&Actions=Y&Committee%26nbspVotes=Y&Floor%26nbspVotes=Y&Memo=Y&Text=Y&LFIN=Y&Chamber%26nbspVideo%2FTranscript=Y).
34 "N.Y. Police Commissioner Calls for Tougher Gun Laws at Hearing," Video, June 9, 2022, www.officer.com/command-hq/video/21270555/ny-police-commissioner-calls-for-tougher-gun-laws-at-hearing.
35 "Role of Body Armor Scrutinized in Mass Shooting Debate," *ABC News*, Video, June 16, 2022, www.youtube.com/watch?v=70WglzuglIU&t=1s
36 See Mary Alice Parks, Patty See, and Nathan Luna, "Buffalo Shooting Renews Calls for Body Armor Regulation," *ABC News*, June 17, 2022, https://abcnews.go.com/US/buffalo-shooting-renews-calls-body-armor-regulation/story?id=85437343.
37 See "Body Armor," New York State Department of State, accessed September 1, 2022 https://dos.ny.gov/body-armor#:~:text=Effective%20July%206%2C%202022%2C%20when,of%20body%20armor%20is%20prohibited

CONCLUSION

From the outset, *Bulletproof Fashion* emerged as a narrow and broad project at the same time. I examined the specific topic of ballistic apparel through a wide lens: security. Given my focus on the United States, it was important to consider the shape that security takes in that context, including the convergence of the following factors: the idiosyncratic place of guns in U.S. society; culturally valorized notions of personal responsibility and self-sufficiency; ingrained consumer cultures pointing to the market for solutions to social problems; and the incorporation of militarized logics, technologies, and values into civilian life. Within that frame, I identified bulletproof fashion as a niche market that nevertheless embodies broader trends of neoliberal securitization. As this book shows, paying attention to this specific "security solution" helps illuminate more than the particularities of an apparel of choice; it sheds light on wider social processes involving subjectivities, emotions, bodies, power, politics, and inequality. From that perspective, this study encourages us to think about how we define security, what the implications of different approaches to security are, what the limitations of technological and market-based responses are, and how non-state actors such as private businesses intervene in the security field. This work also demonstrates that rather than an area characterized solely by rational considerations, security is steeped in emotions, including but not limited to fear. Finally, security needs to be understood in relation to social differences and inequalities, which influence experiences, perceptions, and discourses of security.

During the period of the study, amid widespread social suffering associated with the COVID-19 pandemic, the inequalities that pervade U.S. society were thrown into stark relief. Social disparities became visible and tangible in their cruelty; implicated in the loss of lives and livelihoods, health risks and food insecurity, and domestic and state violence, among other indicators. The pandemic hit members of marginalized groups and communities the hardest, even though most people have been affected in one way or another. As mass deaths followed the disease, it became more necessary to think about security in terms other than war preparation, fortified borders, militarized police forces, and outsized military budgets. Also, around the initial stages of my research in 2020, widespread Black Lives Matter demonstrations and denunciations of police brutality challenged assumptions about the police as guarantors of security. Whereas this time of social dislocation and collective upheaval revealed myriad forms of solidarity and mutual aid, it also resulted in individualized security responses, including those reliant on gun purchases and firearm trainings. These trends indicate that fear and distrust of the "other" were part of the emotional climate that characterized the period, exacerbated by a charged and contentious electoral season (culminating in the attack on the U.S. Capitol by Trump supporters on January 6, 2021).

The discourse in some of the bulletproof apparel websites echoed an ominous outlook on society, implicitly or explicitly suggesting that people may turn against each other amid chaos, and therefore body armor was a necessity. It required preparing for "a fight for survival," as a Bulletproof Zone blog post put it.[1] The context of crisis surely facilitated this type of rhetoric, but the mobilization of fear and anxiety through the marketing of consumer products is not new, and it is not limited to security-oriented apparel. According to sociologist Zygmunt Bauman, "[u]ncertainty-generated anxiety is the very substance that makes the individualized society fertile for consumerist purposes [. . . .] More often than not, production of consumers means the production of 'new and improved' fears."[2] The social and political milieu at the time of this study was certainly ripe for feelings of fear and vulnerability, and to those especially attuned to the view of "the world as a dangerous place,"[3] the idea of fortressing the body with arms, or perhaps armor, could find resonance.

This book shows how bulletproof fashion companies, as non-state actors, have promoted notions of security reliant on the construction of a fortress body. This type of response is inscribed within wider perceptions about the seeming inability of the state to protect its citizens. In the United States, many people have decried how political leaders failed time and again to enact gun safety measures that could have helped prevent unnecessary bloodshed. Other critics point to the state as a perpetrator of illegitimate violence, particularly against communities of color, through its repressive apparatus. Among gun owners, there are those who do not wish to wait for law enforcement to protect them, as it might be too late.[4] For ideological and/or pragmatic reasons, groups and individuals may take security matters into their own hands, and the market is there to sell the required gear. Bulletproof apparel companies seek to fill a vacuum of sorts, promising to deliver physical protection and peace of mind. In this way, they appear almost as public servants, partners with security solutions, offering products for not only wealthy adults but also children, teachers, and health care workers, among others. In company messaging and media reporting, bulletproof fashion is often presented in the context of mass shootings and other security threats. In line with neoliberal logic, the state is implicitly rendered inefficient and ineffective, and the market emerges as a vital option to those yearning for security. The market devolves a collective problem to private individuals who, as consumers, have the choice, or even the responsibility, to mind for their own protection and the security of their loved ones.

Fitting within the framework of consumer societies, the protection that the bulletproof apparel industry offers is actually available to those who can pay. Even if there were agreement about the benefits of bulletproof fashion, it is not accessible to large swaths of the population. Also, one may wonder to what extent individual consumer solutions detract from more expansive and transformative approaches. In his critique of consumer culture, Zygmunt Bauman argued:

> To become a consumer means to be dependent for one's survival, even for keeping up simple daily routines, on the consumer market. It means to forget or fail to learn the skills of coping with life challenges, except the skill of seeking (and, hopefully, finding) the right object, service or counsel among the marketed commodities.[5]

In addition to these limitations, there are ethical and political implications embedded in market-based solutions. In *Shopping Our Way to Safety*, sociologist Andrew Szasz challenged the wisdom of consumer strategies aimed at protecting against environmental hazards.[6] His critique was based not only on the exclusionary dimensions or futility of some of these individual practices but also on how they may lessen the impetus to participate in collective strategies to prevent or solve the problems identified. Analogous considerations apply to bulletproof fashion in relation to the social problem of gun violence. For instance, parents may strap their school-aged children into military-grade backpacks, but would they care to address the underlying factors that enable school shootings in the first place, or the threat of gun violence to children in other social settings? Bulletproof fashion may give a false sense of security to individuals who adopt it, while leaving the underlying problem intact.

This study also raises questions about the ambivalent dimensions of technological solutions, in this case, body armor as a technology long used by military and security forces and that percolated into civilian spaces. In addition to the disturbing aspects that the dystopian notion of an armored society presents, some of the perspectives and information shared in this book prompt us to consider how body armor itself might entail security risks, echoing the often-ambiguous effects of other security-oriented technologies. Similar to how permissive access to military-style firearms by civilians has facilitated their use in mass shootings, body armor can also be deployed for destructive purposes, by providing an extra shield and increased sense of invulnerability to perpetrators of gun violence. While companies highlight the defensive qualities of body armor technologies, this type of gear can also be part of an apparatus of violence and aggression. Still, in the case of bulletproof apparel and accessories—which unlike guns are not inherently designed to injure or kill—their regulation through bans can be controversial. Whereas body armor is sometimes part of "tactical" gear, with guns included, many of the garments that companies advertise cannot be used for harmful purposes unless complemented by weapons.

Furthermore, the appearance of bulletproof apparel matters, too. The ballistic gear that raises particular alarm is the type that resembles, not only in function but in form, the garments used by military or police forces. The concern is that such overt body armor can become part of the "spectacle" of a mass shooting.[7] Civilian garments that do not emulate a militarized "look" allow companies to stress the defensive nature of the products more easily. In so doing, they highlight not only the protective qualities of ballistic technologies but also aesthetics, fashion, and style linked to varied groups and identities. Fashionable and inconspicuous bulletproof apparel offers civilians the opportunity to blend in, to pursue a variety of "normal" activities while supposedly protected against random or targeted shootings. The form of the product—the design, color patterns, resemblance to other fashionable apparel—is also a mechanism through which particular emotions "stick" to the objects, to borrow from Sara Ahmed's conceptualization.[8] Feeling adventurous, good-looking, or sexy can be part of the repertoire of the "fashion of fear" that civilian bulletproof apparel represents. Yet fashionable and normal-looking design might not be enough to tame the dissonances filtering through the interstices of companies' messaging (even among the reviews of satisfied customers). Crayons and ballistics, leisure and threat, sexuality and mourning, play and death: These dissimilar elements come together in uneasy tension in some visual and textual discourses about bulletproof products.

In combining security and fashion, bulletproof apparel embodies the concerns and aesthetic trends of a society that has not been able to resolve the problem of gun violence, and in which many people favor individualized strategies of security. This is evident, for instance, in attitudes about self-defense with guns and relatively high rates of gun ownership. As other forms of apparel—interpreted as "social skin"[9]—bulletproof fashion is about more than individual expression and preferences. It is one way in which the social milieu becomes imprinted on the body. This social inscription can be deep: Clothing and accessories do not just shape the contours or surface of our bodies; they can also affect bodily movement, gesture, feelings, and relationships. The fortress body, whether armed or armored, can be thought of in relation to its effects at the level of individuals, and in terms of its social dimensions, including the normalization of an armed society. As we have also seen, the various representations of body armor for civilians reflect and reproduce a number of societal hierarchies and differences, such as those based on class, gender, race-ethnicity, and sexuality. Far from selling a uniform type of body armor, companies offer a variety of product designs catering to different social groups and appealing to their perceived interests, concerns, desires, and lifestyles. Though not economically accessible to many people, the proliferation of designs and products still conveys the "normalcy" of fitting everyone, from children to adults, in bulletproof gear.

While the reviews and testimonials of people who purportedly bought the products are often laudatory (not surprisingly given their publication on company websites), they also provide a clue about the motivations, emotions, and experiences surrounding bulletproof products. In such comments, we can find love, care, sadness, trauma, gratitude, enthusiasm, and aesthetic appreciation, in addition to fear, worry, and a desire for protection. The "fashion of fear," it turns out, is more complex than what first meets the eye. Stakeholder focus groups also yielded important insights; in this case, from potential consumers who connected with the topic of security in specific ways. Indeed, the social roles and occupations of different focus group participants influenced their attunement to various kinds of security matters and concerns. Such perspectives can vary whether one is a gun enthusiast, police officer, gun violence prevention advocate, teacher, parent, health care worker, anti-gender violence advocate, or social justice activist hoping to end police violence. Of course, these experiences are not uniform even within groups but shaped by broader social identities, political and ideological orientations, and systems of social inequality.

Focus group discussions about security and bulletproof fashion revealed a variety of emotions and perspectives. While the specific groups' composition may have lent itself to particularly critical views of bulletproof fashion, there are still nuances within and across groups. For example, though grounded in distinct reasons and analyses, a gun rights supporter and a social justice activist may both see some value in civilian use of body armor, or gun ownership for that matter. A police officer may be particularly attuned to security in relation to crime but may also think about security as connected to "job security." Participants elaborated on various dimensions of security that both resonated with their particular experiences and also reflected the broader social and political processes that were unfolding. Thus, they talked about security in the context of the pandemic, policing, protest, and social unrest, as well as in relation to violence in the home, neighborhoods, education sites, health care facilities, and the political sphere. The pandemic operated as a significant interpretative force, as participants in the different groups talked about security, including bulletproof fashion, enmeshed with reflections about life in pandemic times.

These multiple sites of violence and insecurity connect with central questions posed in this study, particularly regarding the meanings of security and how such notions overlap or differ from what we learn through mainstream media and state discourses and priorities. What are the greatest threats to our lives, bodies, and well-being? What does security mean to each of us in our daily experiences? To speak of a "we" can be misleading, for the conditions associated with security and vulnerability vary widely for individuals and social groups, and are marked by social inequalities and power differentials. Yet as members of a political society, it is valid to ask: Do we need more guns, ever more powerful weapons, and all manner of armor to lead lives free from violence and bodily harm? What kinds of worlds might different notions and strategies of security prefigure? Some of these worlds may be considered dystopian—though perhaps as dystopian as already existing worlds of war, gun violence, state repression, and myriad traumatizing collective experiences. Whereas these events are sometimes framed as exceptional occurrences, for many people they are familiar and ongoing situations, though not necessarily accepted as "normal" life.

Among concerned citizens, activists, and political leaders, there are those who advocate for strategies aimed at preventing and uprooting multiple forms of armed violence. These approaches sometimes include measures that seek to reduce arms proliferation, whether at the macro level of nations and/or the smaller scale of communities. Others seem to double down on securitization, promoting an increasingly armed society and supporting the development of more fortresses and fences as the route to security. Under the latter frame, body armor for civilians might appear as a logical and appropriate solution. Even so, imagining a world in which everyone goes about their daily lives in body armor may prompt thorny questions about how a society gets to that point and whether it is the kind of society one would want to live in. If not, what might it take to dismantle the social forces and arrangements that fostered such an outcome? Tackling the problem of gun violence is but the tip of the iceberg.

During the summer of 2022—in large part as a response to the mass shootings in a grocery store in Buffalo, New York, and in an elementary school in Uvalde, Texas—Congress passed the "Bipartisan Safer Communities Act" with a set of measures aimed at reducing gun violence (President Biden signed it into law on June 25, 2022). These initiatives include support for community-based violence intervention programs, strengthened background checks for gun purchasers under 21, resources for mental health services, funding for school safety programs, measures targeting the illegal firearms trade, and the inclusion of dating partners among domestic violence perpetrators who could face gun-related restrictions. While not as far reaching as some proponents wished for, this legislation was hailed as breaking a stalemate of decades and giving a measure of response to sustained efforts by gun violence prevention advocates.[10] Heeding the public call to "do something," President Biden also took executive actions to mitigate the problem of gun violence through a variety of initiatives, including those dealing with the "proliferation of ghost guns," "firearms trafficking corridors," "firearms dealers' statutory obligations," "community violence," and various programs directed at youth education and workforce training, and to survivors of domestic violence, among others.[11] However, on June 23, 2022, the Supreme Court of the United States issued a majority ruling in the *New York State Rifle & Pistol Association v. Bruen* case that struck down New York State's requirement to show "proper cause" as a condition for obtaining a license to carry a concealed gun in public. The National Rifle Association (NRA) applauded the Court's decision, considering it a "monumental win for NRA members and for gun owners across the country," as the ruling could prompt changes not only in New York but in other states with similar provisions.[12] New York Governor Kathy Hochul, in turn, signed a number of gun safety measures as a response to the Buffalo mass shooting and, later on, to the Supreme Court's ruling.[13] New restrictions on concealed carry in "sensitive" places were issued, and body armor too was further restricted in the state of New York. These various responses hint at the contested terrain of efforts to address gun violence and regulate gun rights, and the different ideas about security that are at play.

Bulletproof Fashion has explored various perspectives on security, guns, and body armor, while also being informed by holistic notions of human security. This multifaceted approach challenges societal and governmental impulses to militarize and accumulate weapons. Indeed, when thinking about security in the broad and interrelated terms of human security, it brings attention to potential harms against body and life that cannot be addressed with the proliferation of guns or by "forting up" the body. Policy planners, activists, and scholars critical of militarized approaches have developed visions of security that emphasize the obligation of the state to ensure the everyday security of persons and communities through means other than weapons or fences. Some highlight how threats to everyday security—for example, food scarcity or environmental degradation—can breed tension and conflict, and are themselves a threat to security broadly defined. At the same time, others note that such problems have also given way to solidarity and to envisioning new ways of living that are more equitable and sustainable. Some have turned to community and mutual aid, rather than the state, seeing it as a hopelessly violent institution.

The analysis in this book interrogates security approaches based on arming and armoring the body, and instead calls for governmental and societal action that addresses the root causes of violence and insecurity in comprehensive ways and with attention to social justice. It also calls to imagine what cultures of peace might look like, not only in the world stage but in our communities and homes. The Gender and Human Security Network—an international group of women who came together for the Hague Appeal for Peace conference in 1999—engaged in such visioning:

> A culture of peace means we are respected and heard; we have education, health care, and a dependable source of livelihood. We have nourishing food, clean and accessible water, clean air, adequate shelter with a good place to sleep, clothing, and physical and psychological safety. We have love and a sense of belonging, and participate in all decisions that affect us. We have time, exercise, rest, peace of mind and spirit. We have music, dance, laughter, joy. To live in a culture of peace, we have a code of ethics that denounces all forms of violence. We have spiritual growth and fulfilment and bodily integrity.[14]

This vision, which perhaps seems utopic, is a far cry from the "hardened" approaches to security that sometimes follow high-profile episodes of gun violence. It is also a vision that requires deep social transformations, the kind that would make it more difficult for violence to find fertile ground. In this vision, body armor and guns are not the sources of security. Equitable social relationships, access to needed resources, infrastructures of care, and a healthy environment are what actually sustain life.

Notes

1 Nicolette Erestain, "What Does Body Armor Have to Do With the Coronavirus (COVID-19)?," *Bulletproof Zone*, March 24, 2020, https://bulletproofzone.com/blogs/bullet-proof-blog/what-does-body-armor-have-to-do-with-the-coronavirus
2 Zygmunt Bauman, "Consuming Life," *Journal of Consumer Culture* 1, no. 1 (2001): 9–29, 27.
3 See Harel Shapira and Samantha Simon, "Learning to Need a Gun," *Qualitative Sociology* 41 (2018): 1–20, 7.
4 Shapira and Simon, "Learning to Need a Gun."
5 Bauman, "Consuming Life," 25.
6 Andrew Szasz, *Shopping Our Way to Safety: How We Changed from Protecting the Environment to Protecting Ourselves* (Minneapolis: University of Minnesota Press, 2007).
7 Lindsay Whitehurst, Gene Johnson, and James Anderson, "Buffalo Is Latest Mass Shooting by Gunman Wearing Body Armor," *AP News*, May 26, 2022, https://apnews.com/article/mass-shootings-buffalo-body-armor-f7789ba97dee4d786ac24ec5c642b7ca; Molly Olmstead, "Why Stopping a 'Bad Guy with a Gun' Keeps Getting Harder," *Slate*, May 27, 2022, https://slate.com/news-and-politics/2022/05/mass-shootings-body-armor-rise.html.
8 Sara Ahmed, *The Cultural Politics of Emotion* (Edinburgh: Edinburgh University Press, 2014).
9 Terence S. Turner, "The Social Skin," *HAU: Journal of Ethnographic Theory* 2 (2012): 486–504.
10 To understand different strands and approaches of the gun violence prevention movement, see Jordan McMillan and Mary Bernstein, "Beyond Gun Control: Mapping Gun Violence Prevention Logics," *Sociological Perspectives* 65, no. 1 (2022): 177–95. For some organizational responses to the new policies, see, for example, Brady, "Brady Celebrates Historic Passage of the Bipartisan Safer Communities Act in the House of Representatives," June 24, 2022, www.bradyunited.org/press-releases/brady-celebrates-historic-passage-of-safer-communities-act-in-the-house-of-representatives; Everytown for Gun Safety, "Monumental Victory For Gun Safety: Everytown, Moms Demand Action, Students Demand Action Celebrate Gun Sense Champion President Joe Biden Signing Bipartisan Safer Communities Act Into Law," June 25, 2022, www.everytown.org/press/monumental-victory-for-gun-safety-everytown-moms-demand-action-students-demand-action-celebrate-gun-sense-champion-president-joe-biden-signing-bipartisan-safer-communities-act-into-law/; Sandy Hook Promise, "The Bipartisan Safer Communities Act: What's Next?," accessed September 11, 2022, www.sandyhookpromise.org/blog/news/the-bipartisan-gun-safety-reform-bill-whats-next/. See the full text of the legislation: "S.2938—Bipartisan Safer Communities Act," accessed September 8, 2022, www.congress.gov/bill/117th-congress/senate-bill/2938/text.
11 The White House, "Fact Sheet: The Biden Administration's 21 Executive Actions to Reduce Gun Violence," July 11, 2022, www.whitehouse.gov/briefing-room/statements-releases/2022/07/11/fact-sheet-the-biden-administrations-21-executive-actions-to-reduce-gun-violence/.
12 National Rifle Association, "NRA Wins Supreme Court Case, NYSRPA v. Bruen," June 23, 2022, www.nraila.org/articles/20220623/nra-wins-supreme-court-case-nysrpa-v-bruen.
13 See "Governor Hochul Signs Landmark Legislative Package to Strengthen Gun Laws and Protect New Yorkers," June 6, 2022, www.governor.ny.gov/news/governor-hochul-signs-landmark-legislative-package-strengthen-gun-laws-and-protect-new-yorkers; "Gun Safety in New York State," accessed September 8, 2022, https://gunsafety.ny.gov/; "Body Armor," accessed September 8, 2022, https://dos.ny.gov/body-armor.
14 See Gender and Human Security Network, "Gender and Human Security Network Manifesto," pp. 70–72 in *Security Disarmed: Critical Perspectives on Gender, Race, and Militarization*, eds. Barbara Sutton, Sandra Morgen, and Julie Novkov (New Brunswick: Rutgers University Press, 2008), 71.

INDEX

9/11 7, 10, 11, 12, 31

ableism 37, 51
accountability 41–42
active shooter drills 31, 50, 53, 91, 122–123, 126–127, 135, 141
active shooter events 65–66, 68–69, 74, 91, 92; *see also* active shooter drills; mass shootings; school shootings
aesthetics: of concealment 95; and fashion 88; "of security" 86–111
Afghanistan 7
age 73, 89, 94, 108, 142; *see also* children; teens; youth
A Girl & A Gun Women's Shooting League (AG & AG) 47
Ahmed, Sara 15, 33, 40, 64, 80, 122, 152
airport security 11–12, 90
alcoholic beverages 45
Alhadeff, Alyssa 71
anger 32, 33, 35, 37, 121; and mass shooting incidents 72; and security 43–44; shields against 72–74
Anker, Elisabeth 8, 9
ankle monitors 102
anti-rape garments 15, 128
anxiety 46, 61, 65–70, 87, 89, 126, 150
armed forces 9, 31, 80, 105
armor 12–13; *see also* body armor
ArmorMe 9, 79, 100
Aspetto 10, 91, 107
attitudes 117; towards guns 4, 123, 135–136

autonomy 104–106; bodily 100
AVS (Active Violence Solutions) 65, 74, 76, 79

Back to School Shopping (art exhibit) 1, 95, 111
Bac-Tactical 73
Baker, Catherine 88
ballistic products 1–3, 5, 8, 15, 72, 96, 118, 125, 130, 138; *see also* bulletproof garments; bulletproof products
Bauman, Zygmunt 62, 150, 151
Bericat, Eduardo 14
Betts, Edxie 108–110
Biden, Joseph 18, 35–36, 38, 154
biometrics 11
Bipartisan Safer Communities Act 154
Black communities 46, 48, 66, 108, 131–132; *see also* Black men; Black people; Black women; people of color; race
Black Lives Matter (BLM) 18, 34–35, 37, 49, 109, 132, 150
Black men 107–108
Black people 3, 8, 18, 43, 48–49, 66, 108–110, 132; *see also* Black communities; Black men; Black women
Black women 100
Blake, Jacob 43
Bleiker, Roland 32
bodies 11–15; fortressing 8, 12, 86, 96–97, 124, 150, 152, 155; gendering of 97; hyper-visible 90; militarization of 8,

12–13; and security 11–12; vulnerability of 89; *see also* bodily autonomy; "bodily capital"; body armor; body scanning
bodily autonomy 100
"bodily capital" 13
body armor 5, 10; availability 143; covert 2, 89, 90, 132, 143; demand for during the pandemic 45–46, 66–67; legislation 8; standards of performance 2; as a symbol of protection 11; used by perpetrators of shootings 3, 8, 143; testing 65; *see also* bulletproof garments; bulletproof products
body scanning 11, 90
border-crossing 7, 11
boundaries 13, 86
Boutilier, Sophia 33
Bovone, Laura 88
Brando, Marlon 107
Bullet Blocker 9, 66, 75, 76, 78, 92, 93, 94, 104, 105, 106
bulletproof accessories 1–3, 10, 14, 16, 17, 61–63, 89, 94, 103, 106, 122, 151, 152; for children 94, 120, 125; for men 103; for women 100–101; and "peace of mind" 66; and pride 66; as "social skin" 86; *see also* bulletproof backpacks; bulletproof products
Bulletproof Backpack (play) 1, 20n3
bulletproof backpacks 1, 2, 63–64, 66, 69–72, 76, 80, 105; design features 91–94, 96
Bulletproof Everyone 103
bulletproof garments 1–3, 8–11, 61–81; companies producing 17; cost 13–14, 16, 94, 129–130; "DIY" 108–110; and emotions 61–81, 117–118, 124, 133–134, 138, 153; global market 10; normalization of 63, 76, 80, 137; and social disparities 14; terminology 20n1, 11; testing 65, 79; *see also* bulletproof vests; jackets; lab coats
bulletproof inserts 1, 66, 69, 76–77, 91, 94
bulletproof products: for children 63–64, 75–78, 91–95, 120–122, 125, 127, 139–141; and pride 77–80; as tokens of love 75–77, 101; *see also* bulletproof accessories; bulletproof backpacks; bulletproof garments; bulletproof inserts; bulletproof vests; jackets; lab coats
Bulletproof Vest (book) 11
bulletproof vests 1, 2, 8, 11, 70, 103–104, 107, 131–132; demand for during the pandemic 45; hidden 13, 96–97; for women 98, 101–103

Bulletproof Zone 45–46, 66, 67, 70–71, 73, 75–78, 90, 92–93
bullet-resistant garments 1; *see also* bulletproof garments
bullet-resistant materials 2
Butler, Judith 6, 49
Buzan, Barry 7

Caldeira, Teresa 86
camouflage 13, 88, 96, 105, 108
Canada 33
capitalism 9, 61, 74, 133–134
cárdenas, micha 108, 110
care: and security 53–55; bulletproof products as tokens of 75–77; *see also* health care
Carlson, Jennifer 48, 97
Center for Disease Control 49
change 33, 52
children: bulletproof products for 1, 9, 14, 63–64, 75–78, 91–95, 120–122, 125, 139–141; of color 94–95; emotional impact of gun violence on 127; parental love for 75–76; protection of 119–122; as sources of threat 73; as victims of firearm use 4; *see also* bulletproof backpacks; school shootings
"choke hold" 42
class 13, 14, 16, 41, 51, 87, 89, 99, 100, 131; inequalities 43, 90, 94, 110
climate change 74
clothing 87–88; brands 88; as demarcation of boundaries 13, 86; militarization of 13, 78, 88, 96, 104; and securitization 11–12; and social phenomena 89; tailor-made 13; *see also* bulletproof garments
cognitive assessments 63
Colombia 9
Columbine High School 68, 73
commercialization 3, 5, 9, 61–81, 89
commodification 61–62, 80; of security 61, 119, 133
communities of color 4, 48; stereotypes of 102; *see also* Black communities; people of color; race
compassion 51, 52
consumer culture 151
co-resistance 52
corporate opportunism 118–119
corsets 14
COVID-19 pandemic 4, 5, 17, 66–67, 69, 89, 120, 134, 145, 149; and alcohol sales 45; and demand for guns 44–45; and social unrest 43–50
Crane, Diana 88

Crawford, Neta 32
crime 41–42, 48, 53, 66, 95, 140
criminal behavior 42, 102
criminality 49, 102
criminal justice system 42, 102
Cullors, Patrisse 108
Cultural Politics of Emotion, The 15
"culture of fear" 66
Cvetkovich, Ann 34

danger 13, 15, 45, 69, 87–88, 92–93; and anger 72–73; and body armor usage 142–143; construction of 12; emotions as sources of 73; perception of 47, 142–143; power to define 7; schools as sites of 92; sense of 40; unforeseen 69, 98
date rape 15
decision-making 31, 62, 127
defense sector 10
democracy 43
DemolitionRanch 65
De Wilde, Jaap 7
"diaphragm law" 42
Diphoorn, Tessa 13
"DIY bulletproof clothing" 108–110
"DIY security ethos" 10
Downes, Stephanie 64

economic disparities 37
embodiment 6
emotions 14–15; as sources of danger 73; and bulletproof garments 61–81, 117–118, 124, 133–134, 138, 153; and change 33; and commodification processes 61–62, 80; gendered 32; "negative" 33, 50, 52, 67; and politics 34–37; "positive" 33, 50, 52, 75, 98; racialized 32; relation between objects and 64–65; and security 15, 31–56; "stickiness" of 40, 80, 122, 152
empathy 32, 50–52, 121
Enloe, Cynthia 3
entrepreneurship 9
Entwistle, Joanne 86, 87
environmental crisis 43
environmental degradation 51
environmental disaster 74
environmental hazards 151
ethnicity 13, 16, 74, 87, 89, 94, 131; *see also* race
ethnocentrism 51
ethnoracial profiling 11

face masks 89
far-right groups 34, 39, 132

fashion 88, 111; and aesthetics 88; "of fear" 2, 12, 13, 15, 16, 33, 86, 152–153
Fassin, Didier 5
fear 65–70, 87, 133, 144–145; culture of 66; "fashion of" 12, 13, 15, 16, 33, 86, 152–153; guns as a source of 46; and political participation 39–40; politics of 10; and security 15, 32, 45–46
Fear and Fashion in the Cold War 89
Feel Tank Chicago 34
feelings 64–65, 144; public 34, 118; *see also* emotions
Feeling Things 64
feminism 5–6, 42
Femme Fatale 14
firearms: acquisition 3–4, 48; and homicide 49; training 46–47; *see also* guns
Floyd, George 18, 51, 53, 132
focus groups 17–18, 34–55, 117–145
Ford, Allison 68
"fortress body" 8, 12, 86, 96–97, 124, 150, 152, 155
Foucault, Michel 12
freedom 103–105
free market 8
frustration 33, 42

Gambetti, Zeynep 12
Garelick, Rhonda 89–90
gated communities 8, 12
gender 13, 14, 51, 87, 89, 91, 100; identity 54; inequality 37; and insecurities 32; and mass shootings 74; normativity 93–94; profiling 11; violence 18, 42, 119, 125–129; and vulnerability 41; *see also* gender-nonconforming people; men; trans people; women
gender-neutral products 91, 102
gender-nonconforming people 109
Ghertner, D. Asher 15, 86
Glassner, Barry 66
Godoy-Anativia, Marcial 12
Goldstein, Daniel M. 15, 86
Goldstein Market Intelligence 10
Goss, Kristin 4
Grewal, Inderpal 7
grief 49, 50, 70–72
Guard Dog Security 64, 70, 75, 91, 128
gun control 4; *see also* gun violence prevention
gun culture 3, 80–81, 127, 137
Gun Goddess 14
gun organizations 4, 14, 47
gun ownership 3–4, 9, 10, 14, 47–48, 127, 138, 152; among women 14, 47

gun rights 3–6, 33, 43, 47–48, 127, 137–140; demonstrations 4; *see also* gun culture
guns: attitudes toward 4, 123, 135–136; demand for during pandemic 44–45; and individual autonomy 106; proliferation 2; and social unrest 43–50; as a source of fear 46; visibility 4; *see also* gun control; gun culture; gun organizations; gun ownership; gun rights; gun violence
Guns Down America 64
gun violence 1–4, 8, 9, 44, 66, 95, 120, 140, 151, 154; and Black communities 48; impact of 127; normalization of 70, 80; and people of color 129–130; prevention 4, 17, 48–50, 129–132, 142, 154; and race 48–49, 66; types of 129; victims of 4, 71–72, 125–126; *see also* active shooter situations; mass shootings; school shootings
Gun Violence Archive 4

Harris, Kamala 1
Head, Chris 108
health care 52–54, 134–137
hegemonic masculinity 104, 107
Hirsch, Marianne 51–52
Hispanic people 48–49
Hochschild, Arlie 51
Hochul, Kathy 8, 154
holistic protection 108
Holloway, Sally 64
home security 15
homicides 49, 129
human rights 51
Hutchinson, Emma 32

identity: gender 54; national 32; personal 54; social 15
Illouz, Eva 61
immigrants 15
incarceration 41–42; *see also* prisons
independence 104
individualism 9, 12, 68
inequality: class 42, 90, 94, 110; gender 37; and neoliberalism 9; racial 42, 94–95; and security 7; systemic 5
injustice: challenging 33; racial 18, 36–37, 47, 51, 131
Innocent Armor 68, 76, 91, 96, 97, 98, 101–105
insecurity 8, 37, 121; emotional response to 45; and fear 39; gendered 32; and institutions 6; and militarization 6; and racism 37, 50

institutions 6–7
international policies 118
international relations 31
intimate partner violence 4, 126
Iraq 7
Israel 9, 79

jackets 1, 13–14, 67, 76, 78–79, 94, 98–99, 101–102, 105–106
Jasper, James 118

Katz, Cindi 10
Kawash, Samira 12
Kelley, Robin D.G. 51
Kevlar 2, 20n6, 74, 109
khaki fabrics 13, 88
Kwolek, Stephanie 2

lab coats 2, 101–102, 106, 139
law enforcement 10, 37, 39, 48, 140–143; criticism of 40; *see also* policing
Leatherback Gear 9, 100, 101, 103
Light, Caroline E. 10, 47
love 33, 75–77, 99; parental 75–76

MacLeish, Kenneth T. 12
Make Our Schools Safe 71–72, 75
marginalized communities 7, 8, 37, 40, 49–50, 69, 77, 109–111, 149
Marjory Stoneman Douglas High School 71–72
marketing 62; *see also* commercialization
masculinity 79, 88, 90, 97, 103–108; aggressive 105; hegemonic 104, 107; militarized 105; toxic 128
mass shootings 1, 3, 4, 8, 154; definition 4; and emotions 31, 65–66, 68–69, 71–74; fear of 10, 33, 46, 61; *see also* active shooter events; school shootings
MC Armor 2, 67, 68–69, 99, 103, 106
McFann, Hudson 15, 86
media representations 63–65
men: Black 107–108; bulletproof garments for 103–108; representations of 91, 103–108; White 48–49; *see also* masculinity
mental health 48, 72, 73, 127, 136–137
metal detectors 12, 53, 94
migrants 7, 33
Miguel Caballero (company) 2, 9, 10, 16–17, 20n8, 99, 103, 106; tests of products 65, 79
militarization 2–3, 7–11, 79, 105, 131; of bodies 8, 12–13; of clothing 13, 78, 88, 96, 104; and insecurity 6

military regalia 88
Millman, Debbie 45
"mobile sovereignty" 8, 9
Moms Demand Action for Gun Sense in America 64
motherhood 100–101

nail polish 15, 128
national borders 7, 90
national identity 32
National Institute of Justice (NIJ) 2
nationalism 78, 79
national policies 118
National Rifle Association (NRA) 4, 47, 130, 154
national security 3, 5–6, 32
Native students 94
neoliberalism 2, 3, 7–12; and inequalities 9
New York State Rifle & Pistol Association v. Bruen 154
NIJ *see* National Institute of Justice
Norgaard, Kari Marie 63
nurses 52–55, 136

occupations 54–55
openness 6
oppression, 54, 140

Paarlberg-Kvam, Kate 91, 95
paranoia 33, 75, 138
parental love 75–76
patriotism 10, 77–78
Pavitt, Jane 89
"peace of mind" 65–70, 72, 81, 122
people of color 7, 33, 36–37, 39, 40, 90; and gun violence 49, 129–130; vulnerability 102, 109; *see also* Black communities; Black people; children of color; communities of color; race; women of color
Peoples, Columba 11
personal identity 54
personal responsibility 9, 10
personal security 2, 5, 14, 15, 73, 74, 98, 123
Pew Research Centre 48
police: brutality 18, 53, 55, 150; demands of abolishing 40–41; violence 37–38, 42, 45, 47, 119, 131–134; *see also* policing
policing 9; and political protests 37–43; *see also* police
political action 34
political debates 41
political decision-making 31
"political depression" 34

political participation 32, 39
political polarization 34–37
political protests 33; and fear 39–40; and policing 37–43; *see also* protests
political rallies 4
political silencing 39
political speech 31
politics: and emotions 34–37; of fear 10; rationality in 31–32
poverty 140
power 7, 12, 63
"precarity" 9
pride 77–80, 102
prisons 40, 128; *see also* incarceration
private initiative 9
privatization 8–9
protests 133; anti-racist 40, 46, 133; social justice 38–39, 133; *see also* political protests
Proud Boys 34–35
public events 34
public feelings 34, 118
public health 4, 45, 136
public mourning rituals 50
public safety 40, 66

queer 54, 77, 109

race 13, 14, 16, 37, 41, 51, 87, 89, 91, 99, 100, 131; and firearm homicide 49; and gun violence 48–49, 66; and mass shootings 74
racial inequality 42, 94–95
racial injustice 18, 36–37, 43, 47, 51, 131
racial justice protests 43, 47
racial minorities 48
racial violence 18, 37, 45, 110
racism 55, 94, 131, 140; and insecurity 37, 50; systemic 36, 50; and trauma 48
racist stereotypes 94
rage 72–74
Randles, Sarah 64
rape 15, 128
rationality 31–32
Reed, Ron 63
research approach 16–19
retail stores 2
rights: human 51; workers' 54; *see also* gun rights
Rittenhouse, Kyle 43
Robb Elementary School 8
"Robocop" aesthetics 90
Rocamora, Agnès 88
Rosen, Kenneth 11
"Run. Hide. Fight" strategy 66, 69

sadness 49, 70–72, 121, 130, 144–145
safe communities 41, 48
Safeguard Clothing 70, 96
Sandy Hook Elementary School 1, 46, 95
Schell, Terry L. 4, 129
Schick, Kate 52
schools 50, 53; security 53; as sites of danger 92; *see also* active shooter drills; school shootings
School Safety & Survival Pack 92
school shootings 1, 9, 46, 72–73, 92, 95, 123–125, 129, 151; and emotions 67–68, 119–122; *see also* active shooter drills
Seager, Joni 3
securitization 7, 11–12, 149, 154
security 5–7; aesthetics of 86–111; and bodies 11–12, 90; and care 53–54; commodification of 61, 119, 133; companies 9; cultures 3; and emotions 15, 31–56; false sense of 63, 130, 151; and fear 15, 32, 45–46; "genuine" 5, 50–55; gifts of 76; human 5, 11, 53; individualization of 3, 7; and inequality 7; "insecure" 3; market-based approach 2; measures 89, 94; multi-layered dimensions 5–6; national 3, 5–6, 32; ontological 70–92; personal 2, 5, 10, 14, 15, 73, 74, 98, 123; and power 7; privatization of 8–9; products 5, 64, 93, 111; as relational 6; "subjectivities of" 12; technologies of 8; and technology 6, 12; *see also* "security state"
security-oriented clothing 3, 87; *see also* bulletproof garments; bulletproof products; security-oriented products
security-oriented policies 31
security-oriented products 10, 15, 64–65, 72, 78, 80, 86, 92, 128; *see also* bulletproof garments; bulletproof products
security-oriented technologies 3
"security state" 7, 9
self-defense 3, 6, 9, 47, 48, 80, 127, 131–132, 137–140, 152
self-protection 9–10, 33, 67, 138
"self-sufficient citizen" 68
self-worth 77
sexism 37, 51
sexuality 14, 100, 101, 103
sexualization 99–100
sexual minorities 48
sexual violence 14–15, 100, 119, 125–129
Shapira, Harel 80–81

Shopping Our Way to Safety 151
Sinatra, Frank 107
Small Arms Survey 3
Smart, Rosanna 4, 129
Smelik, Anneke 88
social control 88
social disparities 14, 129, 149
social hierarchies 13
social identification 77
social identity 14, 89
social inequality 3, 16, 153
social justice 38–39, 51, 108, 133, 142, 153, 155
social norms 88, 117
social order 12
social problems 6, 42, 52, 63, 70, 87, 110, 133
"social skin" 86, 152
social status 90
social unrest 43–50, 71
solidarity 52
South Africa 13
sovereignty 8, 9
state: expenditures 9; failure to protect citizens 10, 95, 134; social welfare provision 9; violence 7, 9, 42, 66, 109
stereotypes: Black women 100; communities of color 102; people with mental health issues 73; Native Americans 94; racist 94
Stroud, Angela 48
subjectivity 12
suits 1, 91, 107
surveillance 11, 31, 89, 102
survival 51, 65, 67–68, 150
systemic change 52
systemic inequality 5
systemic oppression 53, 140
systemic racism 36, 50
Szasz, Andrew 151

tailor-made clothing 13
Talos Ballistics 66, 69, 78, 96, 98, 101, 104, 105
tattoos 100
teachers 2, 122–125
technologies of security 8
teens 73, 92–93; *see also* youth
terrorism 10, 31, 32, 89; *see also* 9/11
Thinking through Fashion 88
Thyk Skynn 46, 66, 90, 98, 99, 102, 107–108
transmisogyny 110
trans people 109

trans women 109–110
trauma 45, 48, 144
Trump, Donald 18, 34–36, 38, 44
TuffyPacks 64, 68, 73, 76, 77, 92, 94
Turner, Bryan S. 6
Turner, Terence 86

Unstoppable 109–111
U.S. Capitol 18, 31, 34–35, 45, 150
U.S. Constitution 3; Second Amendment 4, 43
U.S. Supreme Court 5, 154

Vaughan Williams, Nick 11
Vestal, Shawn 64
vigilantism 18, 39, 43, 131, 142
violence: gender 18, 42, 119, 125–129; in health care settings 52–53, 134–137; intimate partner 4, 126; police 37–38, 42, 45, 47, 119, 131–134; political debates on 41; in prisons 128; racial 18, 37, 45, 110; sexual 14–15, 100, 119, 125–129; "slow" 6; state 7, 9, 42, 66, 109; structural forms of 6; against women 42; *see also* gun violence
Volsky, Igor 64
vulnerability 6–7, 108–109; of Black men 107–108; of the body 89; Butler on 6; construction of 14; gendered 41; of people of color 102, 109; to violence 66

Wæver, Ole 7
war 6, 32; "on terror" 7; reporting 11; zones 3, 6, 9, 13
Watts, Shannon 64
Well Armed Woman, The (organization) 14
WhIsBe 95
White men 48–49
women: Black 100; bulletproof garments for 98–103; of color 42, 54, 100, 102–103; gun organizations for 14, 47; gun ownership 14, 47; objectification of 99–100; occupations populated by 54–55; representations of 98–103; trans 109–110; as victims of firearm use 4; violence against 42
Wonder Hoodie 66, 72, 74, 75, 91, 94, 96, 100

xenophobia 37, 131

youth 73, 78, 91, 120, 129, 154; *see also* teens

Zoom 17

Milton Keynes UK
Ingram Content Group UK Ltd.
UKHW051538260624
444749UK00008B/62

9 781032 354323